FROM FRIGHT TO MIGHT:

OVERCOMING THE FEAR OF PUBLIC SPEAKING

Ron Reel

Phillip Maynard

Kenneth Klawitter

Carolyn Inmon

Liesel Reinhart

Jeff Archibald

The 7th Edition revisions were conducted by Liesel Reinhart, Ken Klawitter and Jeff Archibald for the Mt. San Antonio College Department of Communication.

DAY&NITE
PUBLISHING

ISBN: 978-1-884155-44-4

Table of Contents

Workbook

Textbook

INTRODUCTION

It's hard to believe it has been almost fifteen years since our first edition of this textbook. Back in 1998, Dr. Ron Reel suggested to our department faculty that we could help students better afford our public speaking course if we pooled our knowledge and created our own textbook. It was a good thing he had that idea. Our previous textbook (the one used at many colleges) is now $125.00. *From Fright to Might* has saved Mt. SAC students almost four million dollars in the last fifteen years.

It's not just a less-expensive book. We believe it's a better book for you, because it's customized for Mt. SAC students by the faculty who are teaching this specific course. This textbook includes references to campus resources that will help you succeed on your assignments – and beyond. Faculty do not make a profit on the book; proceeds are used for academic initiatives here at Mt. San Antonio College, including annual student scholarships, classroom technology and supplies, intramural speech contests, the Speech and Sign Success Center, and the Mt. SAC Forensics Team. Details for all of these programs are found on the next page.

This new edition incorporates feedback from students and instructors. The biggest change is the new workbook section in the first half of the book. This new workbook/textbook format will help you develop your skills through activities and also build your understanding of oral communication principles through interesting reading. There's even space to take notes on the pages of the book. Since many of our faculty members design their class sessions around textbook readings and activities, be sure to bring this book to every class meeting. And since public speaking opportunities occur throughout life, you may want to find a space on your shelf for this book after your class has ended.

In this seventh edition of *From Fright to Might* we are again proud to feature the work of Marco Cianello on our cover and throughout the book. Marco is a graphic novel and animation artist originally from Italy who now works for studios here in the United States.

All of us who teach this course know that, for many, it's an experience that begins with a little dread or even fear. Be assured that more than 80% of students who complete this course report that they enjoyed public speaking much more than they expected, and more than 85% report an increase in self confidence from their experience. All of us who teach SPCH 1A have shared the feelings of nervousness and exhilaration that go along with standing up and speaking to an audience, which may be why a student once told me that public speaking kind of like "doing an extreme sport or being on a roller coaster." I think maybe he's right. Buckle up and enjoy the ride!

Liesel Reinhart
Chair, Department of Communication

SPCH 1A Freedom of Speech, Academic Integrity, and Respect: An Agreement

The purpose of this agreement is to create an environment of respectful, ethical learning during this semester of SPCH 1A Public Speaking at Mt. San Antonio College.

This agreement requires all students to take responsibility for the integrity of the content of their work in this course, with the highest possible standard applied to graded assignments.

This agreement also requires students to demonstrate respectful listening to one another, to the instructor, and to all authorized guests while they are addressing the class.

By signing this agreement, I offer my assurance of the following:

The work I present in this class (including but not limited to written assignments, speech outlines, and oral presentations) will be my original work. I will not plagiarize the work from other sources, fabricate information or sources, or submit another person's work as my own.

I will regularly attend in a timely manner and participate actively in each class section. I will adhere to my instructor's guidelines concerning the use of phones and other electronic devices during class.

I will give my respectful attention to student speakers in our classroom, recognizing that my role as a listener can impact their successful work on graded assignments.

I accept that some viewpoints expressed in this classroom may vary from my own and will listen respectfully to these (and all) views in the spirit of open discourse and learning.

(Additional items for your specific class may be added here): _____

_____

_____

_____

_____

Sign Name: _____

Print Name: _____ Date: _____

Mt. SAC Student Learning Outcomes for SPCH 1A

As of January 1, 2012 the following Student Learning Outcomes (SLOs) are in place for the SPCH 1A and SPCH 1AH courses at Mt. San Antonio College.

SLOs are statements that express what students should be able to take away from a specific learning experience. They do not in any way reflect the full range of learning students may complete in this course, but are meaningful.

1. Students will be able to perform basic speech delivery skills.

2. Students will utilize appropriate speech organization.

3. Students will be able to evaluate the reliability of information sources.

4. Students will deliver an organized verbal response to a prompt with little to no preparation time.

5. Students will critically evaluate public speeches.

6. Students will be able to articulate an argument with reasoning and support.

7. Students will create full-sentence outlines using appropriate, credible research sources and attribution.

8. Students will speak extemporaneously (with minimal notes).

9. Students will perform five speeches.

10. Students will understand the need to adapt communication style to acknowledge the differences in others.

11. Students will be able to use electronic resources to conduct research.

12. Students will feel more confident.

13. Students will create and effectively utilize visual aids.

14. Students will enjoy public speaking.

As part of your experience in this course, you will participate in assessments of your learning in these key areas. The following pages (xi-xii) contain forms you will use for these assessments. Please do not complete them until notified by your instructor.

SLO Assessment Form: Basic Delivery Skills

Note: You will need to provide this form to your instructor to be completed for one of your speeches this term. Copies will not be accepted.

Student Name:_____

Assignment used for assessment: _____

Date of assessment: _____

EVALUATION RUBRIC
(TO BE COMPLETED BY YOUR INSTRUCTOR)

	3	2	1	0
Eye Contact	Sustained	Direct	Partial/ Glancing	Avoidance
Organization	Intro/Body/ Conclusion and Signposting	Intro/Body/ Conclusion	No clear division of three areas	No structure to speak of
Body Control	Controlled body; some purposeful movement and/ or gesture	Solid speaker's stance	Some distracting wandering or fidgeting	Lack of body control, Excessive wandering/ fidgeting
Volume	Commanding, Authoritative, Fills the room	Adequate to be easily heard and hold attention	Not easily heard; does not hold full attention of audience	Not audible

SLO Assessment: Critical Evaluation of Public Speeches

Note: You will need to provide this form to your instructor to be completed with your outside speaker, self, or peer critique assignment. Copies will not be accepted.

Student Name:_____

Assignment used for assessment (circle one):

         Self-evaluation   Peer critique   Outside Speaker Critique

Date of assessment: _____

EVALUATION RUBRIC
(TO BE COMPLETED BY YOUR INSTRUCTOR):

Score	Criteria	Mark One
3	Student evaluation achieved the following objectives: • summarize the observed speech • identify both content and delivery aspects of the speech • consistently utilize terminology consistent with the course text and/or lecture • propose strategies the speaker could utilize to improve the content and/or the delivery of the speech, when appropriate • provide at least one detailed description of the speech as support	
2	Student evaluation achieved the following objectives: • summarize the observed speech • identify multiple areas of excellence and areas for improvement, when appropriate • utilize terminology consistent with the course text and/or lecture	
1	Student evaluation achieved the following objectives: • summarize the observed speech • identify at least one area of strength and one area for improvement, but may omit either content or delivery variables • will not consistently utilize terminology consistent with the text and/or lecture	
0	Student is unable to critically evaluate public speeches	

THE SPEECH & SIGN SUCCESS CENTER (SSSC)

SSSC Referral Form

Student Name: _____

Referred by Instructor: _____ Date: _____

Purpose of Visit (mark all that apply):

☐ Research tutoring   ☐ Outline tutoring   ☐ Record/review speech

☐ Delivery tutoring   ☐ General tutoring   ☐ Other: _____

Note to instructor: Please attach a copy of the associated assignment if you do not currently have it on file at the SSSC.

Note to student: Tutoring appointments are suggested, though drop-in tutoring may be possible. Visit *http://www.mtsac.edu/instruction/humanities/speechsign*

SSSC Attendance Verification Form

Student Name _____

Date of Visit: _____ Length of Visit:_____

Purpose of Visit (mark all that apply):

☐ Research tutoring   ☐ Outline tutoring   ☐ Record/review speech

☐ Delivery tutoring   ☐ General tutoring   ☐ Other: _____

SSSC Staff/Tutor Name_____

SSSC Staff/Tutor Signature _____

FROM FRIGHT TO MIGHT:

WORKBOOK

Self-Critique: Ten Basic Steps

Name: _____ Date: _____

Specific Purpose of Speech:

Evaluate yourself in each of the following areas discussed in Chapter Three: (Place an "X" in the appropriate column, add your comments in boxes below the categories.

	Needs Work	OK	Good	Excellent	Amazing
1. CARING:					
2. ORGANIZATION					
3. STARTING & ENDING STRONG					
4. LOOKING & FEELING GREAT					
5. SHOWING YOUR PERSONALITY					
6. *NOT* DROPPING THE BALL					
7. CONTROLLING YOUR BODY					
8. MAKING EYE CONTACT					
9. CONTROLLING YOUR VOICE					
10. EVIDENCE OF REHEARSAL					

Peer Critique Form

Speaker's Name:_____

Topic: _____

Three strengths you observed:
1.
2.
3.

Two areas for improvement:
1.
2.

Peer Critique Form

Speaker's Name:_____

Topic: _____

Three strengths you observed:
1.
2.
3.

Two areas for improvement:
1.
2.

Peer Critique Form

Speaker's Name:_____

Topic: _____

Three strengths you observed:
1.
2.
3.

Two areas for improvement:
1.
2.

Peer Critique Form

Speaker's Name:_____

Topic: _____

Three strengths you observed:
1.
2.
3.

Two areas for improvement:
1.
2.

Peer Critique Form

Speaker's Name:_____

Topic: _____

Three strengths you observed:

1.
2.
3.

Two areas for improvement:

1.
2.

Peer Critique Form

Speaker's Name:_____

Topic: _____

Three strengths you observed:

1.
2.
3.

Two areas for improvement:

1.
2.

Peer Critique Form

Speaker's Name:_____

Topic: _____

Three strengths you observed:

1.
2.
3.

Two areas for improvement:

1.
2.

Peer Critique Form

Speaker's Name:_____

Topic: _____

Three strengths you observed:

1.
2.
3.

Two areas for improvement:

1.
2.

Peer Critique Form

Speaker's Name: _____

Topic: _____

Three strengths you observed:
1.
2.
3.

Two areas for improvement:
1.
2.

Peer Critique Form

Speaker's Name: _____

Topic: _____

Three strengths you observed:
1.
2.
3.

Two areas for improvement:
1.
2.

Peer Critique Form

Speaker's Name: _____

Topic: _____

Three strengths you observed:
1.
2.
3.

Two areas for improvement:
1.
2.

Peer Critique Form

Speaker's Name: _____

Topic: _____

Three strengths you observed:
1.
2.
3.

Two areas for improvement:
1.
2.

SPEAKER CRITIQUE

Name of Speaker/Event: _____

Location: _____ Date: _____

1. Describe the background and/or credentials of at least one of the speakers for this performance.

   _____

   _____

   _____

2. What was the overall message of this performance? What were the main points?

   _____

   _____

   _____

3. Who was the audience for this performance?

   _____

   _____

   _____

4. Describe the feedback given by the audience and how it may have affected the performance.

   _____

   _____

   _____

5. Describe any interference that occurred during the event and how it may have affected the performance. _____

   _____

   _____

6. Describe the context/environment for this event and how it may have affected the performance.

_____

_____

_____

7. Give the speaker a score from 1-10 (10 being best) in the following categories:

caring	
personality	
body control	
vocal control	
appearance	
preparation/rehearsal	

8. What did the speaker do well in this performance? _____

_____

_____

9. How could the speaker improve?

_____

_____

_____

ATTENDANCE VERIFICATION

_____
(Signature of speaker you observed, event host, or SSSC representative)

10

1-1: Communication Scavenger Hunt

Although people generally associate communication with words, an important concept in this chapter is that almost anything can have communicative value. Form teams and go outside of your classroom to collect one item for each category listed below. You may not use any items in your classroom or that you brought with you to class today. After you have located the items, put together a group presentation about the objects you found. All group members must participate in the presentation!

Something that communicates **love**

Something that communicates **evil**

Something that makes an **argument**

Something that has the goal to **inform**

Something that has the goal to **persuade**

Something that has the goal to **entertain**

Something that is **representative** of your group

Something mentioned in a **song** (Your group must perform at least 10 seconds of the appropriate part of the song).

Additional Rules:

- Time limit =
- No splitting up, and learn each other's names!
- No breaking of laws or school policies.
- All valuable items must be returned after class.
- No repeat use items.
- Be creative!

1-2: Introducing Someone Else

Interview a classmate. Use some of the following questions and some of your own to find out more about the person. Then write a short (under one minute) speech to introduce this person as a guest speaker for a class or other event. Your introduction should make the audience feel excited about the person you introduce!

Some Questions to Ask:

What is your ancestry/heritage? Where were you born?

Are you named after someone?

What is your major?

What do you plan on doing in 10 years?

What do you like to create?

What sports or music do you like?

Do you have any children?

What is your favorite TV Show?

What is your favorite movie?

What are three adjectives to describe yourself?

Write Out Your Introduction Here:

2-1: Diagnosing My Degree of Speaking Anxiety

Part One: Circle the physical and psychological symptoms you feel or have felt before or during a speaking situation:

Racing Heartbeat	Sweating	Nausea	Shaking/Twitching
Breathing Difficulty	Blank Memory	Dry Mouth	Sense of Defeat
Excessive Blinking	Wringing of Hands	Nervous Laugh	Panic
Bathroom Urge	Ums/Non-words	Pacing	Other:_____

Part Two: Mark an "X" by the statements that you feel are **true** for you:

1. _____ I will never be a great speaker.

2. _____ I always arrive early on the first day of class so I have time to park and find my classroom.

3. _____ I feel tired right now.

4. _____ I have experience as an athlete and am familiar with the physical effects of adrenaline.

5. _____ Before a test or presentation I usually do the minimum amount of preparation needed to get the grade I want.

6. _____ I have given at least ten speeches in the past three years that were at least five minutes in length.

7. _____ The people who are watching me speak are waiting for me to screw up and make a mistake.

8. _____ I can think of three things I do well as a speaker.

9. _____ I can remember an instance when I was really embarrassed while standing in front of a group of people.

10. _____ I really enjoy speaking in front of people.

11. _____ I will probably "blank out" during a speech in this class.

Part Three: Use the space below to describe below your scariest imaginable hypothetical speaking situation. Consider writing about the topic, the setting, the audience, the context, and more:

(turn the page to continue...)

Part Four: Review your results.

A.   How many symptoms did you circle in part one?   _____

B.   In part two, how many odd numbered answers did you mark?   _____

C.   In part two, how many even numbered answers did you mark?   _____

D.   Add A and B, then subtract C.   _____

This number (D) indicates your speech anxiety rating. This is not a psychological diagnosis, but does indicate your relationship to anxiety-related conditions and behaviors. What does your rating say about you?

(-5 to 3)   Calm and collected. You are the rare person who has both a natural affinity for speaking and personal habits and experiences that further reduce your anxiety.

(4 to 10)   Very typical. You probably experience manageable symptoms of anxiety that could be further reduced by better habits and preparation.

(11 to 16)   Some cause for concern. You will probably need to follow steps in Chapter 2 to decrease your anxiety so you can successfully complete this course.

(17 to 22)   High anxiety. You may wish to further discuss your anxiety level with your professor. Remember, though, that fears can be overcome! Don't give up!

E.   Review the description you wrote in part three. Which of the following factors that influence speech anxiety are evident in your situation?

_____ Fear of being the center of attention   _____ Low self-esteem

_____ Concern about being judged   _____ High stakes

_____ Feeling subordinate to the audience   _____ Feeling different than the audience

_____ Degree of unpredictability   _____ Excessive self-focus

Part Five: Given what you have learned about yourself in this activity, write yourself a diagnosis for three specific anxiety-reduction techniques from Chapter 2:

#1:

#2:

#3:

2-2: Fear Confession

This activity is to be done in conjunction with the first speaking experience in front of the classroom. First, rate your anticipated fear before your first speaking experience. After your speech, rate your actual fear. Choose a partner and share these results with him or her.

1. Rate your anticipated fear using 1 as "No big deal" and 10 as "I'd rather die than do this again":

Low level fear			Noticeable fear				High level fear		
1	2	3	4	5	6	7	8	9	10

2. Rate your actual fear after your speech:

Low level fear			Noticeable fear				High level fear		
1	2	3	4	5	6	7	8	9	10

3. Share your fear with a friend, asking these questions:

    •   When did you feel the fear?

    •   What were the physical manifestations of the fear?

3-1: Video Self-Analysis

Video one of your class performances, either at home, during class, or in the SSSC. Review the recording three times:

The first time: Watch the tape with no sound. Observe your appearance and body control.

The second time: Turn your head away and just listen to your voice. How is your rate? Do you sound like you care? Is there personality in your voice?

The third time: Watch and listen at the same time. Make observations about your overall effectiveness.

Write a short paper analyzing your performance. Which did you do well? Which still need attention? Give specific examples, and don't be too hard on yourself.

3-2: Speech Performance Preparation Checklist

Mark an "X" in each box for all the items you have completed to prepare for your upcoming speech. If you haven't completed an item, be sure to do that step and then mark an "X" in the box.

❑ Prepared a speaking outline or manuscript

❑ Prepared speaking notes or note cards

❑ Performed the speech for a live person or people at least once

❑ Timed the speech at least four times within the time limits for the assignment

❑ Memorized the first and last line of the speech

❑ Included personal touches or a sense of my personality in the speech

❑ Imagined the speech performance from start to finish with no mistakes

❑ Care about my topic, my audience and/or my grade and will clearly show it during speech

❑ The work I have done on this speech reflects the overall grade I hope to earn in this class

Congratulations! You are ready to give a great speech! Now relax and soon it will be your turn to speak.

4-1: Class Observation

Ask a professor on campus if you can sit in on 20-30 minutes of one of his/her classes during a lecture session. Sit near the back of the class and discreetly observe the listening behaviors of the students in class. Afterwards, answer each of the following questions:

1.   What percentage of the students did you feel were listening actively and supportively?

2.   What negative listening behaviors did you observe?

3.   What positive listening behaviors did you observe?

4.   What could be some of the likely outcomes of the listening behaviors of this class?

5.   Why didn't the assignment ask you to observe students in a class in which you are enrolled?

5-1: Topic Evaluation

Imagine that you have been asked to give a 6-8 minute informative demonstration speech for a third grade class in your community. You have come up with some possible topics, but aren't sure which is best. Complete the following chart to find the best topic(s) for this speaking occasion:

TOPIC IDEA:	Is it APPROPRIATE FOR THE SITUATION/ASSIGNMENT?	Is it RESEARCHABLE?	Is it INTERESTING TO YOU?	Will it be INTERESTING TO MY AUDIENCE?	Is it IMPORTANT AND RELEVANT to my audience?	Can it be covered within my TIME LIMIT?	If it meets all the criteria you have a GREAT TOPIC!
The history of the United States							
Don't drink soda							
How to play soccer							
Preparing your own tax returns							
My vacation to China							

5-2: Evaluating Your Own Speech Topic

Use this sheet to evaluate your potential topics for a speech assignment in this class. You professor may also ask you to use it to evaluate your classmates' topics prior to a speech.

Goal of speech: _____

Audience: _____ Length of speech:_____

TOPIC IDEA:	Is it APPROPRIATE FOR THE SITUATION/ASSIGNMENT?	Is it RESEARCHABLE?	Is it INTERESTING TO ME?	Will it be INTERESTING TO MY AUDIENCE?	Is it IMPORTANT AND RELEVANT to my audience?	Can it be covered within my TIME LIMIT?	If it meets all the criteria I have a GREAT TOPIC!

My BEST topic is:_____

6-1: The Difference Between Stereotyping and Audience Analysis

Complete the following table to help clarify some of the differences between stereotyping and sound audience analysis. An example has been provided.

Observed or studied audience characteristic	A stereotype of this group that would be harmful to use in your speech preparation	A reasonable conclusion you might draw for shaping your speech
Mostly 60-year old people	They will all be hard-of-hearing so I will have to say my speech really loud!	I could use examples in my speech from the mid-1950's when they were teenagers.
All women		
Mostly Republicans		
All Latinos		
All Video Gamers		
Mostly college students		

6-2: Audience Data Collection

Imagine that a guest speaker will be coming to your class in a few weeks and wants to prepare thoroughly for the occasion. He/she needs your help in understanding the audience and speaking context. For this speech, the audience is your class and the setting will be your classroom.

Your professor will assign you a category of audience analysis from the list below. If the class is large, some students may need to work in pairs.

Number of students	Employment status	Seating arrangement
Gender	Employment type	Stress level of students
Ethnic background	Socio-economic status	Taboo topics
Religious affiliation	Education level	Formality of attire
Degree of religious involvement	Relationship status	Temperature of room
Nationality	Age	Lighting & acoustics
Political affiliation	Memberships of students	Size of room

Determine an appropriate method for collecting data about your classmates in your category of analysis. You may wish to use visual observation, a sampling of your classmates, or a census (asking everyone in the class). You will need to decide if you will ask yes/no, open-ended, or closed-ended questions. Some topics may be sensitive. How can you tactfully collect accurate data?

Collect your data and review your findings, then prepare a very short statement of your findings for a potential guest speaker in your classroom.

FOLLOW-UP QUESTION: If a guest speaker for your class wasn't able to get information like you have just provided from students in the class, what other options would he/she have for conducting audience analysis for this occasion?

7-1: Evaluating Sources of Information

For this activity, you will need to refer to a copy or printout of a source you are planning to use for an upcoming speech.

PART 1: Document the Source

1. Title/name of source: _____

2. Type of source (periodical, book, website, interview, etc.): _____

3. Date: _____

4. Author (organization or person): _____

PART 2: Assess Source Credibility

1. Is the source from a recognized publisher or organization (New York Times, Wall Street Journal, American Cancer Society, etc.)?   YES   NO

2. What experience, education, or credentials does the author/interviewee have?

   _____

   _____

3. Is the information consistent with information found in other sources?   YES   NO

4. Was the source accessed through a library database?   YES   NO

PART 3: Assess Source Recency

1. Was the source published within the last 3 years?   YES   NO

2. If the source is web-based, is the site regularly updated? Are the links current?   YES   NO

3. Is recency important for the specific topic discussed in the source?   YES   NO

PART 4: Additional Questions

1. Who is the intended audience or reader of this source?

   _____

   _____

2. (For websites) What is the purpose of the site? Does it express a bias?

   _____

   _____

3. Is the source attempting to sell a product?   YES   NO

PART 5: Evaluate the Source

1. On a scale of 1-10 (10 being the best), rate the relevance of this source to the topic (or its

   adequacy to prove the point) _____

   What contributed to your rating?

   _____

   _____

2. On a scale of 1-10, rate the recency of this source _____

   What contributed to your rating?

   _____

   _____

3. On a scale of 1-10, rate the credibility of this source _____

   What contributed to your rating?

   _____

   _____

7-2: Incorporating Research

For a persuasive speech on capital punishment, you have found the following excerpt from an editorial titled "Doubts on the Death Penalty" from the Los Angeles Times of December 17, 2011.

"We bring this up now, three months after the debate in question, because new data have emerged showing that despite a certain bloodthirsty element in some parts of the conservative base, support is steadily eroding for the ethical, legal and financial morass that is capital punishment. The Death Penalty Information Center's annual report on capital punishment in America, released Thursday, showed that executions continued to drop in 2011, to 43; that's down from 85 in 2000 and 46 last year. More significantly, the number of death sentences across the country fell dramatically this year, to 78 from 112 in 2010. And perhaps most significant of all, the percentage of Americans who say they support the death penalty, which was 80% in 1994, fell to 61%, the lowest ever.

In California, one number in particular stands out: There were only 10 people sentenced to death in the Golden State in 2011, compared with 29 last year. That may be a statistical anomaly, or it may indicate that prosecutors and courts are finally concluding, correctly, that death sentences have become largely pointless; legal complications have prevented anyone from being executed here since 2006. A continuing conflict over the state's method for lethal injection and a shortage of a key drug often used to perform it, mean this situation won't be resolved any time soon."

In your speech, you intend to prove the following claim: "Public support for the death penalty is decreasing."

1. Choose a *direct quotation* from the article that you could use to support this claim:

2. Now *paraphrase* that quotation and write it below:

3. Which would be better to use in your speech? Why?

4. Write a full sentence(s) *including proper citation*, for how this would sound in your speech:

7-3: CREATING MLA CITATIONS

Create a properly formatted MLA works cited page for the following sources (use today's date for date accessed for web sources):

1) A book called The Tortilla Curtain, written by T. Coraghessan Boyle, published in New York by Viking Penguin, copyright 1995.

2) The Warner Bros' film titled Casablanca, made in 1942 and directed by Michael Curtiz. It stars Humphrey Bogart and Ingrid Bergman.

3) The word "fungible." (Hint: you will need to look at a dictionary for this one)

4) An article written by Molly Hennessy-Fiske titled Digital Artifacts of an Uprising. It was published in the July 7, 2011 edition of the Los Angeles Times. The article appears on pages A1 and A5.

5) An essay written by Lee Sandlin titled Losing the War. The essay appeared in the book The New Kings of Nonfiction, edited by Ira Glass and published by Riverhead Books in New York in 2007. The essay appears on pages 315-361.

6) An article titled "Mississippi most obese state, Colorado least" written by Lisa Baertlein. The article was published on July 7, 2011 through Reuters on Yahoo.com.

7) An uncredited article titled "Four Ways to Deal with Stress" last updated on June 20, 2011 and taken from the American Heart Association's website.

8) An entry titled "Hendrix, Jimi" written by David Henderson and taken from the Encyclopedia of African-American Culture and History. The encyclopedia was edited by Colin A. Palmer and published in Detroit by Macmillan Reference in 2006. The article was located in the Gale Virtual Reference Library and accessed on June 30, 2011.

9) An article titled "How to Catch Rainwater" from eHow.com.

10) A blog post titled, "The 10 Greatest Comedy Movies of All Time" written by MovieChick23 (real name Jennifer Sanchez) on her LiveJournal page on April 19, 2010.

7-3: ANSWER KEY

(Note: answers are given in the order of the assignment. Actual works cited page would have the entries *alphabetized*.)

Works Cited

Boyle, T. Coraghessan. *The Tortilla Curtain*. New York: Viking Penguin, 1995. Print.

Casablanca. Dir. Michael Curtiz. Perf. Humphrey Bogart and Ingrid Bergman. Warner Brothers, 1942. DVD.

"Fungible." *The American Heritage Dictionary*. 3rd ed. 1997. Print.

Hennessy-Fiske, Molly. "Digital Artifacts of an Uprising." *The Los Angeles Times* 07 July 2011: A1, A5. Print.

Sandlin, Lee. "Losing the War." *The New Kings of Nonfiction*. Ed. Ira Glass. New York: Riverhead Books, 2007. 315-361. Print.

Baertlein, Lisa. "Mississippi Most Obese State, Colorado Least." *Reuters*. Yahoo.com, 07 July 2011. Web. [today's date].

"Four Ways to Deal with Stress." *American Heart Association*. American Heart Association, 20 June 2011. Web. [today's date].

Henderson, David. "Hendrix, Jimi." *Encyclopedia of African-American Culture and History*. Ed. Colin A. Palmer. Detroit: Macmillan Reference, 2006. Gale Virtual Reference Library. Web. 30 June 2011.

"How to Catch Rainwater." *eHow.com*. eHow, n.d. Web. [today's date].

MovieChick23 [Jennifer Sanchez]. "The 10 Greatest Comedy Movies of All Time." *LiveJournal.com*. LiveJournal, 19 April 2010. Web. [today's date].

7-4: IMPROVING MLA CITATIONS

Find the errors in MLA formatting in the following works cited page. Circle the errors, then correct the errors to format the entry correctly, if possible. Errors may include:

missing dates	missing publication type	punctuation error
missing names	missing publication info	indentation error
alphabetization error	capitalization error	italicization error

---

Bibliography

Anthony, Sharon, Thomas W. Brauch, and Longley, Elizabeth. What Should We Do About Global Warming. Beloit College and the Regents of the U of California, 12 Aug. 2008. Web. 13 Sept. 2010.

Center for Marine Biodiversity and Conservation. *Ocean Acidification*. Scripps Institution of Oceanography, UC San Diego, 2007. 13 Dec. 2010.

Denny, Mark W., and Steven D. Gaines, eds. *Encyclopedia of Tidepools and Rocky Shores*. 2007. Print.

Flannery. *The Weather Makers: How Man is Changing the Climate and What it Means for Life on Earth*. New York: Atlantic Monthly. Print.

Docksai, Rick. New Greenhouse Gas Threat. The Futurist 43.2 (2009): 10-11. *ProQuest*. Web. 19 Oct. 2010.

Hawksworth, David L., and Alan T. Bull, eds. *Vertebrate Conservation and Biodiversity*. Dordrecht: Springer, 2007. *NetLibrary*. 5 Dec. 2010.

Mercola, Joseph. "Critical Alert: the Swine Flu Pandemic Fact or Fiction?" *Original Internist* 16.2 (2009): 79-85. *Health Reference Center Academic*. Web. 19 Aug. 2009.

United States. Environmental Protection Agency. *The EPA Climate Change Kids Site*. Web. 13 Oct. 2010.

7-4: ANSWER KEY

Works Cited

Anthony, Sharon, Thomas W. Brauch, and Elizabeth J. Longley. *What Should We Do About Global Warming*. Beloit College and the Regents of the U of California, 12 Aug. 2008. Web. 13 Sept. 2010.

Center for Marine Biodiversity and Conservation. *Ocean Acidification*. Scripps Institution of Oceanography, UC San Diego, 2007. Web. 13 Dec. 2010.

Denny, Mark W., and Steven D. Gaines, eds. *Encyclopedia of Tidepools and Rocky Shores*. Berkeley: U of California, 2007. Print.

Docksai, Rick. "New Greenhouse Gas Threat." *The Futurist* 43.2 (2009): 10-11. ProQuest. Web. 19 Oct. 2010.

Flannery, Tim. *The Weather Makers: How Man is Changing the Climate and What it Means for Life on Earth*. New York: Atlantic Monthly, 2005. Print.

Hawksworth, David L., and Alan T. Bull, eds. *Vertebrate Conservation and Biodiversity*. Dordrecht: Springer, 2007. NetLibrary. Web. 5 Dec. 2010.

Mercola, Joseph. "Critical Alert: the Swine Flu Pandemic Fact or Fiction?" *Original Internist* 16.2 (2009): 79-85. *Health Reference Center Academic*. Web. 19 Aug. 2009.

United States. Environmental Protection Agency. *The EPA Climate Change Kids Site*. EPA, 30 Oct. 2008. Web. 13 Oct. 2010.

8-1: Developing Main Points

Develop main points for each of the following topics. Be sure to carefully phrase and order the points.

1. **An informative speech about "Your favorite restaurants in Los Angeles"** using the spatial sequence.

2. **A memorable experience speech about "Fashion disasters"** using the topical sequence.

3. **An informative speech about "The Civil War"** using the chronological sequence.

8-2: Visualizing the Structure of a Speech

Speeches often sound fluid, like a continuous flow of ideas. However, underneath there is typically a structure much like the outlines that you have studied and created. But can you identify that structure? The following paragraphs are from a main point in a student speech. They are two subpoints in the first main point. Take this paragraph, identify the ideas and their support, and place them in the speech structure below.

"So what are bed bugs? They are small parasites, less than one quarter of an inch long, and about the size of an apple seed. They are reddish brown, flat, wingless insects that feed on human blood, typically when we're asleep. They get their name bed bugs, because they most often live in our mattresses and box springs.

But lately, bed bugs are being found in more places. Cnn.com of July 2, 2010 reports that several New York clothing stores were closed because of infestations, including Abercrombie & Fitch, Hollister, and Victoria's Secret. They have also shown up in hotels, banks, grocery stores, movie theaters, and dentists' offices. Dormwise, your essential college resource of July 14, 2011 also notes that bed bugs have gone to college. They've shown up in dorms and libraries of schools including Ohio State, Texas A&M, Stanford, and Florida. They are becoming a big nuisance as they can spread quickly in the close living quarters. According to CBS News August 30, 2010, New York ranks as the most bed bug infested city, followed by Philadelphia, Detroit, and Cincinnati. Los Angeles ranks at number 10."

I. Let's conduct an overview of the bedbug epidemic.

    A.

        1.

        2.

        3.

    B.

        1.

        2.

        3.

            a.

            b.

        4.

            a.

            b.

9-1: Write an Introduction

Attention device: _____

_____

_____

_____

Topic revelation statement:_____

_____

_____

_____

Significance statement (use a *source citation*): _____

_____

_____

_____

Preview of main points:_____

_____

_____

_____

Now, explain how you will achieve the goals of *rapport* and *personal credibility* during your

introduction: _____

_____

_____

_____

9-2: Attention Devices

Work alone or with a partner to come up with possible attention devices for the following two topics in each of the categories given.

Attention Device Category	Topic #1: How to play basketball	Topic #2: Illegal Immigration
Rhetorical question		
Real question		
Provocative or stimulating statement		
Reference to a recent event		
Humor		
Quotation		
Startling statistic		
Real-life story		
Hypothetical situation		

10-1: SCRAMBLED OUTLINE

Listed below are sentences taken from the body of an actual student outline for an informative demonstration speech about managing your credit. First, identify which statements are main points, which are subpoints, and which are supporting materials. Then organize them correctly by placing them in the blank outline provided for you.

Cars are also easily recovered collateral for the lender.

What is credit?

First, pay all of your bills on time.

Once you build credit, you must maintain it.

Simply put, credit is debt.

How does one get credit?

Credit allows you to purchase something before you have the ability to pay for it.

It is also important to monitor your credit.

Credit is a structured system to manage debt.

A good place to start is by obtaining a credit card.

A Consumer Credit Report tracks your credit rating.

Second, verify everything on the report is correct.

Do not apply for too many credit cards.

Car loans are an excellent way to build credit.

One way to manage your credit is financial responsibility.

Get a report from a national credit agency.

Car loans typically have lower interest rates than credit cards.

I.

   A.

      1.

      2.

   B.

II.

   A.

   B.

      1.

      2.

III.

   A.

      1.

      2.

   B.

      1.

      2.

10-2: Informative Outline Preparation Checklist

Before you turn in your speech outline, use the following checklist to make sure you have followed the principles and formatting for outlines that you've learned in class. Your instructor may have different or additional criteria for your outline, so pay close attention to his/her instructions!

Formatting

❑ All numbering and lettering is consistent

❑ Each I, A, 1, or a has a corresponding II, B, 2, or b

❑ Introduction, Body, and Conclusion are labeled

❑ All outline items are complete sentences

Content

❑ All four parts of my introduction are included (and labeled) and they will captivate my audience

❑ Both parts of my conclusion are included (and labeled) and they will wrap up my speech

❑ All transitions are included

❑ The required number of sources are cited and are formatted as they will be spoken in my speech

❑ Each of the major ideas in the outline are adequately supported

❑ The length and amount of information in each of my main points is balanced

❑ Each part of the outline contains one idea per letter/number (simplicity)

❑ Each part of the outline follows the principle of subordination

Works Cited

❑ The works cited page/section is labeled properly

❑ The citations are formatted correctly (indentation, alphabetization)

❑ The type of source (Web/Print/Film/etc) is noted for each source and all date(s) published and accessed (for web sources) are present

Other

❑ My outline is completely typed

❑ My outline is stapled

❑ My outline has been checked for spelling and grammatical errors

❑ My name is on the outline

❑ _____

❑ _____

❑ _____

10-3: Persuasive Outline Preparation Checklist

Before you turn in your speech outline, use the following checklist to make sure you have followed the principles and formatting for outlines that you've learned in class. Your instructor may have different or additional criteria for your outline, so pay close attention to his/her instructions!

Formatting

❑ All numbering and lettering is consistent

❑ Each I, A, 1, or a has a corresponding II, B, 2, or b

❑ Introduction, Body, and Conclusion are labeled

❑ All outline items are complete sentences

Content

❑ All four parts of my introduction are included (and labeled) and they will captivate my audience

❑ Both parts of my conclusion are included (and labeled) and they will wrap up my speech

❑ All transitions are included

❑ The required number of sources are cited and are formatted as they will be spoken in my speech

❑ Each of the major ideas in the outline are adequately supported

❑ The length and amount of information in each of my main points is balanced

❑ Each part of the outline contains one idea per letter/number (simplicity)

❑ Each part of the outline follows the principle of subordination

Works Cited

❑ The works cited page/section is labeled properly

❑ The citations are formatted correctly (indentation, alphabetization)

❑ The type of source (Web/Print/Film/etc) is noted for each source and all date(s) published and accessed (for web sources) are present

Other

❑ My outline is completely typed

❑ My outline is stapled

❑ My outline has been checked for spelling and grammatical errors

❑ My name is on the outline

❑ I appeal to **ethos** in the following ways_____

❑ I appeal to **pathos** in the following ways_____

❑ I appeal to **logos** in the following ways_____

11-1: Slang and Jargon

Create a glossary of three slang and five jargon words you know, including the term itself, a sample usage, and a definition.

Example: <u>Stat</u>. "Get that gurney in here stat." A medical term meaning immediately. (Jargon)

Slang Words

1. _____

2. _____

3. _____

Jargon Words

1. _____

2. _____

3. _____

4. _____

5. _____

Name:_____

11-2: Connotative and Denotative Meanings

Circle the words below you perceive to be positive. Draw a **line** through the words you perceive to be negative. Work quickly and don't leave out any words:

Family	Money	Broccoli	Freeway
Marijuana	Brown	Red	Age
Fast	Organized	Skinny	Children

When you have finished, compare your responses to the words with two or three classmates. Why were some of your responses different?

12-1: Critique a Visual Aid

Your instructor will show you a sample visual aid from a previous public speaking class. Even though you don't know for sure how it was used during the previous speech, critique the quality of the visual aid using the criteria explained in Chapter 12. Use this analysis to develop a one minute presentation in which you evaluate the visual aid. Be sure to use good techniques for handling the visual aid during your presentation!

Answer these questions about the visual aid:	YES	A Little Bit	NO
Does it have only one major idea?			
Does it look professional?			
Is it large enough for every audience member to easily see it?			
Is all the text legible to audience members in the back row?			
Is it attractive?			
Is there a consistent color scheme?			
Is it interesting?			
Is it creative?			
Is there too much text?			
Is it too cluttered or crowded?			

13-1: The Advantages and Disadvantages of Speech Delivery Styles

Complete the following table below using information from this chapter and your own thoughts:

Delivery Style	Advantages	Disadvantages	Appropriate situations for this style
Impromptu			
Extemporaneous			
Manuscript			
Memorized			

14-1: Informing vs. Persuading

The fine line between informative and persuasive speeches can be confusing at times. First, indicate which of the following specific purpose statements could be strictly an informative speech (INFO), or if they sound like they are instead persuasive topics (PERS).

Second, for the truly informative topics, identify whether they are best described as speeches of (1) description, (2) demonstration, (3) explanation or (4) revelation.

INFO	PERS	Topic	1	2	3	4
X		How a dialysis machine works to clean blood.			X	
		Why people should donate blood.				
		The different protocols of blood donation sites in the community.				
		Which local donation site is the best for donating blood.				
		Reasons why Jehovah's Witnesses do not accept preoperative autologous blood donation.				
		The risks and benefits of blood donation.				
		Types of people who are not eligible to donate blood.				
		Changes that should take place regarding the storage of donated blood.				
		The blood type classification system.				
		A new blood transfusion process.				
		How donated blood is used in our community.				
		Reasons why Medicare should pay for dialysis.				

15-1: Persuasive Topics

Come up with some possible topics for different types of persuasive speeches:

Desired Influence	Sample Topic	Your Topic Idea
Value-Changing or Reinforcing	Capital punishment is wrong.	
Belief-Changing or Reinforcing	Smokers have rights too.	
Action-Changing or Reinforcing	Set aside 10% of your paycheck in a savings account.	
Policy-Changing or Reinforcing	Let's maintain federal funding for the arts.	

15-2: Enhancing Ethos, Pathos, and Logos Appeals

Place each listed concept into one or more of the boxes below if you think it could build your ethos, pathos, and/or logos as a speaker. Keep in mind whether or not this is a content factor or a delivery factor. Items may be used more than once. Be prepared to explain your choices!

Appropriate Language

Articulation

Attire

Avoiding fallacies

Body control - solid stance

Caring

Clear language

Controlled Rate

"Don't drop the ball."

Facial expressions

Organization of ideas

Personality

Posture

Pronunciation

Source citation-publication

Source citation –date

Start strong, end strong

Support – Literal Comparison

Support- Definitions

Support- Explanations

Support- Facts/statistics

Support- Interactions

Support- Stories/specific examples

Support- Testimony

Support- Visual aid

Sustained eye contact

Transition statements

Preview & review statements

Transitional walking between main points

Vivid language

Vocal Variety

	Content Factors	Delivery/Speaker Factors
Ethos Builders		
Pathos Builders		
Logos Builders		

15-3: Problem/Cause/Solution Worksheet

General Goal:

Specific Purpose:

Introduction

Attention Device:

Topic Revelation Statement:

Significance Statement (Use a source):

Preview of Main Points:

Body

TRANSITION into **first main point** (I), an explanation of the problem:

I.   First Main Point:

    A.   Definition of the Problem:

    B.   Scope of the Problem (Who is affected? Where?):

    C.   Harms of the Problem*:

        1.   Economic (cost to society, individuals, etc.):

        2.   Environmental (conservation, safety, aesthetics, etc.):

        3.   Societal (justice, freedom, equality, sovereignty, etc.):

        4.   Psychological (pain and suffering, depression, rage, guilt, etc.):

        5.   Physiological (death, illness, injury, etc.):

* Does not need to include all types of harm, only those which are supported with sound evidence and reasoning.   continued

TRANSITION into **second main point** (II), the causes of the problem:

II.   Second Main Point

    A.   First Contributing Cause to the Problem:

    B.   Second Contributing Cause to the Problem:

TRANSITION into **third main point** (III), the solutions to the problem:

III.   Third Main Point

    A.   Policy Changes Needed to Solve the Problem (if any):

    B.   Personal Action Changes Needed to solve the Problem (if any):

    C.   Attitude or Belief Changes to Solve the Problem (if any):

Conclusion

Statement to Review Topic and Main Points

Lasting Thought:

Final Call for Action:

Works Cited

List all works cited:

16-1: Brainstorming

Instead of just envisioning your future as a public speaker, let's time warp to the future and brainstorm a few lists about speeches you might one day give:

Possible presentations your desired profession might require	Possible speaking occasions your personal life or education might require	Possible speaking occasions your involvement in clubs, community groups, church or other groups might require

See the "Time Warp Speech" assignment in *Appendix A* for a related speaking assignment.

17-1:Impromptu Speaking Brain Archive

Choose four major categories of knowledge (ex: US history, Literature, Movies, Famous Inventors). For each category, pick four specific examples about which you can speak for a minute or so. List several major themes or topics related to your examples. When you prepare your Impromptu speech, refer to this list to help you generate ideas for supporting materials!

Sample Category: Movies

The Lion King	Family, destiny, revenge, leadership, "hakuna matata"

Category 1: _____

Example	General themes/topics related to this example

Category 2: _____

Example	General themes/topics related to this example

Category 3: _____

Example	General themes/topics related to this example

Category 4: _____

Example	General themes/topics related to this example

17-2: Impromptu Speech "Notecards"

Use the following blank templates to help prepare your practice impromptu speeches or your graded speech in class. This is only a suggested format. Be sure to follow your instructor's model for impromptu speaking that you learned in class.

Attention Getter:

Topic revelation statement:

My opinion on the topic:

Preview

POINT/EXAMPLE #1:

    Explanation/Support:
    Link to Topic:

POINT/EXAMPLE #2:

    Explanation/Support:
    Link to Topic:

Review
Lasting Thought:

Attention Getter:

Topic revelation statement:

My opinion on the topic:

Preview

POINT/EXAMPLE #1:

    Explanation/Support:
    Link to Topic:

POINT/EXAMPLE #2:

    Explanation/Support:
    Link to Topic:

Review
Lasting Thought:

FROM FRIGHT TO MIGHT:

TEXTBOOK

LEGEND

As you read the book, look for these helpful graphics to orient you to special information:

 **Fright to Might Moment**

 **Important Concept**

 **Reference to Other Chapters**

 **Speaker's Secret**

CHAPTER ONE

AN INTRODUCTION TO SPEECH COMMUNICATION

The mind is a wonderful thing. It starts working the moment you're born and doesn't stop until you speak in public.

-George Jessel

In May of 1851, activists from around the country gathered in Akron, Ohio for the second National Women's Rights Convention. The activists spoke about womens' right to education, the right to own property and, perhaps most importantly, the right to vote. Several members of the clergy had also come to the event, mostly to heckle the speakers. None of the women could quiet these protestors who booed and hissed at their opposition. Then, an older African American woman came forward to speak. She was 54 years old and a former slave who had chosen the name Sojourner Truth. She turned to the man who had just ridiculed women as too weak to be given the right to vote and spoke these words:

"The man over there says women need to be helped into carriages and lifted over ditches, and to have the best place everywhere. Nobody ever helps me into carriages or over puddles, or gives me the best place – and ain't I a woman?"

Later on in the speech, Truth stated:

"If the first woman God ever made was strong enough to turn the world upside down all alone, these women together ought to be able to turn it back , and get it right side up again! And now they is asking to do it, the men better let them."

Sojourner Truth's "Ain't I A Woman" speech was so powerful it not only silenced the hecklers and brought several audience members to tears but would also go on to be considered one of the most influential civil rights speeches in the history of American public address.

As you deliver speeches in this course, you will become part of the vivid history of American public address. For many of you, this class also marks your first venture into the field of communication studies: an academic discipline that examines the way human beings use words, body language, and countless other forms of symbolic expression. Perhaps this is the first time you will receive training in a specific type of communication called public speaking. As you begin, realize that public speaking is only one form of communication. Scholars also examine the way we communicate in one-on-one interactions, how we communicate in our rituals and performances, how we transmit messages in businesses and other institutions, and the many ways we are affected by mass media like television and the Internet. Communication is a huge part of our lives, but what exactly does the word mean?

WHAT IS COMMUNICATION?

Think about how often we use forms of the word communication in everyday conversation:

We just don't communicate anymore!

Let's keep the lines of communication open.

Communicate with your kids about drugs.

Communication is the means by which we interact with our world and is the basis for all of our learning and relationships. Even though the word is central to our lives, we rarely stop to consider what it means. Even among scholars, the word communication has been interpreted and defined in literally hundreds of different ways.

A Definition of Communication

Communication: An interactive process of sharing symbols in order to construct meaning.

Let's break down some of the concepts in this definition. The word **interactive** suggests an active engagement between two or more individuals or points of view. While we might think that this requires two people to be involved, many scholars expand this definition to include the possibility of communication with animals (interspecies communication) and even with ourselves (intrapersonal communication).

Communication is also a **process**, which means that it is ongoing or continuous. In fact, there is an old saying in the communication field that, "You cannot not communicate."

A **symbol** is anything that stands for something else. In speech communication symbols can be **verbal**, since words represent ideas or concepts, or nonverbal. **Nonverbal** symbols include gestures, facial expressions, posture, clothing, and even the distance between the participants.

Finally, we put these symbols together to form messages that allow us to make sense of the world around us and **construct meaning**. When we construct meanings, we interpret the symbols from the communication interaction through the lens of our own experience to gain understanding.

A Model of the Communication Process

One way to get a clearer grasp on the concept of communication is to consider an operational "model" of the various elements present in the process.

A Model of the Communication Process

Sender

Message

Channel

Receiver

Feedback

Interference

Context

One of the most vital elements in the communication process is the **sender**. The sender originates the **message**, or the content of the communication.

The **channel** is the way the message is conveyed between the participants. For instance, when you watch a televised sporting event, the channel, or medium, is television.

The **receiver** is the recipient of the message, who may respond with **feedback**. Recognize that feedback is essentially another message, which demonstrates the interactive process described in our definition.

Sometimes messages are altered or obstructed in the communication process because of **interference** — factors that get in the way of or change the intended message.

Finally, **context** is the term for the environment in which communication occurs. The context can include the time of day, location, recent events, and the relationship of the participants, all of which can shape the communication act.

Identify the elements in the communication model in each of the following examples:

81

- A young woman yells at her boyfriend in a busy shopping mall. He says nothing, turns around, and walks way.

- Stella walks into class wearing her Air Force uniform. A classmate stands and salutes.

- You are lost in the desert. You build a fire and send smoke signals for help.

- A father sings to his baby in a busy airport, tying to make her fall asleep.

- Samantha, the family doberman pinscher, barks and whines until her owner lets her outside.

- A young child carries on an imaginary conversation with a teddy bear.

- After watching American Idol, you text your vote for your favorite singer.

Public Speaking Defined

The specific type of communication you will study in this course is **public speaking**. In their 2007 book *Mastering Public Speaking*, George Grice and John Skinner explain that public speaking occurs, "when one person speaks face-to-face with an audience." They add that, "the audience may be as small as your public speaking class or as large as the masses of people who fill stadiums."

Even though the focus in a public speaking situation is on the **speaker** (the sender), the **audience** (the receiver) plays an important role in providing feedback during the presentation. Since communication is an interactive process, we must remember that participation by both the speaker and the audience is essential for effective communication in public speaking.

The Impact of American Public Address

In the 5th century B. C. a Greek man named Corax published the first book designed to educate students in the art of public speaking. Skill in oratory, or public speaking, was considered essential in ancient Greece as well as many non-Western cultures. West African history, for example, has been remembered and recorded for centuries in the speeches of a griot, or public storyteller. The vast oral traditions of the Winnebago, Lakota, and other Native American tribes attest to the historic power and richness of live performance as a means of sharing information and teaching values.

Today, public speaking remains an important activity in many cultures throughout the world, but it is not always equally valued and protected by those in power. The United States stands out as one of the few nations that has fortified the right to speak as one of its founding principles. When the first amendment to the U.S. Constitution was adopted in 1791, it guaranteed every citizen the freedom to speak and express opinions. While this right has not always been extended equally to everyone, this nation's history is full of vivid reminders of the power of public expression.

American presidents have used public address to help change the course of history. President Abraham Lincoln gave speeches like his famous "Gettysburg Address" to argue for the abolition of slavery and to help our nation overcome the ravages of civil war. During the 1930s, President Franklin Delano Roosevelt delivered his "fireside chats" over the evening radio to encourage legislation that would help usher in the New Deal—a variety of programs designed to create jobs, grow the economy, and reform the financial sector. In the 60's, President John F. Kennedy ushered in a new era of personal responsibility by urging Americans to consider "….not what your country can do for you, but what you can do for your country." In 1986, President Ronald Reagan was scheduled to give his annual state of the union address when news broke that the Space Shuttle Challenger had exploded and its seven-member crew had perished. Reagan used the moment to deliver a moving tribute to the astronauts lost in the tragedy. Current political leaders continue to build upon this legacy of speechmaking. Then-Senator Barack Obama's 2008 address "A More Perfect Union", whose title references the preamble to the United States Constitution, addressed race and inequality in our country. It is considered one of the key speeches that eventually led to his election as President.

> **Have you ever visited or lived in a country that did not allow for free expression? How, if at all, was is different than the U.S.?**

The power of speechmaking has not been reserved only for this country's presidents. For example, Susan B. Anthony was a teacher who became an important civil rights leader by publicly advocating for women's right to vote during the late 1800s. Perhaps our country's most renowned orator, Martin Luther King Jr., began his journey as a reverend before leading the African-American Civil Rights Movement during the 1960s with famous speeches like "I Have a Dream" and "I've Been to the Mountaintop." Using King as his inspiration, farm laborer Cesar Chavez championed the rights of his fellow workers through strikes, non-violent protests and speeches like "Breaking Bread for Progress," delivered in 1968. In the 1970s, small-business owner Harvey Milk got on an actual soapbox in San Francisco to fight for the rights of gays and lesbians with speeches like "Tired of the Silence." Milk's speech argued that invisibility was the gay community's greatest hindrance and motivated hundreds of people to "out" themselves in response.

There is no doubt that the history of our nation would be significantly different were it not for the public speeches of these important leaders. But just as important as these leaders are the average citizens who exercise their right to free speech in classrooms, courthouses, town halls and public spaces across the nation. Although these everyday speeches may not be written about in textbooks, they still hold the power to shape people and communities. The power of **free speech** and expression is often evidenced by the ways in which it is regulated and patrolled. Students at the University of California at Davis found this out the hard way when they were pepper-sprayed by police while taking part in the Occupy Movement at their school in 2011. Despite the potential hazards, however, the history of our nation will certainly continue to be defined as well as shaped by the influence of public speaking.

GOALS OF PUBLIC SPEAKING

People speak in public for a variety of reasons, such as to teach a lesson, sell products, commemorate an occasion, inspire an audience, or remember a loved one. Even though there are many purposes for giving speeches, most can be categorized as having one of three primary goals: to **inform**, to **persuade**, or to **entertain**.

Certain speeches are designed to fulfill one of these goals. For example, a classroom speech discussing how to create a web page is primarily a speech to inform. Other speeches may achieve multiple goals, such a speech that uses humor to convince listeners to exercise regularly. It may be designed primarily to persuade, but it may also entertain. Understanding your primary goal is helpful when preparing a speech. In speaking, as in life, clear goals lead to more successful outcomes.

Identify the primary goal of each of the following speech topics:

• My most embarrassing moment

• Immigration

• Changing your car's oil

• Flu vaccinations

• Racism

Is it possible that any of these topics could be adapted to meet two or even all three public speaking goals? It is important to remember that you, the speaker, will determine the objective of each speech you deliver.

GOALS OF THE PUBLIC SPEAKING COURSE

Your classroom speeches may sound and look different than speeches you will encounter in the real world. You will be required to give verbal source citations for your research, use limited notes, and follow strict guidelines for preparing your written outlines. Since it is impossible to address all the specific public speaking situations that you will encounter during your life, these rigorous standards and skill building speeches will best prepare you for speaking in the real world.

BENEFITS OF PUBLIC SPEAKING

Many of you may be here simply because this course is a requirement. That is a pretty good reason to take it, but it is not the only benefit to be gained from studying and practicing public speaking. There are also academic, career, and personal benefits.

Academic Benefits

Public speaking is not the only class where you will be asked to deliver a speech. Many professors require oral presentations in courses as diverse as art history, French, or even physics. Your professors know that if a student has the ability to explain material in a speech, he or she truly understands the information. Be sure to apply all that you learn in this course when completing speaking assignments in other classes. All of your presentations should be logically organized, supported with relevant research and content, and delivered in a clear and engaging style.

When choosing a major and/or minor, you may wish to consider speech communication as a field of study. Many attorneys, counselors, entertainers, and business people major in communication before pursuing specialized training. The table on page 86 lists just some of the careers related to a major in communication.

Also, if you want additional experience with public speaking, consider joining a club or organization that offers performance opportunities. According to their website, as of July 2011 **Toastmasters International** had more than 12,500 clubs in 113 different countries where group members gather to perform speeches and hone their communication skills. You can find a local organization at www.toastmasters.org. Your college likely has many groups that also offer speaking opportunities such as student government, mock trial, and drama. The most comprehensive training in public speaking is available to you if your school has a forensics team, which has nothing to do with crime scene investigation. In this usage, forensics is another name for competitive speech and debate. However, it is worth noting that Anthony E. Zuiker, the creator of the forensic investigation television show CSI, competed for several years on his college's forensics team.

Jobs in Communication

Speechwriter

Journalist

Mediation Specialist

Non-Profit Director

Political Analyst

Press Secretary

Media Critic

Television Reporter

Trainer

Lobbyist

Motivational Speaker

Sales Representative

Diversity Consultant

Public Relations Coordinator

Speech Instructor

Sports Promoter

Reporter

Editor

Author

Public Defender

District Attorney

Corporate Lawyer

Private Practice Lawyer

... many others!

Career Benefits

Unless you win the lotto or retreat to the wilderness to hunt and fish for your survival, one day you will likely enter the work force (if you have not already). No matter what your employment, chances are that effective communication skills will be vital to success in your career.

Most members of professional organizations, from CEOs to entry- and mid-level employees, are expected to speak both within organizations and to the public. In fact, according to Julia Wood in her 1998 book *Communication Mosaics*, during any given 24 hour period of the work week, professionals will deliver more than 30 million presentations. The November 1, 2001 issue of *Career World* cites a report from the National Association of Colleges and Employers that claims, "The top ten qualities employers seek have little to do with technical skills and a lot to do with personality and attitude. Employers want team players with great verbal and written communication skills."

Even if you enter a profession in which you will not be expected to deliver speeches or interact with the public (which is highly unlikely), everyone must interview for a job. The skills you acquire in this course as well as other communication courses can help you land a job and succeed once you are hired.

Personal Benefits

Public speaking can also provide the personal benefits of improving your overall knowledge and confidence. Putting together an effective speech makes use of a variety of critical thinking skills including researching, organizing, analyzing an audience, and writing. Expect these skills to improve as you progress through the course. You will also gain valuable knowledge about the topics you cover in your speeches and the topics covered in your classmates' speeches. All in all, this class is a fantastic opportunity to improve skills and gain knowledge about a number of compelling issues and topics.

Public speaking can also improve your **confidence**. As discussed in the next chapter, most people have anxiety about speaking in public. Learning to control that anxiety will make you a more confident speaker and will also build self-esteem that may help you overcome other obstacles in your life.

Becoming an effective speaker will also help you become a more dynamic member of your community. We live in a democratic society that depends on truly informed and active citizens. Whether you're running for political office or just speaking up at a city council or school board meeting, the power of public speaking will help you shape and direct the community in which you live.

CONCLUSION

In this chapter, we have introduced the concept of communication – a concept as old as recorded history. We have also looked at the importance of public speaking both to our society and its citizens. We have considered the goals of public speaking as well as its academic, career, and personal benefits. This is just the beginning.

Speaker's Secret

As you begin work in this course, don't be intimidated if you feel you are not a "born speaker." Remember that no one is born as a good speaker, or a speaker at all for that matter. All communication skills are learned, and we can improve our communication skills throughout our lives. This course can be an important step in that process.

FROM FRIGHT TO MIGHT MOMENT

As your first speech approaches, there is a strong likelihood that you are feeling a little apprehensive or nervous. Take a moment to talk to some of your new classmates and you may discover that you have a very sympathetic audience for your first speech.

CHAPTER TWO

SPEECH ANXIETY

There are only two types of speakers in the world: those who are nervous and those who are liars.

— *Mark Twain*

Academy Award-winning actress Reese Witherspoon feels it. Television host David Letterman admits to it. Even your public speaking professor has probably felt it many times. According to *Communication Quarterly*, February 2006, public speaking tops the list of fears in the minds of most people.

Speech anxiety, sometimes called stage fright, speech phobia, shyness, and performance anxiety, is a very common phenomenon, but for newer speakers, it can be overwhelming. In the academic world, this fear is called **communication apprehension**.

Feelings of anxiety can show up as late as the last point of your speech or as early as the moment the speech is assigned. You may have already felt it in this class. If so, you aren't alone. Public speaking is probably the class that students fear more than any other.

Communication researcher James McCroskey advanced our understanding of communication apprehension over three decades ago, identifying two types of stage fright: **trait apprehension** and **state apprehension**.

Human Communication Research, Volume 4, 1977, reveals that trait apprehensive individuals are those who are nervous in many types of situations and are often identified as shy. State apprehensive individuals are only nervous immediately before and sometimes during a speech. Even professional speakers, McCroskey found, felt the symptoms of state apprehension which included shaking hands, a pounding heart, sweaty palms, chest pain, dizziness, or butterflies in the stomach. Sometimes the symptoms can be even more severe. Feeling nauseous, having to go to the bathroom, and even fainting are known to occur in speakers.

Some Symptoms of Speech Anxiety
Racing Heartbeat
Sweating
Nausea
Breathing Difficulty
Dry Mouth
Shaking/Twitching
Wringing of Hands
Nervous Laugh
Panic
Pacing
Procrastination
"Blanking"
Negative Self-talk

Psychologically, speech anxiety may cause everything from **procrastination** (putting off preparing a speech) and **negative self-talk** (convincing yourself about all of your flaws) before the speech, to **"blanking"** (forgetting what to say next or forgetting a portion of your content) during the speech.

As you prepare to speak, your brain tells your body it needs assistance to get through the task at hand. Because you may view public speaking as an emergency, your brain sends the signal to your body that causes the release of a hormone called **adrenaline**. This hormone causes increased heart rate that leads to increased muscle tension and accelerated body systems, called the **fight or flight reaction**. If you *fight*, you're going to respond to the challenge to the best of your ability by preparing and delivering the best speech possible. If *flight* is your choice, you will avoid the causes of this anxiety by missing the speech, withdrawing from the course, or even dropping out of college.

Unfortunately, many students consider dropping public speaking classes or changing majors to avoid public speaking. People with speech anxiety are known to receive poorer grades in school, and many of these students are more likely to drop out of college. They also cannot perform certain jobs. Perhaps this is why public speaking is widely known as one of the top human fears.

REASONS FOR SPEECH ANXIETY

Speech anxiety can be caused by a number of different factors, most of which are in our control.

Often, our **lack of speaking experience** is to blame. Remember the first time you rode a bike, rode a roller coaster, or drove on a freeway? Perhaps you felt anxiety. In most instances, the more times you do something, the less nervous you will feel. No one expects you to be good at something the first time you try it. The same is true with public speaking. Most people in college have not had the opportunity to give many formal speeches in their lives. Much of the nervousness you feel may simply be from doing something unfamiliar to you. Additionally, most of us have never taken a class such as this one to help reduce anxiety. Mike Aoki, a corporate public speaking coach, writes on his website **Reflective Keynotes** that, "if you've never been trained to research, write, and deliver a speech, you should feel scared."

Other factors can also enhance anxiety. Perhaps you had a **prior negative experience,** such as a classmate laughing at you during a class presentation.

Actor James Earl Jones, who was tormented as a child because of his stuttering, credits public speaking for allowing him to overcome this problem. Even though there may just be one brief episode in our past, it can impact us for years to come.

Almost all young children want attention. However, as they grow older, things can change. They may find themselves avoiding the spotlight and experiencing **the fear of being the center of attention**. If you have speech anxiety, search your past. When was the first time you recall not wanting people to pay attention to you? **A prior negative experience** could be a factor in your anxiety.

Reasons for Speech Anxiety

Lack of Experience

Prior Negative Experience

Fear of Being the Center of Attention

Low Self-Esteem

Concern about Being Judged

High Stakes

Feeling Subordinate to the Audience

Feeling Different than the Audience

The Degree of Unpredictability

Self-Fulfilling Prophecy

Excessive Self-Focus

Low self-esteem increases anxiety. If you don't feel good about yourself, then you may not feel you have anything meaningful to share with an audience (even though you probably do). People who are not confident about their abilities often have **concern about being judged by the audience**. Often we let what others think about us mean more than what we think about ourselves.

The **high stakes** of a speaking situation can make even the most confident speaker quiver. Stakes are the potential outcome of a speaking situation, such as a job (for a job interview), a grade (for a class speech), or an award (for a speaking contest). The higher the stakes, the more nervous we may become.

Feeling subordinate to the audience implies feeling "less" than them in some way. If you had to defend yourself in front of a judge and jury, you might feel intimidated because of their positions and power. A similar concept is **feeling different than the audience**. This occurs when you realize that those individuals listening to you are not your peer group. For instance, a male speaking to an all female audience might be more nervous than he would be speaking to a group of mostly men. Other types of perceived differences between you and your audience that might impact your confidence level include age, income, ethnicity, economic status, and even being less well-dressed than audience members.

The **degree of unpredictability** of a speaking situation can enhance anxiety. This fear of the unknown happens when you find yourself in unfamiliar circumstances or in a situation where you don't feel in control. This might include being asked to speak at a moment's notice, having a speech location moved to a new venue, or even being asked an unexpected question during a job interview. This is why some people become especially nervous about giving impromptu speeches.

91

Some speakers act out the **self-fulfilling prophecy**. Speakers who are afraid they will fail tell themselves from the onset that there's no reason to prepare because they won't do well anyway. Because of this lack of preparation and negative attitude, they are not successful and therefore confirm in their mind their prediction of a poor performance.

Overall, probably the single biggest factor in speech anxiety is our **excessive self-focus**. Simply put, we spend way too much time thinking about ourselves and not enough time thinking about our audience. People often obsess about how they will be perceived by the audience - smart or stupid, attractive or awkward, funny or silly. Your speech is not about you. It's about your topic. You don't "speak for yourself," you speak for your audience.

There's an old wives' tale that suggests to get rid of speech anxiety, you should picture your audience naked. That's terrible advice. Instead, picture your audience dangling from a cliff, and imagine that the words of your speech are the information they need to pull themselves to safety. If you are focused on your audience and constantly obsessed with whether or not they understand what you are saying, you won't have a chance to worry about yourself.

It's natural to worry about how we appear to others, but confidence is one of the most important life skills we can possess. Learning to manage anxiety and achieve success as a speaker is a great way to build your personal confidence level. Remember, you present yourself to people all the time, every day. Speech is just an extension of the kind of communication you do on the phone, in person, or over the Internet. If you can push through your anxiety, you'll have the power to help, influence, and entertain your audiences much more effectively, and without fear.

STRATEGIES FOR ANXIETY REDUCTION

There are many things you can do before delivering your speech that may reduce your anxiety. Consider some of the following techniques.

Before the Speech

Prepare for the speaking event. Singers don't sing in public until they know the words to their song. Speakers should speak only when they have clarified their ideas, perfected the content, and practiced their delivery. The more you have prepared, the less anxiety you will experience.

Know your own strengths and weaknesses. Each public speaker has strengths and weaknesses. If you are a great storyteller, make sure to use that strength while giving a speech. By using what we know we do well, there is less to fear. Also, know your weaknesses. If you are uneasy with statistics, don't fill your speech with numbers. If numbers are needed, choose them wisely and place them where absolutely necessary. The more you know about your strengths and weaknesses, the better your speech will be.

Familiarize yourself with the speech situation so you can be in control of as many elements as possible. Arrive early to the room where you will be giving the speech before the audience is seated. Walk to the area in which you will be speaking and practice your delivery. Examine how far away the audience will be from you. Adjust the lectern, if needed. Practice with the microphone if you are using one. You will eliminate potential fear that might cause you to be less effective.

Get ready to speak physically and mentally. Before you give any public speech, you need to make sure you are physically and mentally ready. Get enough sleep the night before. In particular, be cautious about the amount of caffeine you consume, since too much may give you the jitters. Deep breathing can also relax your body. Take a few deep breaths before you are called upon to speak.

Many professional trainers **prepare mentally** as well. They call this "visualizing" – an exercise in which you picture yourself performing a task successfully before you attempt the task. To try it, close your eyes and imagine yourself giving a perfect speech. Notice your delivery, the organization, and the response you want from the audience. This type of visualization can help overcome the fear that you won't be able to complete the speech because you have already "seen" yourself do it.

Realize your audience wants you to do well. Because you are enrolled in a beginning public speaking course, all of the other audience members or students will be giving speeches, too. They are less apt to judge your mistakes because they can relate to your situation and will likely be more compassionate. In most beginning public speaking classes, audience members are very supportive of each other.

Know that it looks worse from inside. We are our own worst critics. You are going to feel more nervous than you look. Your audience cannot see everything you feel. Because of the higher energy level we experience while speaking, we lose some perspective. A pause that is only two or three seconds in length may seem like an eternity when standing before the class. After you finish your speech, a classmate may comment on how effective the pause was in the speech. It may have been enough time for that person to catch up and understand the point you were making. Audiences tolerate a few mistakes from beginning speakers because it demonstrates they are learning the process of speech-making.

During the Speech

Sometimes anxiety flares up during a speech performance. Consider the following advice to reduce your anxiety while you are speaking.

Accept that you are experiencing some level of fear. Don't dwell on the fright. Acknowledge it and move on. Don't forget that some fear is beneficial to public speakers. As discussed earlier in this chapter, when we experience fear, adrenaline causes us to become energetic and more alert, giving us the extra strength needed for gesturing, projecting, and being involved in our speech. Adrenaline is the same hormone that athletes depend on, and you can make it work for you in the same way. Many advanced speakers claim that the only time they worry about a speech is when they don't feel any fear.

Engage in positive self-talk. Each time a negative thought enters your head, dismiss it with positive affirmation. If you think, "I cannot do it," replace it with, "I can and will do it." Tell yourself that you have prepared properly for the speech. Affirm that your topic is worthy of sharing with your audience.

Breathe. While you are speaking, remind yourself to keep taking regular, deep breaths. Many speakers are afraid to stop talking long enough to breathe regularly and this can create a tense feeling in the chest or even make a speaker feel faint.

Don't apologize for being nervous. By calling attention to your nervousness, you ask the audience to notice an issue that would probably go unnoticed otherwise.

Focus on the audience, not yourself. If you concentrate your energies on how the audience is reacting to your speech, you will have little time to worry about yourself. Instead of wondering if the audience likes you or thinks you are a good speaker, focus on whether or not the audience understands your message. Many speakers feel an immediate improvement in their anxiety level if they can get past thinking about themselves and instead think about the audience.

After the Speech

After the speech is over, you should **evaluate yourself** to help build your confidence for future speaking situations. It is very healthy to evaluate your performance once it has been completed. This evaluation must be done in relation to where you are as a public speaker. We would not expect a beginning public speaker to evaluate his or her performance in the same manner as a professional motivational speaker.

CONCLUSION

In this chapter we have discussed what some consider to be one of the top fears of Americans - public speaking. We have examined the reasons for speech anxiety and how to overcome it. If, as you progress through this course, you experience anxiety, revisit this chapter for assistance in managing your fear. Also take note of "From Fright to Might Moments" at the end of most chapters where the authors have given you additional ways to build your confidence as a speaker.

Speaker's Secret

Gain experience by speaking as often as possible. Volunteer as a public speaker, reader, trainer, or guide. Seek opportunities where you can give presentations. Every time you give a speech, you will become a better, more assured speaker. You will stop feeling afraid of public speaking and begin to look forward to the opportunity provided to you.

FROM FRIGHT TO MIGHT MOMENT

Give yourself permission to grow. Many people feel they are the same today as they were yesterday. However, a quick check will show that not to be true. Even if you feel afraid of speaking today, keep an open mind about how you might change in the next few weeks or months. You may just surprise yourself.

CHAPTER THREE

PREPARING YOUR FIRST PUBLIC SPEECH

I'm speechless. I have no speech.

— *George Costanza, Seinfeld*

Your professor is probably about to assign your first public speech. Perhaps you've done some ice breaker activities, but now the first speech is coming up. Carefully preparing the content of the speech is very important. The Boy Scout motto is, "Be prepared." It's a philosophy just as important in public speaking as it is in camping and hiking.

Preparation is all the work you do prior to a speaking event to shape your content and delivery. Preparation time for an impromptu speech can be very short — one minute, 20 seconds, or even less. Preparation for an important speech can also take hours, weeks, or even months. For instance, it is not unusual for the President of the United States and his or her staff to prepare for more than a month for the annual State of the Union address. Unfortunately, many student speakers do not prepare sufficiently for their speeches, and the result is often a disappointing performance.

The importance of preparation in public speaking cannot be overemphasized. There are many advantages of preparation, including:

• Preparation can improve your speech content and delivery.

• Preparation may increase your **credibility**, the perceived authority that you have to speak about your topic.

• Preparation decreases your anxiety.

An old Chinese proverb says, "The journey of a thousand miles starts with a single step." The road to becoming a great communicator never ends. There is always something to learn, but for now, you need to start somewhere. This chapter addresses the beginning steps to start you on your journey.

97

THE TOP 10 MOST IMPORTANT STEPS FOR BEGINNING PUBLIC SPEAKERS

STEP 1: CARE

The first step is to **care**. It sounds so simple, but you must care when you stand up in front of the room. Your professors see so many students who walk up to the front of the room who look like they just don't care and would rather be somewhere else. Maybe they are trying to look cool, or perhaps they chose a topic they find uninteresting. For whatever reason, they seem bored or distant.

This completely ruins a performance. An audience must invest valuable time to listen to your speech. Showing you care proves to them you appreciate the investment they are making in you. Marco Benassi, a professor at the College of DuPage in Illinois, writes in *Six Keys to Effective Public Speaking*:

"Your audience will NEVER care more than you do."

Find something to care about in every speech you give. If you don't care about your topic, your audience, or yourself, you can't possibly get a message across to others.

Audiences can tell if you care through the energy in your voice, the expressiveness of your face, the confidence of your body language, and the preparation and quality of your work. Caring actually smoothes over mistakes you make. If your audience knows your speech is important to you, they will want you to succeed.

STEP 2: ORGANIZE YOUR THOUGHTS

Organization is the process of planning out the information and ideas in your speech so there is a clear, logical structure that the audience can easily identify. A speaker who rambles or drifts from idea to idea is difficult for an audience to follow. Every time you speak, establish a clear pattern for your thoughts. Consider your speech a journey that requires a beginning, middle, and end.

Speeches should all include three major areas: an **introduction** (beginning), **body** (middle), and **conclusion** (ending). The body is typically the longest part of the speech.

Within the body, you should delineate separate **main points**. To determine your main points, you can brainstorm all the interesting ideas you hope to include, then group related ideas until you have just a few major areas to discuss.

You will learn many more ways to organize the body of your speeches in Chapter 8 and learn more about writing introductions and conclusions in Chapter 9. For your first speech, though, be sure to plan out each segment of your presentation. Your professor may give you a specific structure to follow.

STEP 3: START STRONG / END STRONG

You have probably heard the adage that, "you never get a second chance to make a first impression." Perhaps you have also been advised to always leave a "lasting impression." The importance of the first and last impression we make as speakers is due to a phenomenon known as the **primacy and recency effects** of communication. Our brains tend to recall things that occur at the beginning and ending of a presentation more easily than what occurs in the middle. This is why the first and last moments of a speech are so crucial.

When it comes to the start of your speech, *Business Week Online* of September 12, 2006 quotes an interview with talk show host Oprah Winfrey in which she explains that, "a powerful beginning will stick with your listeners. Make yourself interesting from the start."

Approaching the front of the room, or **taking the stage,** should be performed with confidence and professionalism. Don't stall or shuffle your feet. Make eye contact with audience members as you walk up, and move confidently to the center of the room. Pause before you start to let the audience visually orient themselves to you. Smile. Breathe. Begin.

When it comes to the content of your speech, pay special attention to the first and last lines of your presentation. Your first line grabs the audience's attention, and your last line will create their final impression. Know exactly what you plan to say. You may even want to memorize the beginning and ending lines of your speech so you can look directly at your audience during these sections.

At the end of your speech, exit in a professional way. Don't run off hastily. Hold your eye contact, and then leave slowly and with confidence. Never end a speech by saying, "That's it" or "I'm done." Even though you hear it done a lot, also avoid saying "thank you." The fact that it is done often makes it a **cliché**, a phrase that has lost its meaning from overuse. It is best to let a meaningful idea resonate in their minds, rather than a meaningless phrase like "thank you." Instead, practice the delivery of your last line so that your speech has **closure**. Raise your pitch and volume slightly near the end of the line, then pause and drop your pitch at the end of the sentence. This is a nonverbal cue to your audience that the speech has finished, and can help avoid the awkward moment when an audience isn't sure if they should applaud or not.

STEP 4: LOOK GREAT / FEEL GREAT

Your audience will make a number of determinations about you by your appearance, just as you probably do when you visit an airport or mall and "people watch." If you were to stand in front of an audience silently with no expressions at all, what would your appearance communicate?

The audience sees you before they hear you, so make that first impression a positive one. Strive to speak in professional and class settings wearing **professional attire**. In America, professional attire usually includes a jacket and tie for men and dress pants or a skirt paired with a collared blouse or jacket for women. Even if you can't afford expensive clothes, you should still make sure what you are wearing is clean and ironed.

How you dress for a speaking event is another way in which you communicate caring. When you have a big date or are attending an occasion like a wedding, you probably dress up to show others that the event is important to you. You may wear a suit or a nice dress to a funeral out of respect for the person who has died. You will communicate to your audience in the same manner by dressing in the best professional clothes you can afford for your speech performances.

You can also make sure you look good by avoiding **appearance distractions**. The table below summarizes some common appearance problems that distract your audience from your message.

Not only is it important to look great, you should also *feel* great. Your physical well-being is key to a great performance and can also impact your outward appearance. Make sure you are well-rested, have eaten, and have had plenty of water before giving your speech. You may want to bring a bottle of water with you to class. If you do, make sure to leave it at your desk when it is your turn to speak.

Common Appearance Distractions

Loud, shiny or flashy jewelry (especially on or around the face)

Poorly fitted clothing

Chewing gum

Hats, sunglasses, or glasses which conceal the eyes

Prominent fingernails

Revealing shirts and skirts

Clothes with logos and messages

Being less well-dressed than your audience

STEP 5: SHOW YOUR PERSONALITY

The next step is hard for some people while easy for others: **show your personality**. Each person has a unique personality. Some may be shy while others are outgoing. Of course, even people described as shy can be expressive when you get to know them. Even if you don't think you have an especially dynamic personality type, you can use this opportunity to develop and define your own style.

Often, because of anxiety, speakers freeze up when they get in front of an audience and speak softly or without much animation, even though this isn't how they talk with their friends and family members. Showing your personality means that you talk with your audience with the same natural enthusiasm you show to those who are close to you.

Greg Dolph, a former professor at Mt. San Antonio College, always advised his students to "make friends with your audience." When speaking, we are spending several minutes communicating with the people in the audience and should let them get to know us a bit during that time, just like we would if we met them at a social gathering.

The number one way to show your personality in a speech is with your **smile**. Smiles communicate feelings of goodwill and invite the audience to listen to what you are saying. Even if you have a negative or sad message to share with them, find a few opportunities to smile so that the audience will like and relate to you. An audience can dislike a message, but still like the speaker.

Another effective way to show your personality is by incorporating your **sense of humor**. Try to add a little humor to every performance. Audiences respond very well to humor if it is natural and stems from your personality. Be careful, however, to avoid making remarks that could be interpreted as being offensive, or your humor could have a negative result.

Finally, use your facial expressions and vocal inflections to **communicate how you feel about what you are saying**. If you say during your speech, "I ate a big piece of broccoli," the audience should be able to tell based on your delivery whether you love eating broccoli or hate it. It is vital that you don't just let your words alone do the work of communicating your ideas. It is very uninteresting for an audience to listen to a speech that is mechanically recited from a manuscript without feeling.

STEP 6: NEVER DROP THE BALL

Just like in sports, an important rule for new speakers is to never drop the ball. **Dropping the ball** happens when you make a mistake while speaking, but it is not the mistake itself. A ball is "dropped" the moment that you verbally or nonverbally call attention to your mistake.

Naturally, people stumble or even blank out occasionally, but how they handle it in the moment makes a big difference. A speaker who drops the ball may roll her eyes, make a twisted face, verbally apologize, lose her confident posture, giggle, or even walk away.

When you make a mistake, it is very hard not to comment on it, but try. When you stop talking about your topic and start talking about yourself, the speech loses focus and becomes about you. Dropping the ball also causes you to lose credibility.

A speaker who holds on to the ball will not comment on the mistake. She will simply stay "in the moment," maintaining eye contact, holding her last expression, and concentrating until she is ready to start speaking again.

Finally, never ask, "Can I start over?" If your audience has already seen you begin your speech, there is no starting over. They can't erase the impression they already have of you. Just stay focused, and pick up at the next place you remember. By the end of your speech, the audience will hardly remember the mistake.

STEP 7: CONTROL YOUR BODY

Excessive, unintentional, or repetitive body movements can distract your audience. Judith Hall and Mark Knapp write in the 2005 book *Nonverbal Communication in Human Action* that, "Body language has a substantial effect on the way others perceive you." Fidgeting, shifting, wiggling, leaning, tapping, and even wandering around the room without purpose takes the attention of the audience away from the speaker's face and can communicate to the audience that a speaker is nervous, even when they aren't. Therefore, it is essential that you work to control some basic physical elements.

Learning to control your legs is an important first step. It's actually pretty easy, once you learn the **speaker's stance**. In the speaker's stance, your legs are shoulder width apart with your feet firmly planted and your toes pointing slightly outward. Your legs should be bent just a little bit (to avoid odd-looking locked legs), and your weight should be evenly distributed over both legs, not leaning toward one hip. This is a solid stance that communicates credibility and is not distracting.

If you have trouble keeping your legs planted firmly when you speak, practice by standing with your toes on two sheets of paper. Check back occasionally to see if you have moved off the paper. Also, choose your shoes carefully. Uncomfortable shoes, high heels, noisy shoes, and shoes that are too small can all make the problem of uncontrolled legs even worse.

Controlling your arms and hands is often the most difficult type of body control for beginning speakers. Avoid placing your hands behind your back, clasping them below your waist, or putting them in your pockets. Arms should be relaxed and at your sides.

It is not necessary to keep your legs and arms completely motionless during a speech. In fact, using **purposeful movement**, the term for intentional gestures and transitional walking, can be extremely effective. These techniques will be discussed later in Chapter 13. For the time being, though, it is important to make sure that your body is simply in control.

STEP 8: MAKE EYE CONTACT

Eye contact is a challenge for some speakers, particularly among those who have come to the United States from cultures in which direct eye contact is rarely made. In the United States, we are expected to make eye contact with people when we are communicating with them. Here, looking someone in the eye shows respect and builds trust. If you avoid people's eyes, you may be perceived as uninvolved, rude, or even untruthful.

Ultimately, your goal is to make **sustained eye contact** with individual audience members for a complete thought before moving on to the next point. For now, work on looking into the eyes of audience members while you are speaking. Be sure to look to both the left and right sides of the room, and not just at your professor.

STEP 9: CONTROL YOUR VOICE

Your voice is the primary way you communicate your message. The speed with which you verbalize words is considered your **rate** of speaking, and the relative loudness of your voice is considered your **volume**. Controlling your rate and volume are essential parts of getting your message to your audience.

Many new speakers find themselves talking too quickly to be understood. Take your time as you speak and control your rate. Remember to pause and breathe. Of course, you don't want to speak too slowly, but speeches delivered at a moderate pace are more likely to be understood and believed. Varying your rate during your speech will also add interest to your presentation.

When it comes to volume, it is not enough for your audience simply to be able to hear you. You need to **project** your voice past people in the front of the room so it reaches the back and sides of the room, as well. Your voice should be the dominant sound in the room, able to easily command attention even in the presence of interference from other sounds, like an air conditioner or a vibrating cell phone. The authors of this book agree that in all of our combined years of teaching, we have rarely heard a student in a public speaking class who spoke too loudly. Usually students are far too quiet to command the continuous attention of their classmates.

More advanced vocal techniques will be covered in Chapter 13, but for now focus on controlling these basic aspects of your voice.

STEP 10: REHEARSING YOUR SPEECH

Rehearsing is one of the most important and neglected parts of public speaking. Can you imagine performing in a play without ever rehearsing your lines? Or playing a competitive sport without ever practicing with your teammates? Practicing your speech is just as important. Unfortunately, students often arrive on speech day having practiced very little or sometimes not at all. If you have not practiced your speech before you come to class, then you are essentially practicing your speech in front of your professor and classmates. This is bound to increase your anxiety as well as the number of mistakes made in your speech.

Students often ask, "How many times should I practice my speech?" There is no stock answer. For some, ten times might be enough to be prepared, whereas for other students it might take thirty or forty rehearsals to be fully prepared. The best advice is to practice until you feel you are truly confident to deliver a strong speech. Remember, delivering your speech in the comfort of your own home can give you a false sense of security. A classroom environment is much different than delivering your speech in front of the mirror in your bedroom or while sitting in traffic.

Most speaking opportunities have strict time limits, and audiences do not usually respond favorably to speakers who exceed their maximum time. Unfortunately, humans are not equipped with an internal stopwatch and it can be very hard to gauge how long you have been speaking during an actual speech. Because of this, it is vital to time yourself several times with a stopwatch or a watch with a second hand when practicing. If you don't have a stopwatch, you can use another electronic device with a digital clock, like a cell phone or microwave oven. If you can rehearse your speech at least four times in a row while meeting the minimum and maximum time requirements, chances are you'll be in time during the performance.

Finally, try to **duplicate the classroom environment** as much as possible. Practice in empty classrooms to hear how your voice sounds in that environment. Most importantly, practice in front of people, especially if you are feeling anxious about the speech. Rehearsing in front of a live audience not only reduces your anxiety when your speech day arrives, but also gives you the chance to get constructive feedback on your speech. More importantly, it can improve your grade. An experiment reported in *Communication Quarterly* of February 2006 showed that students who practiced their speeches in front of an audience received higher evaluation scores from professors than students who practiced without an audience.

In 2009, Mt. San Antonio College opened the Speech and Sign Success Center (or SSSC), offering private videotaping rooms and speech tutoring. Ask your instructor for more information about using the SSSC to rehearse your speeches for this course. Use the SSSC forms on page xv of this workbook for verification.

The Top 10 Most Important Steps for Beginning Public Speakers

1. **Care**
2. **Organize Your Thoughts**
3. **Start Strong/End Strong**
4. **Look Great/Feel Great**
5. **Show Your Personality**
6. **Never Drop the Ball**
7. **Control Your Body**
8. **Make Eye Contact**
9. **Control Your Voice**
10. **Rehearse Your Speech**

CONCLUSION

This chapter has covered some of the basic elements for preparing and delivering your first speech. Work to master these basic steps with each speech you give. Later in the term, you will begin applying more advanced techniques to your speaking style.

Use these ten steps as a progress check for yourself throughout the semester. If you keep working on them, they can be a good way to track your progress from fright to might.

Speaker's Secret

Some popular ways to practice learning the content of your speech include:

- Using a smart phone or webcam to record your speech and watch it back several times
- Writing your speech or outline several times by hand
- Drawing a diagram of your speech so you have a visual picture of its content

FROM FRIGHT TO MIGHT MOMENT

There is no substitute for practicing your speech in front of real people. It's one of the best ways we know of to decrease speech anxiety. Find a practice audience (friends, family members, even classmates) and deliver a few solid run-throughs before coming to class. If you have prepared enough beforehand, speech day can actually be a very enjoyable and fun day.

CHAPTER FOUR

LISTENING

"Courage is what it takes to stand up and speak.
Courage is also what it takes to sit down and listen."
— *Winston Churchill*

An entire chapter devoted to the topic of listening may, at first, seem out of place in a textbook about public speaking. However, if you remember the communication model detailed in Chapter 1, the role of a receiver or listener is a necessary part of any communication scenario. In fact, without listeners, a speech really isn't a speech at all. Also, think about all the time outside of this class you spend listening to music, listening to family and friends, and paying attention to professors. These are just a few examples of moments when we find ourselves as the receivers of information. Research reported in a 2009 *International Journal of Listening* article confirms that listening remains our most-used communication skill, comprising almost 25% of our waking hours. Developmentally, most children listen first and then use the skill to learn to speak, read, and write. Even as early as our days in the womb, we listen to our mother's heartbeat.

You might think that with all this time spent listening, we would be effective listeners. Unfortunately, many people are poor listeners. The authors of the 1983 book *Effective Listening* report that 48 hours after hearing a ten-minute speech, an average listener comprehends and retains only 25% of the information they heard.

DANGERS OF POOR LISTENING

Poor listening, sometimes called **non-listening** has several detrimental results. One of these is the **negative impact on the speaker.**

When a speaker looks into an audience and sees faces that are clearly distracted and uninvolved, he or she can be very disheartened. This unresponsiveness may even increase the speaker's anxiety. Often, audience members forget that they can be seen by the speaker and imagine themselves to be invisible "observers" of communication.

However, watching a public speaker is not like watching television; your involvement (or lack thereof) matters.

Poor listening also has a **negative impact on the success of the communication event as a whole.** Without good listeners, the entire communication process breaks down. You have probably heard about Martin Luther King, Jr.'s "I Have a Dream" speech delivered at the Lincoln Memorial in Washington, D.C. at the height of the civil rights movement. Despite his outstanding speech content and delivery, the event might have been a total failure had the audience not listened attentively, understood his message, and responded passionately.

Finally, poor listening has a **negative impact on the listener.** Poor listeners are often perceived as being rude, self-involved, or even less intelligent.

It's easy to understand why. If we lose 75% of the content shared with us, we end up with some pretty distorted information. **Message distortions** occur when the messages that are received are fundamentally different than those that were sent.

There are three common types of message distortion.

Omission means that the listener did not comprehend the entire message and is missing key elements. **Addition** occurs when the listener adds information and details from his or her own imagination. Finally, **substitution** occurs when the listener confuses the portion of the message they have heard with a different set of information and ideas.

Message Distortions

Omission

Addition

Substitution

We can easily embarrass ourselves on exams, at work, or in social situations when we fail to listen effectively and distort the messages we hear. The consequences are often more damaging than just momentary embarrassment. It sometimes makes our personal relationship with another person strained. It can cause us to perform a task at work incorrectly, jeopardizing fellow-workers or clients. When dating, it may cause what would have been an outstanding date to end early without a chance of ever seeing that person again. Clearly, a listener must begin the process of accepting the responsibility to listen and not just hear what people are discussing.

Listening is a vital element in the communication process, one which often needs improvement. To begin this improvement, we must first understand the process of listening itself.

THE FIVE STAGES OF LISTENING

Listening is not as simple as it may seem. Often it is confused with hearing, but that can be clarified. Once a speaker sends a message to a receiver, a five-stage process begins.

STAGE 1: HEARING

Hearing is the first stage in the listening process. Hearing is the natural, involuntary, physiological, passive process by which we take in sounds from the outside world and filter them through the inner workings of the ear.

Our listening skills can break down in the hearing stage. **Physical impairments** such as hearing loss may impact the hearing stage of listening. Another influence can be external noise. External noise can include auditory and visual interference from outside the communication transaction. We've all heard the sound of a siren cut through a conversation. Because of this interruption, we didn't hear what was actually being said.

Hearing	Listening
Involuntary	Voluntary
Passive	Active
Sounds	Sounds with meaning

STAGE 2: SELECTION

In **selection**, we consider all the sounds we hear and then choose certain messages on which to focus and others to disregard.

During the selection process several factors impede effective listening. **Preoccupation** with concerns about family, employment, or even an upcoming social event can prevent a listener from selecting to focus on the message of the speaker. Researchers contend that at least once per minute we stop focusing on the immediate message and take a mental vacation.

Another challenge during the selection stage is rapid thought. According to the 2010 book *Business Communication: Process and Product* by Mary Ellen Guffey, Patricia Rogin, and Kathleen Rhodes, while the average individual speaks at approximately 125-250 words per minute, the mind of the average listener can think up to 1000-3000 words per minute. This gives the listener a false impression that he or she can focus on other thoughts or messages and still follow the speaker. However, if you have ever tried to carry on a conversation with someone who is texting on a smart phone, you know this is extremely challenging and hard to maintain for more than a few minutes.

Message overload can also impact selection. When the brain has reached its limit of information, like too many complicated statistics or technical terms, the listener may stop paying attention to the message and focus on something else.

Finally, the **avoidance of difficult things** can be another obstacle to the selection process. If the speaker is discussing a topic that is too emotional for the listener to handle, or if the discussion appears to be too intellectual or complex, the listener may retreat to thinking about other things or go on a "brain vacation."

STAGE 3: INTERPRETATION

During **interpretation**, listeners assign meaning and begin to understand the speaker's message. We assign meanings through the filter of our particular life experiences, which are never exactly the same as others' life experiences.

Five Stages in the Listening Process

Hearing

Selection

Interpretation

Evaluation

Responding

An obvious example of a problem during this stage is listening to a speech in an unfamiliar language. While we may hear and select the speaker's message, our life experiences have not given us the language tools to interpret and understand the content. However, problems with interpretation extend beyond language barriers.

Sometimes listeners use their life experiences to make inferences about what a particular type of person will likely say, or how a particular type of speech will always sound. They decide how the content of a particular topic will unfold because they have heard the topic before and assume the speaker is conveying the same information. These listeners **jump to conclusions** - interpreting only a portion of the message and making faulty or even biased assumptions about the speaker or the content of the speech.

Even when we have the best intentions and try to interpret every detail, fact, and statistic presented, we listen too intensively and can miss the major concepts.

STEP 4: EVALUATION

In **evaluation**, the listener goes beyond simply interpreting messages and begins to draw conclusions based on certain questions: Is this information important? Is it appropriate? Is it true?

Gullible listening is accepting information at face value and not applying any critical thinking to what has been said. This can create disastrous results. A student in one class gave a speech encouraging the class to obtain credit to establish a consumer credit history, without warning the audience of the potential dangers. Another student, without questioning or considering the potential outcome of the total message, signed up for several credit cards. By the end of the semester, this particular listener was overextended and could not make his credit card payments. He should have listened more critically to the message being presented.

Evaluating the overall merit of a speech and a speaker is important. However, if you spend all your time focusing on the speaker's appearance and delivery or if you mentally argue and disagree with everything he or she says, then you are guilty of **overly critical listening**. If you are overly critical, you may start to rehearse arguments in your mind and stop paying attention to the speaker's words and ideas.

Also keep in mind that most audience members are **self-centered**. Audience members think about what benefits "self." If it's not apparent or if a speaker does not explain why the information presented is important to listeners, the lack of apparent advantages for listening can cause audience members to evaluate messages negatively and stop listening altogether.

STAGE 5: RESPONDING

The final stage of listening is **responding**. Ideally in this stage, listeners respond to speakers with verbal and nonverbal cues that demonstrate their comprehension of the message presented. Remember that communication is a constant transaction between the sender and receiver, so we are responding at all times while we are listening. This term was defined in Chapter 1 as "feedback."

Unfortunately, our responsiveness can break down in two key ways. First, listeners can send the speaker **negative feedback**. Frowning, snickering, or talking to a classmate while someone is speaking sends the message that the speech (or the speaker) is not important. This lack of respect may cause the speaker to perform poorly on their assignment.

Second, even though most research suggests that we are poor listeners, we seem to be quite talented at fake listening. **Fake listening** occurs in part because we are expected to pay attention and be courteous audience members. We all know the fake listening cues: the head nod, the smile, and the courtesy laugh. These may give the impression that we are listening. While it may seem more polite at certain times to fake listen, if our minds are elsewhere, then we miss out on a chance to receive potentially valuable information. Most importantly, when we participate in this type of unacceptable behavior, we risk the chance of getting caught "faking it" when we are asked to vocalize our response.

GENERAL LISTENING PROBLEMS

There are two final ways in which listening breaks down which can have an impact in any of the five stages of listening. First, **physiological listening problems**, including hunger, tiredness, or an upset stomach, can prevent the receiver from listening at maximum capacity. Second, our **lack of listening training** contributes immensely to our poor listening habits. According to an article in the *Washington Post* of February 20, 2001, less than 2% of adults have had any formal training in listening skills. Yet, listening requires instruction and practice in order to be successfully developed.

IMPROVING LISTENING SKILLS

Decades of watching television and interfacing with computers have made Americans into more passive participants in communication settings. If you talk to your television, it won't talk back. **Passive listening** is listening without being engaged. This type of listening has few benefits because we do not force ourselves to grow and learn.

Active listening is listening that is engaged. This interactive participation is vital for effective communication in class. Don't hide behind someone or sit in the back. Turn your phone off. Consider some self-improvement of your listening skills in two areas: the mind and the body.

Active Listening in the Mind

Psychologically, you can optimize your ability to hear, select, interpret, evaluate, and respond to a message through a few simple steps. First, when a message is presented to you, simply **decide that it is time to listen**. Deciding to listen to the message eliminates some of the distractions in the selection stage. Every time you find yourself on a "brain vacation," force yourself to return to the moment at hand.

Improving Listening Skills

Decide that it's time to listen

Focus your listening

Avoid jumping to conclusions

Look for common ground

Place yourself in a listening position

Use positive, responsive facial expressions

Follow basic rules of courtesy

While the speech is underway, you can also **focus your listening**. Compare and contrast ideas and issues and engage in a mental review of the speaker's main points. Examine the similarities as well as the differences presented by the speakers. Use the "extra" mental energy you have because of rapid thought to stay involved in the speech and avoid daydreaming. Also, pay careful attention to a speaker's evidence. This allows you to listen critically without sacrificing comprehension or being too gullible.

Finally, **avoid jumping to conclusions**. Delay or avoid judgment so you can fully hear the speaker's content. You can also **look for common ground**. Identify common interests you have with the speaker and/or the message to help account for the weight of your personal bias in the evaluation stage.

Active Listening in the Body

When we are listening we are also communicating nonverbally, so it is essential to monitor our physical responsiveness. A simple technique is to **place yourself in a listening position**, which includes facing the speaker, making eye contact, and keeping your body position open by avoiding crossed arms or a hunched back. Additionally, **use positive, responsive facial expressions** to encourage the speaker and send the message that you are open to new ideas.

People who send positive and encouraging nonverbal messages to speakers are considered **supportive listeners**. As you give your speeches in this class, you will undoubtedly be grateful when you see friendly, interested, and smiling faces looking back at you from the audience.

Of course, we must also **follow basic rules of courtesy**. Turn off cell phones and other personal electronic devices, refrain from side conversations, and avoid distracting noises that impede hearing and selection.

CONCLUSION

In this chapter we have discussed the vitally important, yet often neglected, skill of listening. In the end, remember that just as it is important to care about speaking, you must also care about listening. *The Journal of Instructional Psychology*, December 1999 states that, "Good listeners stand out in the crowd; they are cherished by employers, teachers, friends, and others. They get promotions and are better informed than are poor listeners. The benefits of listening improvement are tangible and vital to success and self worth." Remember, you don't just hear a speech. You need to actively listen to the speech to understand the presentation.

Speaker's Secret

Get adequate and regular sleep. A tired mind is an unfocused mind. Listening is key to learning, yet too many students are too tired to listen effectively.

FROM FRIGHT TO MIGHT MOMENT

Listening to your classmates' speeches is one of the best ways to reduce your nervousness on a big speech day. If you allow yourself to become involved in their messages, you won't be as likely to obsess about your own speech that is coming up.

CHAPTER FIVE

TOPIC SELECTION AND CLARIFICATION

The secret to being boring is to say everything.

– *Voltaire*

One of the greatest fears of speakers is that they will be perceived as boring. Enthusiastic and polished delivery can help you be more interesting. But above all, you need to have something interesting to tell your audience. Choosing the right topic is essential for an exciting speech.

Selecting and clarifying a topic for a speech is an important step in the speech making process. In certain instances, you will have little or no choice in the process. Your professor, for example, may assign you a topic for certain speeches. In the workplace, employers will often dictate the content of a presentation. For events like funerals or graduation, the nature of the occasion often calls for a speech about a predetermined topic. Sometimes, however, the choice is all yours. Given the opportunity, beginning speakers often choose topics about which they are already knowledgeable. But just because you are familiar with a topic does not necessarily mean it is the best topic for the assignment. In this chapter, we will discover the three steps in choosing a topic and then investigate strategies for clarifying the topic you have chosen.

TOPIC SELECTION

In an effort to help you decide on the right topic for each speaking occasion in a reasonable amount of time, we have identified a simple three-step process to help you choose a topic.

STEP 1: COMPILE A LIST OF POTENTIAL TOPICS

Three Steps in Choosing a Topic

1. Compile a List of Potential Topics
2. Evaluate Each Topic
3. Commit to One Topic

With the goal of the speech in mind, generate a list of as many potential topics as possible. First, brainstorm a list of topic ideas. Consider your interests, beliefs, hobbies, educational experiences, jobs, and cultural background; reflect on classes you have taken, and even places you have traveled. You may not find enough possible topics through **brainstorming** alone, though, so consider researching to find topic ideas. Browse magazines, bookstores, libraries, and web sites in general areas of interest to you and collect even more possible topics for your speech. Finally, you may discover some great potential topics by simply asking around. Ask friends or family members for ideas. Your professor for this class or in your other classes may have ideas to share with you, too. When creating this list, try not to limit the number of topics. Soon enough, you will have to start crossing some off the list, so give yourself as many options as possible.

STEP 2: EVALUATE EACH TOPIC

Evaluating a Topic

Is it appropriate for the situation/ assignment?

Is it researchable?

Is it interesting to me?

Will it be interesting to my audience?

Does the topic have impacts for my audience?

Can it be covered within my time limit?

Reduce your list of potential topics by asking the following questions for each topic. If you answer "no" to any of these questions for any topic on your list, cross that topic off and move to the next one.

1. **Is the topic appropriate for the speaking situation or assignment?** If you are asked to speak at a family reunion, you probably should not deliver a serious persuasive speech about a controversial topic. The topic should be more entertaining and personal. Similarly, if your professor asks you to prepare an informative demonstration speech, you would not want to select a persuasive topic. Be sure that the topic you choose is right for the general goal of your speech.

2. **Can I find enough research on this topic?** To prepare a speech, you will need a good understanding of your subject area. Your professor will even assign you a minimum number of sources for some of your speeches in this class. Before you commit to a topic, be sure to investigate to see if you can find enough information about your topic to prepare a complete and supported speech.

3. **Is the topic interesting to me?** Clearly, you will be more motivated to work on topics that interest you. However,

do not limit yourself to speaking only on topics that you already know or care about. The best speakers search for new topics and develop an interest in fresh subject areas.

4. **Will a speech on this topic be exciting or interesting for my audience?** Have you ever had to sit through hours and hours of someone else's vacation slideshow? If so, you probably understand the importance of choosing a topic that has some interesting and exciting elements for your audience. Speeches are delivered for the benefit of audiences, not the speaker. Try to select topics that will interest most of the people to whom you are speaking. Also avoid topics that have been discussed over and over again. If audience members feel like they have heard your message before, you will have a much harder time keeping their interest. Sometimes, great topics do not always sound so interesting at first. A few years ago, Mt. San Antonio College student Brandon Nakawaki won a national informative speaking championship with a speech about kudzu— a weed growing out of control around the world. While this may seem like a dry and uninteresting topic, he used humor, fascinating stories, visual aids, and unexpected facts to keep the audience glued to their seats.

5. **Does the topic have a direct or indirect impact on my audience?** A good topic will go beyond just being interesting and will also be relevant to the lives of audience members. Be sure there is a reason why your audience **needs to know** the information you are presenting. For instance, you could consider whether the topic will help your audience live a safer, happier, or healthier life. Will it help them make more money, have better financial security, or get a better job? Will it give them insights into a new culture or increase their understanding and acceptance of others? Will it challenge them to think about a timely issue or teach them about an important new development that will influence their lives in the future? Be sure you can clearly explain in one to two sentences how your topic will have a significant payoff for your audience by the end of the speech. You do not want to speak and then immediately be forgotten.

6. **Is the topic area too large to cover in my allotted time?** A common mistake that speakers make is to select topics that are too broad. Could you really talk comprehensively about "television" in an eight-minute speech? You could speak for hours and not thoroughly inform your audience about "television." Choose a topic that you can cover thoroughly. Narrow your focus to a subset of the original area. For instance, more suitable topics in the area of "television" might include "violence in children's cartoon shows," or "how a television works," or "advances in high definition television." You will probably find it much easier to write a speech with a narrow topic area.

Scrutinize each possible topic idea you have using this list of six questions. If you answer "no" to any of them, go back to step one until you find a topic that meets all six criteria.

STEP 3: COMMIT TO YOUR TOPIC

Although it might be scary, commit to your topic as early as possible. Your professor may also want to approve your topic. Try to complete this step as early in the speech making process as possible to give yourself plenty of time to develop the content of the speech and to practice your delivery. Also, you should not switch topics late in the process. Some speakers find a new topic idea just a few days before a major assignment and change their topic — often with disastrous results.

TOPIC CLARIFICATION

Once you have made your choice of topic, the time has come to clarify exactly what you will be speaking about by writing out your speech goal, specific purpose, and topic revelation statement.

Speech Goal

The first step in topic clarification is to write out the **speech goal**. This is fairly easy since, as you might recall from Chapter 1, there are only three goals: to inform, to persuade, or to entertain the audience. After committing to one topic, we recommend revisiting the instructions your professor has given you for this speech and to make sure your topic fulfills the assignment. Mistakenly choosing a persuasive topic for an informative speech (or vice versa) is a frequent problem in basic public speaking courses. For example, if you want to inform your audience about the importance of wearing seat belts, your goal is actually to influence the behavior of your audience, and you should probably save this speech for your persuasive presentation.

Specific Purpose

The second step in topic clarification is to write out the **specific purpose**. Writing out a specific purpose statement can help you narrow and focus your topic. The specific purpose explains in detail what you will accomplish during your speech. Be realistic and describe only what you can cover in the allotted time. You may use the following formula to write your specific purpose:

> **Your speech goal + the audience to whom you are speaking + a precise description of your topic area = specific purpose**

For example:

> **Specific Purpose: To persuade my classmates to complete their drivers' license organ donor cards.**

Remember, the objective you state in this specific purpose statement must be accomplished by the time the speech has ended.

Topic Revelation Statement

Finally, the topic revelation statement (TRS) of your speech is a summary sentence explaining the specific content area you will discuss during your speech. Here's a sample TRS:

> **Today, I hope to convince you to complete your organ donor card, a generous, life-saving action for people of all ages.**

Four Features of a TRS

Conversational voice

Time indicator

Communicating verb

Vibrant adjectives

This example contains the **four features of a TRS** that distinguish it from the specific purpose. First, the TRS is written in a **conversational voice** using words and phrases that sound like a person speaking. Writing in a conversational voice is important since the topic revelation statement will actually appear in the text of your speech introduction. Second, the TRS begins with a **time indicator:** words or short phrases that create a sense of immediacy and alert your audience to the urgency of your topic. Some examples of time indicators include "Today," "In the next few minutes," or "This afternoon." Third, the TRS must always be a complete sentence with a subject (in this case "I") and a strong **communicating verb:** a verb that actively expresses your function as a speaker. The easiest choice might seem to be the verb from your speech goal. For instance, "I will *inform* you about..." However, be cautious of telling an audience that you "will *persuade*" them as this might create some defensiveness. Try a more accessible option: "I will argue that..." or "I will make the case that..." or even "I hope to persuade you that..." Some other good communicating verbs include:

Describe	Present	Demonstrate	Offer
Reveal	Assert	Tell	Compel
Express	Challenge	Show	Defend
Teach	Urge		

Finally, consider adding a few **vibrant adjectives** to make your topic sound more vivid. In the preceding example, the topic of organ donation sounds a lot more exciting after the speaker describes it as "generous" and "life-saving."

The topic revelation statement is possibly the most important sentence in your whole speech. If the audience doesn't recognize it when they hear it, they may struggle to understand the whole point of your speech. Therefore, you should spend some time crafting the most accurate and most exciting wording for this portion of your presentation.

CONCLUSION

To help you review the process of topic selection and clarification, let's consider the example of an actual student named Herman.

Herman was assigned an informative speech. He created a long list of topics (step one) by brainstorming and speaking with one of his biology professors. One of the topics on the list was "bugs."

Next, he evaluated the topics (step two). Although he decided that "bugs" was a topic of potential interest to his audience, and he liked them personally, he found that the topic was not suitable for his time limit of eight minutes. It was just too broad. Imagine how long it would take to actually cover the topic of "bugs" thoroughly! It's not possible to name every bug on earth in eight minutes, or even eight hours.

Herman narrowed his focus to cockroaches. Because he was speaking to a general audience, he decided to steer clear of complicated anatomical and biological aspects of the cockroach and instead commit to one topic (step 3): how scientists are using cockroaches to solve crimes, a branch of science known as forensic entomology.

Now he was ready to clarify his topic. First, he wrote his speech goal.

Speech Goal: To inform.

Herman made sure that his topic was indeed informative and not persuasive in nature. If he chose instead to speak about why cockroaches should be a protected species, he would need to revise his topic in light of that persuasive speech goal.

Next, he wrote his specific purpose.

Specific Purpose: To teach my classmates about the role cockroaches can play in helping forensic scientists solve crimes.

Now Herman had to explain the topic area of his speech in language suitable for his audience - his topic revelation statement:

Topic Revelation Statement: Today, I will introduce you to an unusual new detective on the crime scene investigation team: the cockroach.

After you have selected a topic and composed your speech goal, specific purpose, and topic revelation statement, you are ready to start your own detective work. Even though it's just one step in the speech making process, topic selection and clarification sets the stage for all that's to come.

Speaker's Secret

Here are some insider tips about places to find great topics. For informative speeches, try scienceblog.com which reports on the latest scientific inventions and discoveries. Persuasive topics can be found on the editorial page of newspapers. You can also tune your radio to NPR (National Public Radio) and your television to the Discovery Channel for coverage of fascinating and important topics. Ask at the Speech and Sign Success Center (SSSC) where they keep a list of hot topics for student review.

FROM FRIGHT TO MIGHT MOMENT

Choosing a great topic can actually help you overcome speech anxiety. A topic that is interesting and relevant to the audience will help ensure that they are focused on your message instead of you.

TOPIC IDEAS: INFORMATIVE SPEAKING

Automotive developments

Aeronautic developments

New surgical procedures

New medications & cures

Genetic discoveries

Space exploration and research

New security techniques

New trends in education

Unexplained phenomena

Military developments/technology

Unfamiliar cultures & traditions

Archaeological discoveries

Criminology developments

Good places to look for informative topics:

- Science Publications: *Science, Scientific American, Popular Mechanics, New Scientist, Discover...*

- Cultural/Anthropological Publications: *Smithsonian, National Geographic*

- Newspaper science and technology sections.

- Websites: scienceblog.com, popsci.com and technology sections of cnn.com, msnbc.com and abcnews.com, just to name a few

- Your professors in other classes. Ask them about the latest developments in their fields!

TOPIC IDEAS: PERSUASIVE SPEAKING

Dangerous things…

Eating & Driving

Gambling Addiction

Sleepy Doctors

Danger of Railway Crossings

Dangerous Playgrounds

Plastic Surgery Consequences

Unjust things….

Genetic Discrimination

Online Cheating

Racial Profiling

HMO Mistreatment

Desperately needed things…

Run for office

Minority Sports Coaches

Cruel things…

Elderly Abuse in Nursing Homes

Endangered Species Poaching

Controversial things…

Bilingual Education

School Vouchers

Term Limits

Prisoner Rights

Good places to find persuasive topics:

- Opinion pages in newspapers and weblogs

- Political publications: *New Republic, National Review, The Nation, Congressional Quarterly*

- Environmental/activist publications: *The Utne Reader, Sierra, Amnesty International*

- Browse pending legislation. Try starting at: http://dir.yahoo.com/Government/Politics/

CHAPTER SIX

AUDIENCE ANALYSIS AND ADAPTATION

There are apathetic, sleeping audiences that must be awakened; there are hostile audiences that must be defied and conquered; there are alienated or sullen audiences that must be won back; there are frightened audiences that must be calmed. There are loyal, affectionate audiences that must be further inspired. There are cool, skeptical audiences that must be coolly convinced. There are heterogeneous audiences that must be molded into some kind of unity.

–Houston Peterson

Just as the good host knows whether her dinner guest would prefer a juicy ribeye steak and a frosty margarita, or a fresh garden salad with a glass of pomegranate juice, the good speaker knows what type of information and delivery their audience would find most palatable. If your message is not audience-focused, you will probably lose the attention of your audience and, with it, your potential to have an impact with your speech.

Audience-focused communication exists all around you. Compare the advertisements in magazines such as *Vogue* to those in *Maxim*, *Teen*, or *Better Homes and Gardens*. The difference you notice in the photos and text is the result of thorough research. Advertisers engage in careful audience analysis that helps them adapt their message according to the needs, interests, values, and knowledge of their target audience.

Laurie Rozakis' 1999 book *The Complete Idiots Guide to Public Speaking*, cites the Volvo car campaign as an excellent example of audience analysis and adaptation, explaining that, "Its ads emphasize different benefits for different audiences: economy and durability in America, leisure and status in France, performance in Germany, and safety in Switzerland." Public speaking is no different. If you hope to accomplish your speech goal and actually inform, persuade, or entertain your audience, you will first need to understand them.

Perhaps you have heard the saying, "knowledge is power." That is the idea behind audience analysis — that knowledge of the audience gives you power to communicate effectively to them. If you are lucky, you have the luxury of surveying your audience. In other situations, you will only have your general knowledge of audiences to draw upon. Regardless, just knowing about the audience is not enough. It is the application of your knowledge that really makes you an outstanding communicator. This chapter will focus on both audience analysis and audience adaptation.

AUDIENCE ANALYSIS

Early in the preparation process for a speech, it is important to acquire as much information as possible about the anticipated audience for your speech in a process known as **audience analysis**.

Useful Audience Information

There are many types of information that are useful to you as a speaker that you will want to know. Consider the following questions about your audience and speaking situation:

1) Who is the anticipated audience for the speech?

It's hard to know exactly who will show up to an event, since traffic, illness, and other issues can always intervene. Still, a prepared speaker will know as much information as possible about the anticipated, or likely, audience for their speech.

The first type of information that you should consider is the demographic make-up of the anticipated audience. There are several demographic characteristics to consider.

Ethnic/cultural background and nationality. Your speech audience may be more diverse than your own neighborhood and may include people from backgrounds who are unfamiliar to you. As the ethnic composition of the

United States continues to change, more people have mixed ethnic heritage, as well, so simple designations of ethnicity often fail to take in the full complexity of an audience. Also, remember that individuals in your audience will not necessarily all be Americans. Being sensitive to the range of cultural viewpoints in your audience is an essential first step in understanding how best to reach them all with your message.

Age. Students in your classroom most likely represent a wide range of ages, and general audiences outside of school may have an even greater range of ages.

Gender and sexual orientation. Gender refers to a person's cultural, social, and psychological identification as male or female. **Transgender** individuals are people who do not identify with their biological sex characteristics. **Sexual orientation** refers to the nature of an individual's natural attraction to other people, and may be same-gender, other-gender, or both. Others may identify themselves as "**questioning**," a term used to indicate that an individual is exploring their gender identity and/or sexual orientation and is unresolved. While you may have a sense of how you personally view gender and sexuality, understanding your audience fully may involve widening that perspective.

Religious affiliation. The majority of people living in the United States hold religious beliefs, but the degree of involvement in religion and type of spiritual practice vary dramatically. Significant numbers of people are also non-religious. Having a broad understanding of many religions and associated beliefs (or lack thereof) is important for any speaker discussing a topic with a religious or spiritual component. It is closed-minded to assume that the audience shares your religious views or that they should.

Socioeconomic status. Socioeconomic status refers to the relative income level of a person taking into consideration factors such as cost of living. A person who makes $50,000 a year in some parts of the world is very wealthy, while that same person may have trouble buying a modest home in California. People with different economic positions have different challenges in life and different capabilities. Having a sense of their financial standing can help you better understand their needs.

Relational status. The relational status of individual audience members refers to their formal bond with another person, such as marriage, domestic partnership, a long term commitment, being single, or being widowed.

Other demographic factors include work experience, education level attained, political affiliation, and many others. These may or may not be important to consider depending on the type of speaking event and the topic you have selected to discuss.

Homogeneity is the relative similarity among a group of people or items, so an audience that is homogeneous will share many demographic attributes. Audiences in which there is a greater level of variety among individuals in the crowd would be described as **diverse**.

2) What is the audience's relationship to your topic?

Another question worth asking about your audience is about their relationship to your topic, if any. You may wish to consider, for instance, if they have any **previous knowledge** about your topic. If so, understanding what they know can help you determine what you will discuss.

Also, you may want to measure their **involvement** with your topic. For instance, if you have decided to speak about physical education for kindergarten students, it would be useful to know if your audience was likely to include many current kindergarten teachers. They may have different expectations and issues to consider about your presentation than a group of parents, for instance.

Finally, if you have a topic that could be controversial in nature, you may want to get a sense of your audience's **attitudes** toward your topic. You don't want to be caught by surprise to learn that your audience is very opposed to what you are discussing, or find that they already agree with your persuasive speech and you have wasted their time.

3) What is the environment for the speech?

Considerations about your physical environment for a speech, sometimes called **situational factors**, include the temperature, seating arrangement, seating comfort, lighting, and **acoustics**, another word for how the sound of your voice will travel in the speaking location.

Some of the information you may wish to find out in advance includes:

- The number of people anticipated to attend the speech
- How the audience will be dressed/dress code for the occasion
- The seating arrangement and location for the speaker
- Amplification (microphones), if any, that will be available

Also, you should try to find out what topics other speakers will be discussing, if possible, to ensure that you are not duplicating information and to highlight relationships between the presentations.

Finally, be aware that **recent events** could have an impact on your presentation. A big news event or a tragic incident will be in the minds of audience members and may need to be taken into consideration.

4) What are the audience's expectations for your speech?

The last and perhaps most important question you should consider is "Why are people attending my presentation?" Most people who choose to attend a presentation do so because they have expectations of what they will hear. Even captive audiences (like your speech class) in which people are expected to attend will still anticipate that certain outcomes will be achieved during a speech. Audience expectations generally fall into two categories: content and quality.

In terms of **content**, the audience may have heard that you are speaking about a particular topic, which means they will expect that the presentation is true to the description. They may also have an expectation about the length of the presentation or the opportunity for interaction with them (such as a question and answer session).

The audience may also have expectations about the **quality** of the presentation, including the level of preparation by the speaker and the anticipated skill-level of the delivery of the speech.

Questions to Ask About an Audience

1) Who is the anticipated audience for the speech?

2) What is the audience's relationship to your topic?

3) What is the environment for the speech?

4) What are the audience's expectations for your speech?

Collecting Audience Information

It's easy to figure out what you would *like* to know about your audience, but getting a clear picture of that information requires some effort. There are four primary ways to collect audience information: observations, research, interviews, and surveys.

Observations

Observations are the easiest form of audience analysis, but not always the most reliable. Before the speech, you can use your senses to perceive information about your audience. Some things that are best identified in this manner include factors like the seating arrangement, acoustics, and amplification.

Other factors may be harder to determine, including demographic factors and your audience's attitude toward your topic. A great use of observations for audience analysis, however, is during your speech. Use your eyes and ears to get a feel for how the audience is responding to what you are discussing.

Research

Research involves the search for relevant printed information about your audience. For job interviews, for instance, it is essential that you research the company to which you are applying and even information about people who will be interviewing you.

Many clubs and organizations have information available online about their members, and most colleges and government agencies make available demographic data, as well.

Interviews

Interviews with people who are familiar with your audience, or people who will be a part of your audience, can be a great way to get specific information you need to prepare your presentation.

Management communications advisor Jim Lukaszewski is quoted in the 1995 book *Successful Presentations for Dummies* as saying that it is customary for him to interview a few of his audience members briefly before he gives a presentation. He asks them the following questions: "If you could decide the focus of my presentation, what would you have me talk about? What about this topic is important to you?" Most people will appreciate your interest in their interests.

Surveys

In some speaking situations, you may be able to directly question the entire audience and then analyze their responses. In fact, your professor may ask you to create an audience analysis survey for one or more of your speeches. While not always possible because of logistics or time, surveys can be some of the most useful types of audience data you can collect, because they are tailored to your exact needs. Remember that you may need much more than just demographic information about your audience. Consider questions that provide insights about the audience's relationship to your topic, as well as their expectations for your speech.

Depending on the type of speech occasion, nature of the topic, and importance of the speech outcome, you may choose to select a very brief or an extremely detailed audience analysis. Regardless, the work you do to increase your audience understanding is a vital foundation for adapting to your audience.

AUDIENCE ADAPTATION

While knowing your audience better may help you feel more comfortable about speaking to them, it's only half of the process. Adapting your speech content and delivery based on what you have learned in audience analysis is the vital speech preparation step called **audience adaptation**.

Adapting to Audience Demographic Attributes

With the proper perspective, a general understanding of your audience's demographic makeup can be very useful.

Remember from Chapter 5 that your **topic selection** will be impacted by your audience's interests and needs, and demographic information may give you a good idea of what some of those interests are, or are not. For instance, if you discover that your audience is primarily composed of individuals with limited income, a speech about expensive resort vacations may not be an effective choice. A speech about reasonably priced or even budget vacations may be more effective and appreciated.

One of the most obvious mistakes that people make which audience analysis can prevent is the use of ineffective **examples** during a speech. It is always an awkward moment when a speaker makes a reference that the audience doesn't understand because of their age, educational level, nationality, or other factors. Many new professors learn this the hard way when they try to relate a concept to their class by comparing it to *Gilligan's Island*, which was a popular television show in the United States in the 1960s, but may be unfamiliar to younger students or those who did not grow up with American television. Similarly, if you were not born before the early 80s, you probably wouldn't connect with examples involving parachute zipper pants, LA Gear hi-tops, Swatch watches, and *Fraggle Rock*. If you were born in the 70s and raised in the United States, though, such nostalgic references would transport you back in time.

Also use your analysis to incorporate **language** that reflects your understanding of your audience's status, position, and knowledge. Regardless of how much they know about your particular topic, knowledge of their educational status may give you some clues as to how you should address them. You also want to be sensitive to diversity of sexual orientation among members of the audience. It's easy for heterosexual speakers to make the mistake of presuming all listeners are heterosexual. It's critical as a public speaker to be respectful of diversity of the audience members in all areas by avoiding potentially offensive remarks or references.

Of course, it is easier to adapt to audience demographic factors if your audience is more homogeneous. If you have an especially diverse audience, you will need to choose examples, language, and even speech topics with broad, general appeal.

Avoiding Stereotyping

While understanding and adapting to your audience is indicative of a respect for them, it is sometimes possible to mistake audience analysis for a more dangerous behavior: **stereotyping**. A stereotype is an oversimplified picture of people different from us, particularly those from another group, race or culture. You may be wondering, "How can I adapt without stereotyping?" As information is gathered, individual variations within the group must be accounted for so that a unique and fair evaluation takes place. The following suggestions may seem obvious, but sometimes speakers do or say things that unreasonably stereotype audiences. If we are not careful, our actions could seriously offend. Be sure not to make stereotyped references, use racial slang terms, or tell sexist or racist jokes. Although politicians sometimes try to emulate their audience (i.e., wearing a cowboy hat when visiting Texas), it is not a good idea to mimic or try to look like the members of a cultural group to which you don't belong.

In their 2005 book, *Presentations in Everyday Life: Strategies for Effective Communication*, Engleberg and Daly urge that you should not make universal assumptions about your audience such as, "they will live in mostly white neighborhoods if they are white and in mostly black neighborhoods if they are black; they will like chow mein if they are Chinese and fried green tomatoes if they're Southern; the husband is more likely than the wife to be the decision maker when buying a car." Avoiding stereotyping requires a deep understanding and respect for others; to that end, don't be afraid to learn as much as you can about your audience and acknowledge the differences you discover.

Adapting Based on the Audience's Relationship to your Topic

As discussed in Chapter 5, audience attitudes toward your topic and involvement with your topic area can influence your **selection of a topic** for your speech. Remember that a good topic needs to be both interesting and relevant to your audience.

Additionally, the audience's relationship to your topic can **alter the focus of your specific purpose** as well as the **complexity of content** that you develop during the body of your speech, especially when it comes to their knowledge about the topic area. You need to find the balance in your speech that avoids telling them what they already know, while also giving them information they will be able to comprehend.

For example, a student was preparing a speech about investing, and his survey data showed that few of his classmates understood the difference between a Roth IRA and a traditional IRA. He changed the focus of his specific purpose to investing strategies for beginners and included an area that explained the differences among different types of IRAs.

In another case, a student conducted a survey to determine his classmates' interest in his topic: fair trade coffee (a type of coffee that gives more profits to coffee farmers). Much to his surprise, he discovered that only three of his 25 classmates drank coffee. He kept his topic, but his specific purpose changed from persuading his audience to buy fair trade coffee to persuading his audience that coffee houses should offer more fair trade coffee.

Adapting to the Speaking Environment

Plan ahead. There is a wide variety of situational factors that require advance consideration. Even a seemingly minor distinction such as whether or not to use a lectern can have a dramatic impact on the feel of your presentation. For example, President Clinton was well known for his town hall style meetings in which the audience asked questions and he responded from in front of the lectern almost mingling among the audience. Removing the barrier between the speaker and the audience made him seem more natural and accessible. In some speaking situations, that level of immediacy is the effect you want; in others, you want the separation between you and the audience to be obvious. The seating arrangement is also worth considering. If your room has extra seats and you want to create a more cozy feeling, consider blocking off seats near the back or moving chairs to one area to discourage the audience from spreading throughout the room. Circular arrangements work well in small groups (perhaps a work meeting) where you want to foster a cooperative environment.

It is also imperative to know in advance the types of resources that are available to you (white board, overhead projector, television, radio, easel, etc.) before the day of your presentation so you don't arrive to discover you don't have the tools you anticipated.

Look the part. Your clothes should be neat, professional, and ideally at least as formal as your audience's attire. If you aren't certain what the audience will be wearing, be sure to ask a representative of your audience.

Arrive early. A timely arrival to your destination ensures that you have a feeling for the conditions of the venue. If you are speaking to audience members in the middle of summer in Arizona and the air conditioning in the building stops working, the message may not be as effective as you would hope. If the audience is sitting in such a way that they cannot see your visual aid, the impact of it is lost.

Choose the right speaking style for the size of the audience. The size of the audience makes a difference in how the speech is delivered. Small, intimate speaking situations call for a different style than large, formal groups. Most experts agree that a conversational approach is used when communicating with just a few (1-5) people. For instance, it is probably more appropriate to sit alongside your audience instead of standing in these situations. Conversely, audiences larger than sixty usually necessitate amplification (depending on the type of space in which the speech occurs). Bigger gestures, greater use of the stage, and more vocal variety are also appropriate adaptations for large audiences.

Meeting and Exceeding Audience Expectations

If you are aware of the audience expectations for your speech, be sure you either meet those expectations or explain why you cannot.

For instance, if you discover that there is a rumor that has widely circulated that you are an expert juggler and will demonstrate your skills during your speech, you should consider adding some juggling to your speech. However, if you can't juggle and are not sure how the rumor started, you may wish to **address the expectation** during your speech so the audience knows you didn't forget to juggle or, worse, intentionally leave it out of the presentation. Humor can be an excellent way to help diminish audience expectations when you feel they are too high. For instance, you might say, "While some of you may know I am an expert juggler, what may not be clear is that I am an expert juggler of statistics – which you will see as we review our third quarter earnings."

A good way to ensure that you have addressed all of an audience's content expectations for a speech is to **take questions** at the end of a presentation. Just be certain you are prepared to answer the variety of questions you might be asked, and limit the number of questions in advance to keep the presentation from going on beyond the expected time limit.

Meeting audience expectations is vital, but when possible, you should always deliver a speech that has been **customized** in some way for your specific audience. Let them know you thought of them when you prepared your presentation. In this way, you can often exceed their expectations.

BENEFITS OF AUDIENCE ANALYSIS AND ADAPTATION

Speakers who utilize what they have learned though audience analysis by adapting their speech content and delivery are likely to **maintain high levels of audience interest**, since they are less likely to address content that is inappropriate for an audience's knowledge or involvement level. They are also more apt to **achieve their speech goal**, as well as **meet audience expectations**; speakers who do not engage in audience adaptation may never know what the audience was expecting.

Additionally, the process can greatly help a speaker **handle adversarial audiences**. When addressing a highly controversial topic, an angry crowd, or an audience who has a prior negative perception of you or your topic, it is even more vital to have that information in advance, so you can make appropriate modifications to your speech goal, language, examples, delivery style, and other factors outlined in this chapter. Additionally, establishing rapport (see Chapter 9) and using humor can also be effective ways to help diffuse tension in an adversarial situation.

Finally, it is always unfortunate to see a speaker who delivers a speech without regard to his or her audience. Sometimes it is flatly embarrassing. Applying what you have learned through your audience analysis can help you **avoid embarrassing subjects or remarks**. For instance, suggesting that everyone relax by "hitting the bar for a stiff drink" to an audience with a large number of recovering alcoholics in attendance would not only be ineffective, it could also reveal the speaker to be insensitive and unprepared.

Even speech professors fall prey to this problem. During job interviews for a faculty position in speech at a community college, one candidate repeatedly referred to the school as "this university." The word "university" commonly refers to a school that awards graduate degrees, which a community college does not. A little research and use of the correct terminology for the school might have secured the candidate a position, rather than revealing a lack of preparation and concern for the college.

CONCLUSION

In this chapter, we have discussed the concept of analyzing your audience and adapting your message while preparing a speech. As you continue to work through the chapters of this book, don't forget audience analysis. Every choice you make in preparing and delivering your speech should be filtered through the simple premise of, "Is this the best way to reach my audience?"

As you analyze and adapt to your audience, keep in mind that you have your own unique style of speaking. This chapter is not suggesting that you morph into a totally different speaker every time you speak so you can accommodate your audience. That kind of change would be both silly and anxiety producing. It is simply suggesting that the application of knowledge is power. You know that audiences have varying attitudes, knowledge, personalities, and needs. If you can "stretch" your natural speaking tendencies so they are flexible enough to adapt to your audience, you will find that your audience will appreciate your effort and will, almost always, respond kindly.

Speaker's Secret

A quick and easy way for some last minute audience analysis is to use the "handshake technique," in which you arrive early to an event and meet members of the audience one-by-one. During these brief interactions you can get a feel for their attitude about your topic, their knowledge level, and sometimes even good ideas for humor or other ways you can relate to them.

FROM FRIGHT TO MIGHT MOMENT

Knowing your audience is the key to reducing speech anxiety by ensuring that you are focusing on them, and not yourself. Audience analysis will also make your message more likely to reach your audience, which is the true measure of success for a public speaker.

CHAPTER SEVEN

RESEARCH AND SUPPORT

The best way to sound like you know what you're talking about, is to know what you're talking about.

— *Author Unknown*

Sometimes people speak using only their own personal thoughts and experiences. If you delivered a memorable experience or introductory ice-breaker speech in this class, chances are your own general knowledge was enough to support the ideas in your presentation. More often than not, however, your own thoughts and knowledge are not enough to construct an effective speech, and you must turn to outside research and supporting materials.

Effectively incorporating research and support will ensure your **speaker competence**. When you stand in front of an audience to deliver a presentation, audiences expect that you have a special expertise in that subject area. But for many of your speech topics, you will not have the credentials to be considered an expert. Moreover, if you use outdated information, mispronounce words, include unsupported assertions, or deliver outright factual mistakes, you will damage the audience's perception of your competence. Imagine the difficulties informing or persuading an audience that views you as incompetent to speak on a subject.

Research and support give you the opportunity to build your speaker competence and, at the same time, provide you a chance to learn about new subjects. Once you are familiar with types of support, sources of research, and ways to integrate material into your speech, the process of research should become especially rewarding.

SUPPORT

An important distinction to make is the difference between the processes of research and support. **Research** is the process of reviewing an array of published materials (books, magazines, websites, etc), conducting interviews, and/or conducting field research in a subject area. The information you pull from your research sources to use in your speech is called your **support**. For some types of speeches, support may also be drawn from your own experiences or creativity. Whenever you make a claim or present a major idea in your speech, you must provide support.

Personal experiences are the easiest sources of support to find. Personal experience is the information we have accumulated through our observations and experiences including educational, professional, and family encounters. We often call this first-hand experience. While personal experience can be valuable, you usually need much more to support the claims in your speech. For example, let's say you make the claim that safety regulations for playground equipment are insufficient and then support this claim with a story about how your daughter fell off of a swing and injured her arm. With only one isolated example, most discerning audience members will not be convinced. While the story could be effective, you will need to look to other types of supporting materials to make your speech more believable and convincing.

Definitions can be particularly effective for difficult concepts. If your speech is about a scientific or technical subject, for example, you will probably need to define some terms that are unfamiliar to the audience. Keep in mind, though, not all definitions have to be **denotative**, or the literal definition from the dictionary. You can define through description, example, or just by putting something in your own words.

Descriptions appeal to our senses. They use creative and colorful language to make a concept come alive for an audience. When the audience can experience your spoken words through their senses of smell, touch, sight, sound, and taste, they are more likely to be affected by your idea and remember it when you are finished. If your speech is about the Australian Outback, your audience will be far more affected if you give vivid details about the sights and sounds of this area instead of just offering facts.

Explanations appeal to our curiosity and capacity for reason. They often focus on clarifying the reason something occurs or how an item works. For example, a speech about a new technique for fighting cancer will resonate more with the audience if they know how the treatment actually works in the body.

Examples are an extremely versatile and effective means of support because they show the audience an idea in real terms. They can be used to personalize or make human the point at hand. They also are used to clarify or reinforce a point. Notice that throughout this book, the authors have provided examples for most concepts to show you in real terms how they can be applied to a speech. Examples may be as brief as a mention of a name or idea. They may also be detailed, sometimes taking up a whole main point of your speech. When using examples, make sure they are relevant to your speech, and do not rely solely on isolated examples to prove your point. A single example can support a claim but it does not prove it. But, coupling an example with statistical data, for instance, is an excellent way to prove the scope or importance of a claim.

Factual examples have actually happened. They are stories of real people or real situations. The audience does not have to be familiar with the people or situations involved, but you should relate the example to the audience. For example, actor Michael J. Fox uses his own stories and experiences to urge audiences, lawmakers, and medical researchers to support research into Parkinson's Disease. Sometimes **extended examples** may take up an entire point of a speech, using aspects of the story to make the smaller points. Another common use of an extended example is one that recurs throughout the speech. It may begin in the introduction, return to make a point in the body, and conclude the speech. Creating a theme that is woven throughout the speech is a good way to help your audience remember your information.

Sometimes, you may want to try to get the audience to imagine themselves in a specific scenario. If so, you might want to use **hypothetical examples**—imaginary situations created by the speaker. Hypothetical examples should contain lots of details and description to have the audience truly create a mental picture. If you want to maximize the effectiveness of your scenario, avoid using the words "Imagine yourself..." You break the illusion of reality when you tell the audience to imagine. Also, never ask your audience to close their eyes as you share the hypothetical example. Some audience members don't like being asked to close their eyes, and many speakers forget to tell the audience when to open them. If your words are vivid enough, your audience will already be creating a mental picture.

Even though people may dislike math and numbers, they still like to see concepts put in numerical terms through **statistics and numerical data**. If you tell an audience that something costs "a lot" of money, their natural response will be, "how much?" If you tell them "a lot" of people believe something is true, they will wonder, "how many?" That's where statistics play an important role. They can clarify or expand an idea by adding quantitative backing. Some statistics you may use include ratios, averages, and percentages. Follow these **guidelines for using statistics** in your speech:

1. *Make sure your statistics are from a reliable source.* Any support should be from a good source, but statistics are especially important to check. The way they are generated, compiled, and reported all contribute to your credibility. Is it reasonable to claim that 80% of students at your school want additional physical education classes scheduled just because 8 of the 10 football players polled by the school newspaper said so?

2. *Identify the source of your statistics.* Identifying statistical sources is important so that audiences believe your claim. If one speaker in your class asserts that, "test scores in California public schools are decreasing," without offering the source for the claim, are you likely to believe that speaker? What if a second speaker claimed that, according to the 2010 California Department of Education annual summary report, "70% of public schools improved their academic performance index scores over the last five years?" If you had to choose between the two speakers, which one are you more likely to believe? In the last section of this chapter we will go into further detail about citing sources.

3. *Use numbers and units your audience can understand.* If your audience is primarily American, units such as kilometers, grams, or euros will likely be meaningless to them. Take the time to convert your numbers to familiar units. Additionally, round off numbers. Your audience doesn't need to know that 48.779% of people believe something. Simply saying "almost 49%" or "nearly half" will be easier for the audience to comprehend.

4. *Explain and clarify your statistics.* It is not enough just to present a number and expect audiences to understand what it means. Interpret the information for them. You may want to clarify the statistic for your audience by relating it directly to them (e.g. "Three out of four students receive financial aid. That means that roughly 25 people in this class get some form of assistance."). Another effective technique for adding impact is to put statistics into familiar terms. In his 2004 book *Presentations for Dummies* nationally acclaimed humor consultant and professional speaker Malcom Kushner offers this example of a speech delivered by the CEO of Unocal Corporation:

> Economist Thomas Hopkins estimates that federal regulations are costing American consumers $400 billion every year. How much is $400 billion? It's about ten times the size of our trade deficit with Japan. It is about double the annual cost of public education in America, from kindergarten through the 12th grade. It's about 33 percent larger than our entire defense budget. It's enough to give every household in America $4,000 every year.

5. *Don't use too many statistics.* Since statistics can often be confusing, make sure to use them only when your numbers improve the audience's understanding of your topic. If you need to use multiple statistics, consider using a visual aid to help the audience both see and hear your information. This strategy has two benefits. It makes sharing the information easier for you and digesting the information easier for them.

Visual and Audio Aids can also support a claim. Audiences can already hear your ideas, but visual aids allow them to see your ideas, too. Visual aids may both clarify an idea and make it more vivid for your audience. For much more detail about visual and audio support, refer to Chapter 12.

Testimony includes the use of direct quotations as well as your own rewording or paraphrasing of information. You may choose to use the words of average people, also known as **lay testimony.** You may choose the words of a specialist to prove a point. This is known as **expert testimony**. Any time you use testimony, inform your audience of the person's qualifications, which may include their experience or education. If your audience understands that the person you are quoting is qualified to speak about that subject, they will be more likely to believe the testimony.

Compare and contrast is a form of support that relates an unfamiliar idea to one the audience knows. It may also be referred to as an analogy. In a **comparison**, the speaker points out the similarities between the two concepts. When **contrasting**, the speaker highlights the differences. There are two common forms of comparison:

A **literal comparison** describes actual similarities between concepts that share physical or observable characteristics. This type of comparison is useful when comparing two programs or two policies. It is often used when comparing objects, events, or people. For example, a speaker might say, "The students in Japan are quite similar to American students except that they attend school more hours per day and six days per week."

A **figurative comparison** relates objects or ideas that may appear to have nothing in common. You may know it as a **simile** or **metaphor**. It compares the relationships between the unrelated items and asks the audience to make the connection more concrete. For example, "The student of today is like a juggler trying to keep all her plates in the air at one time. Between work, school, family, and friends she is always struggling to balance her many activities and responsibilities."

RESEARCH

Now that you know a little something about what to look for, let's examine where to look for it. You have many different research sources at your disposal, usually on your own campus and maybe online in the privacy of your home. Understanding and learning to use those sources efficiently will make research much more enjoyable. The suggestions here are by no means comprehensive, but they will cover the basics for three sources of research you should consider.

Web-based Research

The Internet is the most common way to access sources of research. Let's face it, nearly anyone can have a web page, which makes the Internet both a blessing and a curse when doing your research.

The web is a fantastic resource simply because of the amount of information available. Complete versions of most major newspapers and magazines are available on the web, as is a great amount of information from local, state, and national governments. Colleges, universities, and corporations publish tremendous amounts of research and information on their websites as well. These are all excellent places to look for information about your topic.

For every legitimate piece of information on the web, there is at least one suspect or false bit of information. This is largely due to the fact that the open nature of the web makes it difficult to have any kind of editorial control. When a newspaper or magazine is published, its articles are carefully checked and edited for accuracy. Often websites, especially personal ones, lack the careful research and fact checking that makes published materials reliable. Virtually anyone can post anything they want on the Internet. Therefore, the burden of checking accuracy and reliability falls on you.

There are several things to consider when **evaluating websites**:

1. *Look for clues to good information.* Does the website include the date the information was published or updated? Is the author clearly identified? Does the site give any information about the author's credentials or experience? Is the information on the site consistent with other sources you have found? Does the site reference credible sources?

2. *Identify the presenter of the information.* What organization is sponsoring or presenting this material? Is there an obvious bias? What can you find out about that organization's goals? Does the website have something for sale?

3. *Consider the domain name and extension.* These are contained in the site's address and usually provide clues about who is providing the information you have accessed. Some common domain names are listed below:

> **.gov - Websites of local, state, or federal governments, usually containing official information.**
>
> **.edu - Websites of colleges and universities. May contain official college pages, homepages of faculty/staff, and student homepages. Consider who at the college is publishing the information.**
>
> **.org - Websites of organizations that range from charitable to professional to political. Consider the organization's goals when evaluating information.**
>
> **.net - Originally intended for technical websites, this extension is now available to anyone and is often used by Internet Service Providers for personal web pages.**
>
> **.com - Often business or commercial websites, but may also be personal websites set up through internet services.**

While web-based research has become popular, it is not always the best source of information for your speech. For that reason, your professor may have specific guidelines or limits for web based research. Often students use the web exclusively because of its convenience, or their lack of experience using the electronic resources provided by their school. It is your obligation to find the best facts for your audience, not simply the most convenient information available. Once you know how to use the library's resources, you'll understand how truly convenient and effective they are.

Library and Database Research

Though the Internet has made it possible to access amazing amounts of information, it is important to remember that the libraries in our communities and on our campuses provide access to excellent resources for speeches. Article databases are well-organized tools to help you access relevant, credible information. Libraries pay tens of thousands of dollars to allow students access to these databases with full-text versions of magazine and newspaper articles, newswire releases, and television/radio transcripts. Databases such as EBSCO, ProQuest, and others are updated weekly or daily and will contain the most recent information on many topics. Although you access these databases online, it is not the same as searching the World Wide Web. The information you find in the school's databases are published articles by known sources with editorial scrutiny; the information posted on the Web is not necessarily subject to review for accuracy and fairness.

Searching these databases can be a bit tricky, as they can often produce too few or too many results to manage. Usually this is not due to a lack of information, but rather a lack of proper planning. Before you actually embark on significant research, brainstorm a long list of words that is capable of both expanding and focusing your results. To become a real pro at using the databases, consider attending a research class or orientation at your library. In the meantime, employ a few simple tips to make your searching more productive:

1. *Learn some simple Boolean search terms.* Words like "AND," "OR," and "NOT" can connect two ideas and narrow down very broad topics (e.g., baseball AND rules).

2. *Search within a date range.* Most databases allow you to search within a set of dates (e.g., after 2010). Start with the most recent dates and work your way back if you don't find enough information.

3. *Use quotation marks.* If a phrase or group of words is placed in quotation marks, typically a database will only find those articles that have that exact phrase or words. This will reduce the number of articles found and increase the usefulness of the results.

4. *Follow the directions for the database you are using.* Often a few minutes spent learning how to optimize your search will save you hours of time sorting through irrelevant results.

Visiting, calling, or emailing your school or community library is a great way to get help with your research process. You can also visit our library to work directly with many useful resources, since the library houses a large collection of books.

Among the library's books will be reference guides such as almanacs, biographical indices, encyclopedias, and periodical and newspaper abstracts or indices. These can be valuable sources of statistics or background information on your topic, so don't forget to check them out. Your professor may have information on specific reference guides that he or she prefers students to use.

Interviews

In addition to published materials, you may want to consider **interviewing an expert** on your topic as a source of research. An expert may provide you with information not available in published material or give you insight into a facet of your topic you haven't considered. Always brainstorm potential people to interview for your speech topics. Aim high — inventors, authors, and even politicians are often willing to talk to students if they know they are doing research for a class.

If you choose to do an interview, it is important to remember that you are using someone else's time. Consider the best way to contact the person: in-person, phone, or e-mail. Follow these guidelines if you are planning an interview:

1. *Contact the person well in advance of your speech.* You may have difficulty scheduling a time to interview them. Don't leave lengthy messages asking the person to call you. Try another time.

2. *Prepare your questions ahead of time.* Prior to contacting the person, know what you want to ask, in case they say "now" is the best time for an interview.

3. *Be courteous and professional during the interview.*

4. *Dress appropriately and treat the person you are interviewing with respect.*

5. *Ask permission if you plan to record the interview.* It is illegal to record a conversation without permission.

6. *Be sure to thank the person for the interview.* You may also want to send a note after the interview is over.

7. *Organize your notes immediately after the interview.* Write out the parts you want to remember and include in your speech. If you wait to do so, you may forget what the person said.

CITING SOURCES

A critical part of using research in a speech is to give credit in the speech to the source from which you obtained the information. This is called a **source citation** or "cite," for short. Using cites adds credibility to you and your ideas.

When to Cite

If you neglect to give proper credit to your source, you could be guilty of a serious offense called **plagiarism**. The Mt. San Antonio College 2010-2011 Catalog gives a thorough explanation of what some refer to as intellectual fraud:

Plagiarism is a direct violation of intellectual and academic honesty. Although it exists in many forms, all plagiarism refers to the same act: representing somebody else's words or ideas as one's own. The most extreme forms of plagiarism are the use of material authored by another person or obtained from a commercial source, or the use of passages copied word for word without acknowledgement. Paraphrasing an author's idea or quoting even limited portions of his or her text without proper citation is also an act of plagiarism. Even putting someone else's ideas into one's own words without acknowledgement may be plagiarism.

If a student is found guilty of plagiarism, most colleges have severe consequences such as a failing grade, probation, suspension, or expulsion. A widely publicized case involving a New Jersey high school student shows one potential outcome of plagiarism. Blaire Hornstine, an honor student with a 4.68 GPA and a score of 1570 on the SAT, was admitted to Harvard University in 2003. She seemed to be an outstanding student on the road to a bright future. When she got caught plagiarizing a series of articles she wrote for a local newspaper, however, Harvard promptly rescinded their offer. In an article in the June 3, 2003 Courier Post, Hornstine gave this explanation, "I am not a professional journalist. I was a 17-year-old with no experience in writing newspaper articles. Upon reflection, I am now cognizant that proper citation allows scholars of the future to constantly reevaluate and reexamine academic works."

Although you may be able to relate to her reasoning, her claim of ignorance was not acceptable, and chances are it won't work at your school either. It is your responsibility to be sure that you are not plagiarizing. If you are uncertain, talk to your professor. Faculty understand that sometimes it can be confusing to know when a citation is necessary. The following guidelines provided by plagiarism.org may also be helpful. The informative website argues that you must provide a source in each of the following situations:

1. You must cite a source any time you use an idea that someone else has already expressed.

If you are delivering a persuasive speech on healthy eating habits, it would not be appropriate to discuss a low carbohydrate diet as though it was your unique idea. Someone else deserves credit for the information.

Similarly, *Reality TV Magazine* reported that Chris Daughtry, a 2006 American Idol finalist, was called "a dirty rotten song stealer" by fans and the media when they claimed he took credit for a new version of the Johnny Cash song "I Walk The Line" that was actually done by the band Live.

These two very different examples make the same point. It is never okay to let your audience think (directly or indirectly) that what you are presenting is your own idea, if you know that it has already been forwarded by someone else.

2. You must cite a source any time you borrow from someone else's work to develop your own ideas. Changing a few words doesn't make it your own work.

On May 2, 2006, *The Associated Press* announced that 55,000 copies of Kaavya Viswanathan's book *How Opal Mehta Got Kissed, Got Wild and Got a Life* were pulled from shelves, and her two-book deal with the publisher was canceled amid rumors of literary borrowing. Viswanathan was not accused of copying word-for-word from other authors, but it was noted that her book has "comparable material" and "similarities in phrasing" to other books.

For example, in Meg Cabot's *The Princess Diaries*, published by HarperCollins, the following passage appears: "There isn't a single inch of me that hasn't been pinched, cut, filed, painted, sloughed, blown dry, or moisturized... Because I don't look a thing like Mia Thermopolis. Mia Thermopolis never had fingernails. Mia Thermopolis never had blond highlights."

In Viswanathan's book, page 59 reads: "Every inch of me had been cut, filed, steamed, exfoliated, polished, painted, or moisturized. I didn't look a thing like Opal Mehta. Opal Mehta didn't own five pairs of shoes so expensive they could have been traded in for a small sailboat."

3. You must cite a source any time you use direct quotations.

Keep direct quotations to a minimum. It makes your speech easier to remember and deliver, and it makes it more interesting for the audience. Nobody wants to hear a string of quotes sewn together; they want to hear you!

According to a October 2008 article written by a Cal State San Marcos librarian, titled "How to Avoid Plagiarism," it is acceptable to use a direct quotation when, "you need to document that the original author really does say what you claim he or she says, (since it is a surprising or out of character thing for this author to say), or when the original author's phrasing expresses the idea so well that no better expression can be found."

This is an example of a direct quotation. The exact language was used and the source was given credit.

4. You must cite a source any time you paraphrase.

When you re-express someone else's ideas using substantially different words and phrases, you are **paraphrasing**. Much of the research you incorporate in your speech can be paraphrased. To paraphrase properly, it is essential that you accurately convey the information and cite the original source of the information. The following is a paraphrased version of the direct quote used in the previous paragraph.

> *A Cal State San Marcos library publication argues that there are only a few instances when a direct quote is necessary. First, when the author says something unexpected, use a direct quote so that the audience does not think you misconstrued the information. The second instance in which you should use a direct quotation is when the original version is so eloquent that your rewording of it bastardizes its intent.*

Generally speaking, there is **no need to cite common knowledge**. For example, it would not be necessary to cite a source when stating, "Sacramento is the capital of California." This is widely known information. When stating the opinion that, "Sacramento, the capital of California, is one of the 100 best communities for young people," your audience members would need to know the source to evaluate its validity. The question of whether information is considered common knowledge depends on several factors, such as who the speaker is, who the audience is, and the expectations of each of these groups. You may be a dental hygienist, and it may be common knowledge to you that amalgam (mercury fillings) have been proven to be safe. Don't rely solely on your first hand knowledge when informing or persuading your classmates on this subject though. They will be much more likely to accept your claims if you couple your own credibility with the research of others in the field. When in doubt as to whether a concept or fact is common knowledge, provide a citation.

Indiana University's School of Education has set up a comprehensive website to assist individuals in understanding plagiarism. If you would like more help with the subject, visit http://www.indiana.edu/~istd/plagiarism_test.html to complete an interactive test of ten questions designed to help you recognize different forms of plagiarism. Upon receiving a score of 100 percent, you have the opportunity to print a confirmation certificate that demonstrates your understanding of plagiarism and how to avoid it.

How to Cite

It is not enough to know what to cite, you also need to know how to cite. **Citing sources** can be very awkward when you are getting started because they can be hard to remember. They also may not sound very natural at first, but you will soon get comfortable incorporating them into your delivery. Here are a few tips about source citations to keep in mind.

1. *Cites generally should be said before the information.* For instance:

> According to a study conducted by Dr. Frank Hu at Harvard University, reported in the June 2011 Journal of the American Medical Association, people who watch television just two hours a day have a 20% greater chance of developing Type 2 Diabetes.

Yes, you would actually say all of that. It may sound long and difficult, especially to memorize, but it's important. Not all cites are that long, but good cites make a big difference. What if it didn't include Harvard University? What if it didn't include the fact that Frank Hu is a doctor? What if we didn't know that the research is current or in a credible publication like the Journal of the American Medical Association? This might be a hard fact to believe on face value, but the cite makes it credible. Although we don't normally cite our sources in this fashion in everyday conversation, it is an effective method for a public speech. With practice, you will get increasingly comfortable and fluid, and you may even come to like the directness of such an approach.

2. *At minimum, cites should ALWAYS include the date and name of the publication or source being used.* It might also include the name of the person who presented the information and information about their qualifications. It could also include information about where a study was conducted, the scope of the study, and so on. Give as much information as you deem necessary for people to understand and trust the information you are presenting. In fact, you may have noticed that citations in this textbook follow the same pattern your authors suggest.

Source Citation Guidelines

Cites must ALWAYS include:

- The name of the publication, book, website, or person you interviewed
- The date of publication, date the website was last updated, or the date of your interview

Cites often SHOULD Include:

- The credentials of the person who is cited
- How the information was collected (i.e., a study of 50 people)
- The author of the article or book, if relevant

Source Citation Guidelines (cont'd)

Citation Language Suggestions:

- "According to (publication name) of (date)…"
- "As reported in the (publication name) of (date)…"
- "On (date), the (publication name) reported that …"
- "The (publication name) of (date) says that…"
- "In a personal interview on date, with (title/name of/person) …"
- Or find language that is natural for you, but still complete and credible.

CONCLUSION

Ideas alone are not enough to sustain your speech. This chapter has shown you how you can develop your ideas by gathering outside resources and using them to clarify your ideas for the audience. We have covered supporting materials to identify and implement in your speech, the different places you may find research, and how to properly give credit to the sources you use. If the organizational structure of your speech is a skeleton, think of research and support as the muscles. Just as physical exercise is essential to build your muscles and keep them in shape, it is equally important that you exercise your research and analytical skills to find great support for every speech.

Speaker's Secret

Worried about saying an important line "just right" in a speech? Consider borrowing someone else's words from an article, or even a poem or song. Just be sure to give credit to the author with a complete source citation.

FROM FRIGHT TO MIGHT MOMENT

Whenever you are in a library and can't find the information you need, there is one person who can always help: THE REFERENCE LIBRARIAN. He or she really is there to help you. If you need assistance, do not hesitate to ask.

SOURCE CITATION VERBS

Verbs carry so much information. Beginners sometimes don't remember this and just repeat the phrase "according to" to introduce the sources of their information. For clarity and interest, try to use variety when selecting verbs:

adds, agrees, argued, ascertained, asserted, called for, claimed, confirmed, considered, contended, contests, debates, described, detected, determined, differs, discovered, discussed, disputes, encountered, established, estimated, explained, figured, found, further supports, held, hit, informed us that, learned, located, met, noted, noticed, observed, perceived, pleaded, pointed out that, pondered, proudly observed, reported, requested, rescued, retrieved, revealed, reviewed, said, suggested, summed it up best, surveyed, talked about, uncovered, unearthed, viewed, warned us that, wrote…

MLA Style* Guidelines – 7th Edition

Resource and Medium Used	Typical Citation Format	Examples**
Books	For more information about citing books, see MLA Handbook, Section 5.5.	
Book with One Author (MLA 5.5.2)	Author last name, first name. *Title in Italics*. City of publication: Publisher, publication date. Print.	Herrera, Hayden. *Frida: A Biography of Frida Kahlo*. New York: Harper, 1993. Print.
Book with Two or Three Authors (MLA 5.5.4)	Last name, first name of first author, and first, last names of other authors. *Title in Italics*. City of publication: Publisher, publication date. Print.	Tunnell, Michael O., and George W. Chilcoat. *The Children of Topaz: The Story of a Japanese-American Internment Camp*. New York: Holiday House, 1996. Print.
Book with Four or More Authors (MLA 5.5.4)	Last name, first name of first author listed followed by ,"et al." *Title in Italics*. City of publication: Publisher, publication date. Print.	Moschovitis, Christos J.P., et al. *History of the Internet: A Chronology, 1843 to the Present*. Santa Barbara: Moschovitis, 1999. Print.
Book Available via an Online Database (MLA 5.6.2.c)	Author last name, first name. *Title in Italics*. City of publication: Publisher, publication date. *Database Name in italics*. Web. Date of access.	Guerette, Rob T. *Migrant Death: Border Safety and Situational Crime Prevention on the U.S. - Mexico Divide*. New York: LFB Scholarly, 2007. *eBook Collection*. Web. 19 Aug. 2011.
Work in an Anthology (MLA 5.5.6)	Author. "Article/Chapter Title." *Title in Italics*. Editor. City of publication: Publisher, publication date. Page numbers. Print.	Gordon, Mary. "The Parable of the Cave." *The Writer on Her Work*. Ed. Janet Sternburg. New York: Norton, 1980. 27-32. Print.
Reference Book (MLA 5.5.7, 5.5.14)	Author, if given. "Article Title." *Title of Reference Book in Italics*. Editor. Edition. Vol. number (for multi-volume works). City of publication: Publisher, Publication date. Print.	Poulin, Russell. "Distance Learning in Higher Education." *Encyclopedia of Education*. Ed. James W. Guthrie. 2nd ed. Vol. 2. New York: Macmillan, 2003. Print.
Reference Book Available via an Online Resource (MLA 5.6.2.c)	Author, if given. "Article Title." *Title of Reference Book in Italics*. Editor. Edition. Vol. number (for multi-volume works). City of publication: Publisher, Publication date. *Database Name in Italics*. Web. Date of access.	"Global Warming." *World of Earth Science*. Ed. K. Lee Lerner and Brenda Wilmoth Lerner. Vol. 1. Detroit: Gale, 2003. *Gale Virtual Reference Library*. Web. 17 June 2011.
Periodicals	For more information about citing periodicals, see MLA Handbook, Section 5.4.	
Newspaper Article (MLA 5.4.5)	Author. "Title of Article." *Title of Newspaper* Publication date, edition: page numbers. Print.	Markoff, John. "Cyberspace's Most Wanted: Hacker Eludes F.B.I. Pursuit." *New York Times* 4 July 1994, late ed.: A1+. Print.
Journal Article (MLA 5.4.2)	Author. "Title of Article." *Title of Journal in Italics* Volume.Issue (publication year): page numbers. Print.	Green, Elna C. "Relief from Relief: The Tampa Sewing-Room Strike of 1937 and the Right to Welfare." *Journal of American History* 95.4 (2009): 1012-1037. Print.

RESOURCE AND MEDIUM USED	TYPICAL CITATION FORMAT	EXAMPLES**
Journal Article Available via an Online Database (MLA 5.6.4)	Author. "Title of Article." *Title of Journal in Italics* Volume.Issue (publication date): page numbers. *Database Name in Italics.* Web. Date of access.	Green, Elna C. "Relief from Relief: The Tampa Sewing-Room Strike of 1937 and the Right to Welfare." *Journal of American History* 95.4 (2009): 1012-1037. *Academic Search Premier.* Web. 5 Aug. 2009.
Magazine Article (MLA 5.4.6)	Author. "Title of Article." *Title of Magazine in Italics* Publication date: page numbers. Print.	Phillips, Matthew. "Revenge of the Nerd." *Newsweek* 8 June 2009: 51-53. Print.
Magazine Article Available via an Online Database (MLA 5.6.4)	Author. "Title of Article." *Title of Magazine in Italics* Publication date: page numbers. *Database Name in Italics.* Web. Date of access.	Melby, Caleb. "The Zen of Steve Jobs." *Forbes* 10 Oct. 2011: 152-158. *Academic Search Premier.* Web. 2 Nov. 2011.
RECORDINGS	For more information about citing recordings and performances, see MLA Handbook, Section 5.7.	
Video/DVD Recording (Citing an entire recording) (MLA 5.7.3)	*Title in Italics.* Director. Distributor, Year of Release. Medium.	*Odyssey of Life: The Unknown World.* Dir. Mikael Agaton. WGBH Video, 1996. Videocassette.
Video/DVD Recording (Citing a particular individual) (MLA 5.7.3)	Last name, first name, function. *Title in Italics.* Director. Distributor, Year of Release. Medium.	Gore, Albert, perf. *An Inconvenient Truth.* Dir. Davis Guggenhiem. Paramount, 2006. DVD.
Interview (MLA 5.7.7)	Person interviewed. Interview by ____. *Title in italics.* Publication information. Medium.	Wiesel, Elie. Interview by Ted Koppel. *Nightline.* ABC. WABC, New York. 18 Apr. 2002. Television.
Online Video (MLA 5.6.2.d)	Author. *Title of Video. Title of Site in Italics.* Publisher, Publication date. Web. Date of access.	Lifesforsharing. *The T-Mobile Dance. YouTube.* N.p., 16 Jan. 2009. Web. 3 Aug. 2009.*
ADDITIONAL SOURCES	For more information about citing additional sources, see MLA Handbook, Section 5.7	
Personal Interview (MLA 5.7.7)	Person interviewed. Kind of interview. Date.	Perry, Sharon. Telephone and e-mail interview. 13 Apr. 2008.
E-mail Message (MLA 5.7.13)	Name of writer. "Subject/Title of Message." Description that includes recipient. Date of message. E-mail.	Seronick, Sandra. "Re: MLA Style." Message to author. 8 May 2009. E-mail.

Resource and Medium Used	Typical Citation Format	Examples**	
Web Sites	MLA no longer requires the URL be added to web site entries unless other required information is unavailable. For more information, see MLA Handbook, Section 5.6.		
Nonperiodical Publication on the Web (MLA 5.6.2)	Author. "Article Title." *Title of Website in Italics.* Sponsor/ Publisher, Publication Date. Web. Date of access.	"The Magic of Harry Potter." *Time Magazine.* Time, Inc., 25 Dec. 2000. Web. 22 Aug. 2011.	
Scholarly Journal on the Web (MLA 5.6.3)	Author. "Article Title." *Journal Title in Italics* Volume.Issue (publication date): page numbers. Web. Date of access.	Pate, Jennifer E., and Glen O. Gabbard. "Adult Baby Syndrome." *American Journal of Psychiatry* 160 (2003): 1932-1936. Web. 18 Aug. 2009.	

EVALUATING WEBSITES

No person or group checks the information that is published on the Internet for accuracy or authority. *You* are responsible for evaluating the authority and accuracy of any information that you intend to use for research purposes. To do so, consider the following:

1. What are the clues to "good" information?

- **Date** - is the date the information was written and/or last updated clearly marked?

- **Author** who is responsible for the information on the page? Does the page list professional credentials or experience which qualify that person/organization as an expert on the topic? What experience does the author have with the topic being discussed?

- **Affiliations** - is the author identified with any group or organization, which might influence his viewpoint?

- **Contact Information** - is there a way to contact the author (email, phone number, or postal address)?

- **Background** is the information presented verifiable in outside sources?

2. Who is responsible for the information being presented?

- Is it from an individual or an organization?
- What are the goals of the author in presenting this information?
- Are the qualifications that allow the author to speak authoritatively on the topic listed?
- Are the background and expertise of the individual/organization given?
- If you have questions about any of these, email the author and ask.

3. Where is the information coming from?

- **Domain names** give basic information on where the data is originating. The domain name is the first piece of information after the http:// of an Internet address. For example, the domain name for Mt. SAC is www.mtsac.edu.

- **Extensions** are part of the domain name (such as edu) and indicate the type of organization that is responsible for the information. Common extensions include:

  .gov A U.S. government website. Governmental agencies publish most of their information online. — Some level of editorial control over the content.

  .edu A college or university website. The schools publish information, as do faculty, staff, and students. — Limited editorial control of content.

  .org An organizational website. Professional (American Medical Association) to political (NRA). — Some editorial control of content, but must consider organizational goals.

  .net An Internet service company. Internet service companies allow subscribers to publish websites. — Only the author has editorial control of the content.

  .com A commercial website. Commercial websites deserve the most scrutiny by researchers. — Author has editorial control, which is intended to sell you something, whether a product or opinion.

4. Did someone else consider this information to be acceptable?

- Was it reviewed or recommended in a professional journal?

- Was it linked from another site whose authority and reliability you trust? --Most search engines do not screen or evaluate the sites that they index. --Directories and pathfinders are based on the selectivity of their creators.

5. Can you write a 1-2 sentence explanation of why your Internet source is authoritative enough to include in your list of works cited?

—Your audience will be looking at your works cited to determine how credible you are as an author.

Courtesy Deb Distante, Mt. San Antonio College Library

CHAPTER EIGHT

THE BODY OF YOUR SPEECH

Speeches are like steer horns: a point here, a point there, and a lot of bull in between.

— Alfred E. Neuman

Once you have completed your research and identified the speech goal and specific purpose, you are ready to organize the **body** of your speech. Remember there are three parts to every speech: the introduction, body, and conclusion. Your introduction usually comprises about 15% of the speech and the conclusion about 5-10%. That means the majority of the content of your speech will occur in the body, which should be organized into your **main points**. While it may seem out of order to begin in the middle, the body of your speech is the largest content area as well as the portion of your speech where you will share the most information with the audience. After you know what will be covered in the body of your speech, it is often easier to compose a more effective introduction and conclusion (which will be covered in Chapter 9).

Most speeches will have between two to four main points. This is because it is helpful for audience comprehension to divide information into categories, and because audiences may have trouble remembering more than four ideas. By far the most common number of main points in a speech is three, which seems to be an optimal number of ideas for audiences to understand and recall easily.

In some instances, you may choose to have a larger or smaller number of main points; be certain that there is a good justification for the decision and be willing to exert extra effort to ensure that the audience is not confused. For instance, one student gave a wonderful speech about large families using twelve main points – one point for each of her siblings. She helped the audience follow her complex organizational structure by using a visual aid of a family photo to reinforce each main point. Conversely, a few short ceremonial speeches may have just one main point, such as a toast. In general, though, for most speeches, you will need to divide the body into at least two to three main points.

DEVELOPING MAIN POINTS

The best way to come up with the main points for your speech is to review your specific purpose, read through all your research, and then complete a seven-step process:

STEP ONE: Brainstorm a list of concepts that pertain to your specific purpose and/or relate to your topic.

Just as brainstorming was an effective technique for selecting your topic, it can now be a great tool for generating an initial list of areas you feel that you should cover in your speech. You should come up with at least 20 or 25 concepts to begin your list.

STEP TWO: Review your research to add additional concepts to your list.

The books and articles you have collected should have additional information that is pertinent to your specific purpose. As you add these ideas to your list, be sure to note the source of the ideas so you can give appropriate citations later on.

STEP THREE: Ask yourself the journalist's questions to add additional concepts to your list.

Imagine you are a journalist writing a story about your topic. Ask yourself questions that begin with the following words:

Who?	**Where?**
What?	**Why?**
When?	**How?**
How much?	

If you don't already have items on your list that address these areas, add concepts to your list that answer these questions.

STEP FOUR: Use audience analysis to anticipate concepts your audience will expect to hear in your speech.

Imagine that you will be a member of the audience for your speech. Even better, speak with a few people who will be in the audience for your speech, such as your classmates. Identify areas in the realm of your specific purpose that will be of particular interest to that audience. Add these concepts to your list. For instance, if you were delivering a speech about financial aid fraud for your college speech class, your classmates would probably want to know how to protect themselves from fraud, as well as resources on your campus in case they are victims. Don't let them down by leaving out the information they will be hoping or even expecting to hear.

STEP FIVE: Reduce the list.

Keeping in mind your time limit and your specific purpose, you probably now need to *remove* some concepts from your list. Look for items that are redundant, outside the limits of your specific purpose, or otherwise unnecessary. If you find that you still have too many ideas to effectively address within your time limit, you need to narrow your specific purpose so it is more achievable.

STEP SIX: Group the remaining concepts into two to three areas of commonality.

Finally, group items on your list by looking for similarities. Come up with a short phrase for each of group that expresses what all the items have in common. For instance, for a speech about major earthquakes, your groups might be "causes of big earthquakes," "damage they can do," and "famous earthquakes." Your goal is to identify two to four groups, which will become your main points. All of the items within each group will later evolve into your sub-points when you prepare your speech outline.

STEP SEVEN: Improve your main point labels.

Carefully consider the way you phrase your main points since you will be saying each phrase several times during your speech. The language you choose must clearly explain what you will cover in that area and should also interest your audience. The phrases you create are your **main point labels.**

For instance, in a speech about "starting your own garden," you might start out with a first main point label such as "things you do to get the ground ready for plants." You could make this clearer by changing it to "preparing your soil." It might also be more interesting and creative to say, "let's dig up some dirt on soil preparation."

Be sure to **avoid the word "and"** when you phrase a main point. If you use "and" then you really have two areas in that point, not one, which can confuse the audience. Instead, either split the information into two different main points or find another phrase that covers both concepts, as in the example below:

Before: "The history and early problems of airplane construction"

After: "The challenging development of the first airplanes"

Main point labels should also be written in parallel structure, using similar language in each. For example, in her speech on African elephants, one student used the following main points:

I.   African elephants are complicated.

II.   African elephants are able to communicate.

III. African elephants are endangered.

1. Brainstorm a list of concepts.

2. Review your research.

3. Ask yourself the journalist's questions.

4. Use audience analysis.

5. Reduce the list.

6. Group the remaining concepts.

7. Improve your main point labels.

ORDERING YOUR MAIN POINTS

Your first consideration in ordering your points should be **logical sequencing.** For instance, in an informative explanation speech about "understanding how a car engine works," the following organization of points would be slightly illogical because it does not follow a natural progression:

I. The engine burns the fuel.

II. The exhaust system vents the engine.

III. The ignition system starts the car.

Obviously, the main points should be ordered so they make logical sense to your audience members. However, in cases where the information has no clear logical order to follow, there is another consideration in ordering your main points: how interesting they will be to your audience. A general guideline is to begin with a point that will get your audience involved while saving the most interesting point for last. In a three-point speech, it would look like this:

I. Second most interesting point

II. Least interesting point

III. Most interesting point

In the event that you are delivering a speech that is likely to be highly controversial, or if you are speaking to an audience who may be averse to hearing what you have to say, consider the following order for your main points:

I. The point the audience will agree with most

II. The point the audience will agree with somewhat

III. The most controversial point

GENERIC SPEECH STRUCTURES

Occasionally, you may find it necessary to organize a speech very quickly and will not have the time to complete a seven-step process to identify your main points. In these cases, it may be helpful to be familiar with the following generic speech structures that can help you create fast and clear main points for your speech:

The Chronological Sequence

In the **chronological sequence,** points are ordered based on linear time from earliest to latest, first to last. Consider the following chronological main points for a speech about making a cake:

  I. The first step is to mix the ingredients.

  II. The second step is to bake the cake.

  III. The third step is to decorate the cake.

The chronological sequence can also be used to discuss a topic as viewed over a period of time.

  I. Baseball was invented as a simple game.

  II. Baseball had a period called "The Glory Days."

  III. Baseball became a high profit business.

A very simple chronological structure is to discuss the past, present, and future of a topic.

  I. Historically, women were important in politics.

  II. Today, women are in many places of political leadership.

  III. In the future, women will be routinely elected to the highest political office.

The Spatial Sequence

In the **spatial sequence**, points are ordered based on physical location. This may include spatial orientation from east to west, top to bottom, or left to right. These geographical or directional patterns help the audience to clearly see a "movement" from point to point as the speech unfolds.

The following is an example of a spatial sequence organizational pattern:

  I. The core of the earth is in the center of the sphere.

  II. The earth's mantle is the next layer outward from the center.

  III. The crust of the earth is on the outside of the sphere.

The Structure-Function Sequence

Finally, in the **structure-function sequence** points are ordered in a fashion to describe something and then show how it works. It is usually organized in two or three main points. The following is an example of a structure-function organizational pattern discussing to use for a speech about the fascinating e. coli bacteria:

      I.   E. coli is a complex bacteria.

     II.   E. coli can infect the human body.

   III.   E. coli DNA can store computer data.

Additional speech structures will be described in Chapter 15, Persuasive Speaking.

CONCLUSION

The development of your main points provides the overall blueprint for a speech. If you take the time complete this process carefully and thoughtfully, you will already have a thorough and ordered list of all the concepts in your speech, including your sub-points. The next step is to formalize your organization, add your support, and flesh out the body of your speech with your outline.

Speaker's Secret

While you won't have the time to memorize most of your speeches in their entirety, it does make sense to memorize your main point labels for a speech. If *you* find it hard to remember your main points, then your audience will probably have a hard time remembering them, too. If this happens, go back and revise the language so it is more memorable and clear.

FROM FRIGHT TO MIGHT MOMENT

Virtually all speakers will become nervous if they don't have a clear idea of what they will say during their speech. Having a strong, clear structure for the body of your speech will give you confidence in your ability to make it through the speech successfully.

CHAPTER NINE

INTRODUCTIONS, CONCLUSIONS, AND TRANSITIONS

What we call the beginning is often the end. And to make an end is to make a beginning.

— *T.S. Eliot*

Recall from Chapter 3 that it is always important for each speech to "start strong and end strong." This chapter will strengthen your ability to meet that objective. Since you have learned how to develop the body of your speech in Chapter 8, it is now time to focus on the first and last parts of your speech – your introduction and conclusion, and on the flow of ideas between your main points: your transitions.

INTRODUCTIONS

Introductions do not include a lot of information about the *topic* of your speech. That information should be presented in the body of the speech. Instead, an introduction motivates and prepares an audience to receive the entire speech effectively. It is the first main area of your speech, usually comprising around 15% of your overall speaking time. For instance, the introduction for a six-minute speech should last approximately one minute. It is possible that certain highly complex or controversial topics may require more time to introduce, but always be sure that you leave yourself enough time to cover the content of your speech in the body thoroughly.

Six Goals of a Speech Introduction

While introductions do not generally attempt to present a lot of information about a speech topic, they do have several goals critical to the overall effectiveness of your speech.

Introductions must **gain the attention of the audience** so they will be ready to hear the material to follow. Also, they need to **reveal your speech topic clearly**, since there should be no confusion about the subject you are speaking about as you begin the body of your presentation.

Also, it is not enough just to reveal the topic of your speech. You must also use your introduction to **inspire audience interest in your** topic so they are motivated to listen attentively to the rest of the speech.

Another goal of the introduction is to **create rapport**. Rapport is a friendly feeling between you and your audience so they will be open and receptive to what you have to say, even if they initially disagree with your position. Audiences listen differently to speakers they know and like.

Similarly, you must also build another kind of relationship with your audience in the introduction – one of trust. In other words, you must **establish your personal credibility**. It is essential that the audience accepts you as someone who has the authority to speak about your topic, or they may not be receptive to what you have to say for the rest of the speech.

Finally, introductions need to **give the audience a "road map"** so they have a general idea of where the speech is going. While many people newer to public speaking often bristle at the idea of "giving away" too much information about the speech early on, presenting the audience with a broad, general view of the direction of the speech will prepare the audience more effectively to listen to your speech. Remember from Chapter 4 that audiences retain relatively little of the information presented to them. Repeating your main points several times during a speech will help the audience in understanding and remembering your overall speech content; this is the first of many times your audience will hear the main points you will be discussing.

Six Content Areas of an Introduction

In order to achieve the six goals listed above, you can use the following content areas when writing your introduction: the greeting, attention device, topic revelation statement (or TRS), significance statement, credibility statement, and a preview of main points. Please keep in mind, however, that for this class your instructor may not require all of these elements in every introduction.

Six Content Areas of an Introduction

Greeting

Attention Device

Topic Revelation Statement, or TRS

Significance Statement

Credibility Statement

Preview of Main Points

The Greeting

A greeting is perhaps the simplest part of your speech to prepare and deliver, but as the first thing you say to an audience, it is also one of the most important. A **greeting** is a brief and friendly phrase extended to your audience to begin your presentation, such as "Good morning," "Hello everyone," or "How are you doing today?" The most effective greetings are those offered naturally in a conversational tone with a warm smile. Sometimes audience members will even respond with verbal comments and a smile back toward the speaker. This interaction is a great way to create rapport as a speech begins.

If a greeting is not used to start a speech, then a speaker should build rapport with a warm smile and conversational tone during the rest of the introduction.

The Attention Device

The attention device is a short (2-4 sentences) section of your speech designed specifically to draw the attention of the audience to you, your speech, and your specific topic area. It is a great place in your speech to utilize your creativity, since there are several different strategies you can use to gain your audience's attention:

Ask a question. Interesting questions inspire audience members to think of answers, so they immediately involve the audience in your presentation. There are two kinds of questions that you might ask an audience. **Real questions** ask the audience to think of an answer and then respond. However, it can be confusing and take a lot of time to listen to all audience members' answers to a question, so real questions should be phrased carefully and must always direct an audience as to the proper way to answer. For instance:

> "By a show of hands, how many people drove on a freeway to get here today?"

> "Do you like cake? Show me how much by applause."

You can also get the audience's attention by using a **rhetorical question** — a question that doesn't require the audience to verbalize an answer, just to reflect inwardly. For instance:

> "Have you ever held in a secret that you really wanted to tell, but couldn't?"

If you are going to start your speech with a question, make sure the question is interesting enough to grab the attention of the audience. Not all questions are thought-provoking, and overly obvious questions may leave an audience flat, such as asking, "How many people here like money?"

Make a provocative or startling statement. Unexpected statements can be a great way to get the audience to listen. A shocking first line may arouse interest quickly:

> "Despite what you have heard, humans have never walked on the moon. It was all an elaborate hoax."

Refer to a recent event. People like to hear about events that are in the news at the present time. "Two weeks ago, classes at this college were cancelled because of severe weather conditions which caused almost a billion dollars in damage. Today, I would like to talk about violent wind storms."

Use humor. Tell a joke. Humor is a very effective way to begin a speech, as long as you avoid potentially offensive jokes and relate the joke to your topic revelation statement.

Make a reference to the audience. "It is a pleasure to be speaking before such a well educated group of individuals. My research indicates that more of this community college's faculty have earned doctoral degrees than the average at four year universities in California."

Find common ground with the audience. An audience member will always want to know, *what is in it for me?* For instance, "We all buy our books here at the book store on campus where we pay high prices and we get very little when we sell them back. I've got a place where you can save 35% on your textbook purchases and get 40% more when you sell them back."

Make a reference to the occasion. Referencing the occasion acknowledges the current situation and involves everyone in your speech. "As a former member of this school's track team, I am especially honored to be invited back to deliver a speech at the dedication of this new stadium."

Begin with a quotation. Quotations add a personal dimension to your speech. "As Mark Twain once said, `We should never let school get in the way of education'." When you use a quotation, it is important to link the quotation to your topic revelation statement.

Begin with a hypothetical situation. Sometimes you need to create a fictional scenario to prove a point. "Today, take a vacation from your everyday existence. You are a student at the most prestigious college in the United States. You are attending this college because you have earned enough scholarship money to pay for your entire tuition, room, board, and even extra spending money. You have no financial worries."

Begin with a story. A strong story can relate the subject directly to the audience. It can be about someone else or yourself. "Janine Jeffrey was only 20 years old. She carried 23 units each semester of her college life, always attended summer school, and completed her master's degree in one year. Her friends called her an overachiever." A technique many speakers employ with this device is to save the ending of the story for the lasting thought in the conclusion of the speech.

Reveal a startling statistic. A startling statistic will make the audience say "wow." "A 2011 United Nations study entitled "Progress of the World's Women reveals a shocking fact: sixteen percent of American women think it's okay for a man to hit his wife." Remember, make sure you always cite your source for your statistic.

Begin with a visualization. A visualization will put the audience into a particular place or frame of mind. "You are on a white sandy beach, waves crashing to the shore from the beautiful blue ocean. You're swinging in a hammock between two large palm trees, sun in your face, wind in your hair, tropical drink in your hand, loved one at your side, not a worry in the world. Can you picture such a place? Well I've been there and that place is Maui."

This list of attention devices above is not exhaustive. There are even more types of attention devices that could be effective, including examples from popular culture, politics or history, role-plays, or audio or visual aids. In fact, there are countless types of possible attention devices. The key is to draw the attention of the audience to you, your speech, and your specific topic. With so many possible techniques at your disposal, there will never again be an excuse to begin a speech with, "Hi, my name is _____ and my topic is…".

Keep in mind that you should not combine multiple devices and allow this part of your speech ramble on and on. As you end your attention device, you may also need to add a **connecting link** to make a natural connection to the next part of your introduction, your topic revelation statement.

The Topic Revelation Statement, or TRS

Certainly most public speaking instructors would agree that the most important single sentence in your entire speech is the one in which you disclose the exact subject you will be speaking about, otherwise known as your **topic revelation statement**, or **TRS** for short.

The technique for choosing and writing your TRS was discussed at length in Chapter 5, so make sure you review this information as you write your speech introductions.

The Significance Statement

Recall that one of the goals of a speech introduction is to inspire audience interest in your topic. To accomplish this, it can be extremely effective to address this goal with a specific content area: the **significance statement**. Significance is the relative importance of a topic to an audience member. Hopefully you have selected a topic that *has a direct or indirect impact on your audience* (see Chapter 5); now you have to convey this briefly and clearly in a short (one to three sentence) statement.

To construct a great significance statement, use personal language that relates to your specific audience. For instance, you could say in a speech to your classmates:

> "Understanding the dangers of their credit card debt will have a big impact down the road for college students."

However, it is much better to say:

> "Understanding the dangers of *our* credit card debt will have a big impact down the road for *those of us in college*."

Whenever possible, it is also effective to use a **source citation** to strengthen your significance statement. One of the best kinds of support you can use to build significance is a direct or paraphrased quotation from a knowledgeable or respected expert on your subject, known as **testimony**. For instance:

> Not only can debt cost us a lot of money, it could cost us a job. Professional corporate background checker Jim Harris told the *Knight Ridder News* of December 21, 2006 that more and more companies are running credit reports on job candidates and, as he warns, "All things being equal, companies are going to hire the person with less debt." We must understand and address the problem of debt among college students before it's too late.

A secondary benefit of using testimony with a source citation in your introduction is that it can help achieve the goal of establishing your personal credibility on your subject, since it shows the audience that you have done research for your presentation. Be sure to refer back to Chapter 7 for more information about the best use of source citations and support in your speeches.

At a minimum, a significance statement must plainly state why the audience should keep listening to the remainder of your speech. Make a strong and direct appeal for their involvement.

Credibility

Credibility can be added to an introduction in a number of ways. A direct and often effective way to meet the goal of establishing your personal credibility to discuss your speech topic is to present a brief **credibility statement** in your introduction. This statement tells the audience your qualifications. If you have a personal relationship to your topic, such as prior personal experience, it can be effective to mention this directly. One way to accomplish this is with a **complete credibility statement**, which is best used when you have extensive experience and knowledge about a topic. For instance:

> As a certified public accountant with more than 15 years of tax preparation experience for literally thousands of clients, I am confident in sharing my tax advice with all of you here today.

You can also make a **partial credibility statement,** which can be added to another part of your introduction. For instance, this is a partial credibility statement added to the beginning of a TRS:

> As someone who works with many overweight young kids in my job as a teacher's aide, today I hope to convince you about the dangers of feeding children a fast food diet.

Of course, you must be careful not to sound boastful or superior when making credibility statements, which could harm your rapport with your audience. The following statement would probably not be very effective, for instance:

> You may think you know how to get good grades on tests, but unless you are like me and always get the high score in every class you take, you probably don't, so you should listen up.

One of the best ways to include a credibility statement in a speech is to have someone else make it *for you* before you even begin speaking. For some real-life public speaking events you will be introduced by another person. Take this opportunity to ask the other person to make a reference to your title, special qualifications, awards, or experiences that make you qualified to speak on your topic. Before you even begin your speech, the audience will see you as a credible speaker.

Finally, in lieu of a direct credibility statement, you must build your personal credibility through your **language use and speech delivery techniques.** Using the appropriate language and terminology for your subject area and pronouncing names and technical terms with accuracy is essential. Direct eye contact, good posture, body control, a strong and loud voice, and low (or no) dependence on notes will help the audience see you as a more confident and assured speaker, as well.

The Preview of Main Points

The last element of your introduction before you move into the body of your speech should be your **preview of main points.** This is a brief and clear list of the two to four main points you will discuss in the same order in which they will occur during the body of the speech.

If you have selected and thoughtfully labeled your main points, constructing your preview is easy. First, simply state your first point label. Second, state your second point label. Third, state your third point label, and so on for each main point. Order indicators help the audience visualize the structure of your speech and include words in series, such as, "First, second, and third," or "First, next, and last."

Remember to **avoid the word "and"** in labeling any main point, since this will likely confuse the audience and make them hear two ideas, not just one.

An example of a preview of main points is:

> First, I'll discuss the important historical aspects of golf, second, I will introduce you to a few heroes of professional golf, and third, I will share the health benefits of playing golf.

Sample Introduction

I. (Greeting) Good morning everyone!

II. (Attention Device) What do you think is the fastest growing sport in our country right now? Maybe you are thinking NFL football or NBA basketball. Well, if so, you would be wrong!

III. (Topic Revelation Statement) In the next few minutes, I will inform you about the fastest growing sport in America: NASCAR racing.

IV. (Significance Statement with Credibility) NASCAR racing might sound like just another racing series, but as a ten year fan I hope to show you how it is different and more interesting than other forms of motor sport.

According to *Sports Illustrated* of November 30, 2005, NASCAR is America's fastest growing sport. Last year more people watched NASCAR races on Sundays than even NFL football games. The only game to outdraw NASCAR was the NFL Superbowl.

V. (Preview of Main Points) First, I will explain the history of NASCAR racing. Second, I will explain the characteristics of the sport. Finally, I will talk about some of the most famous drivers.

CONCLUSIONS

Conclusions of speeches are also important because they leave the audience with a final summary and impression of your entire presentation. Conclusions are generally not as long as introductions but have two important goals. These goals are the two content aspects of the conclusion.

The first goal of the conclusion is to **review the topic revelation statement and main points** of your speech. Reiterate what your purpose was (or what you wanted to accomplish in giving the speech) *and* the main points you used to achieve your goal. When you summarize, the audience will be more likely to remember these concepts after your speech has ended.

The second goal of the conclusion is to create a **lasting thought** about your speech. This is achieved by sharing an idea or phrase that brings the concepts of the speech together and will remain with the audience after your speech has ended. A good way to create psychological unity for the audience is to tie in your lasting thought with the attention device you used in the introduction. This is easily done when you return and complete the same story you used in the opening of the speech. You may also choose to end with a meaningful quotation, a final call for action, advice, a dramatic statement, or your personal feelings about the topic you discussed.

Remember from Chapter 3 to end strong and end with finality. We should know your speech is over by the last sentence in your speech. Never end with a weak phrase or a cliché like "thank you" or "that's about it." The last line and last word should be powerful, vivid, and memorable. Think of it as the final note at the end of a symphony. It must also be delivered well. You want to allow the speech to resonate well beyond the moment you leave the stage. Always hold the last moment before you walk away from the speaking situation and walk back to your seat with confidence and poise.

Sample Conclusion

I.   (Review of Topic and Main Points): Today, we have discussed the history of NASCAR racing, the characteristics of the sport, and some of the most famous drivers.

II. (Lasting Thought): As you can see, NASCAR is the most exciting and fastest growing sport in America. Next time you are home on Sunday morning and you are bored watching ball and stick sports, turn your channel to the weekly NASCAR race and enjoy the ride! You will soon get goose bumps when you hear, "Ladies and gentlemen, start your engines!"

TRANSITIONS AND SIGNPOSTS

Transitions are the phrases used to connect the major parts of your speech together. Think of them as bridges. Bridges allow us to get from one point to the next without falling into water or going down a path we don't want to travel. The transition allows us to go from one point of the speech to the next without getting lost. In a three-point speech, you will have four distinct transition statements:

INTRODUCTION to FIRST MAIN POINT

FIRST MAIN POINT to SECOND MAIN POINT

SECOND MAIN POINT to THIRD MAIN POINT

THIRD MAIN POINT to CONCLUSION

The transition immediately following your introduction is a **simple transition**. It alerts the audience to your arrival at the first point:

> So let's find out about the ingredients you'll need for your cake.

The remaining transitions should be **summary transitions** which review the previous main point and carry the audience into the next point. For instance, a transition from the first point to the second point might be:

> Now that you know the ingredients you need, I will explain how to make your batter.

Even though they may sound repetitive, clear transitions are necessary signposts for your audience. Listening comprehension is far worse than reading comprehension, so we need to make every possible effort to keep the audience from being lost and confused during speeches.

Signposts are statements that indicate where you are at various places during your speech. A polished public speaker works like a great GPS locator – helping the audience know where they are. The most common signpost is simply a number. Some examples are *first, second, third, next, last, finally, in conclusion,* etc. See the sample outlines throughout this book for examples.

CONCLUSION

Introductions, conclusions, and transitions are vital components of the overall effectiveness of your speech. The introduction will give the audience a *first* impression; the conclusion will give the audience a *lasting* impression. Take time to prepare and practice these critical elements of your speech. Remember, you want to start strong and end strong!

Speaker's Secret

Studies about the beginning and ending of a message (known as the primacy and recency effects) show that both areas have a strong impact in the overall perception of a message. You can take advantage of this knowledge by spending extra time creating your introduction and conclusion and then rehearsing their delivery over and over for the best possible primacy and recency effect.

FROM FRIGHT TO MIGHT MOMENT

If you feel nervous about delivering your speech, take the time to memorize the first line of your introduction and the last line of your conclusion. In addition to reducing some of your anxiety, it will make your speech delivery even more effective.

CHAPTER TEN

OUTLINING

Wishing consumes as much energy as planning
— *Anatole French*

Most important undertakings begin with some type of plan. Before the 2,722-foot Burj Khalifa Tower was erected in Dubai, architects and designers spent several years drafting the blueprints to ensure that the actual building process went smoothly. Just like a skyscraper, each speech you create requires careful design and planning. A crucial step in this planning process is outlining.

THE THREE FUNCTIONS OF OUTLINING

Sometimes students think that a speech class won't involve any written work, complaining that, "I thought it was all just about talking." While it is true that you can speak without writing anything down in advance, the *quality* of your speech will be impacted dramatically based on the preparation work you do. While some speeches will involve the eventual creation of a complete **manuscript** of every word you will say, all speeches can benefit from a process of writing and editing in advance of the presentation. This advance preparation of your speech is usually achieved by outlining the speech, a process with three distinct functions.

The First Function of an Outline: Helping You to Be Organized

The first function of an outline is to help you organize the body of your speech into appropriate main points and subpoints. **Main points** are identified in the outline farthest left on the page. This is a visual cue for the speaker that the speech topic has equal subdivisions. **Subpoints** are the subordinate ideas that develop and clarify the main points. They are indented. If any of the subpoints need further development, you can create and indent your **sub-subpoints**, and so on.

The convention typically followed in outlining is that the most general idea also be identified with Roman numerals, descending to capital English letters, then to numbers, then to lower case English letters, and, if necessary, to lower case Roman numerals. For instance:

I.   **Main point**

    A.   **Subpoint**

        1.   **Sub-subpoint**

            a.   **Sub-sub-subpoint**

                i.   **sub-sub-sub-subpoint**

Often the information conveyed on the furthest indented line of a speech outline is your **support** for your ideas, which you will recall from Chapter 7.

The Second Function of an Outline: Checking for Logical Progression of Ideas

The second function of an outline is to ensure your speech has a logical sequence. To do this, adhere to the following principles when organizing your outline: simplicity and subordination.

Simplicity is the first principle of outlining. This means that each symbol of the outline should be followed by only one idea or statement. You must make your ideas easy to follow, and to do this they must be split into the smallest possible units. The example below illustrates how an idea can de divided into simpler units.

I.   **In order to develop proper study habits, you should create a good study space, get plenty of rest, and organize your study materials.**

This main point has three different ideas. It should be divided so each line contains only one idea.

I.   **There are several steps to developing proper study habits.**

    A. **You should create a good study space.**

    B. **You should get plenty of rest.**

    C. **You should organize your study materials.**

However, you should also not split ideas that are already simple. Only break down information into substructure if there are *at least two sub-ideas* that you can identify. You should avoid, for instance:

I.   **There is one reason why people don't take enough vacations.**

   A.   **Their jobs don't allow it.**

This should be all be expressed on the line above:

I.   **The reason people don't take enough vacations is because their jobs don't allow it.**

Subordination is the second principle of outlining. Splitting information into A-B-C or 1-2-3 is fairly easy, but subordination requires that each idea in your outline support the idea that is superior to it symbolically. In other words, each subpoint must directly support the main point under which it falls. Each sub-subpoint must support the subpoint under which it falls. This example demonstrates a subpoint that *does not* support its main point:

I.   **A lawn mower has many uses.**

   A.   **It cuts grass.**

   B.   **It provides exercise to the person mowing.**

   C.   **There are several maintenance concerns with a lawnmower.**

      1.   **Adjustments must be made to the motor.**

      2.   **The blade must be sharpened.**

      3.   **The engine must be properly lubricated.**

      4.   **The mower must be properly stored.**

The problem with this organization is that the maintenance concerns have nothing to do with the *uses* of a lawn mower. Let's make the maintenance concerns a separate main point:

I.   **A lawn mower has many uses.**

   A.   **It cuts grass.**

   B.   **It provides exercise to the person mowing.**

II.   **There are several maintenance concerns with a lawnmower.**

   A.   **Adjustments must be made to the motor.**

B. The blade must be sharpened.

C. The engine must be properly lubricated.

D. The mower must be properly stored.

The Third Function of an Outline: Practicing the Delivery of the Speech

The third function of an outline is to help the speaker practice and deliver the speech. Classroom speeches, as well as real-life speech situations, are often **extemporaneous**, meaning the speaker prepares the complete content of the speech — including a very thorough outline — but does not write the speech out word for word. The outline helps the speaker practice because the main points are clearly identified. Also, since many people learn information visually, it creates a clear separation between concepts to help a speaker remember where ideas are in their speech.

You will learn that there are three kinds of outlines for every speech that you will give. One is designed as you prepare your materials. One is to be given to the professor. The last outline is the one you will use when delivering the speech.

THE THREE TYPES OF OUTLINES

While preparing speeches in life, you may need to prepare three different types of outlines: the working outline, the formal outline, and the speaking outline.

The Working Outline

The first stage of outlining should begin with a **working outline**. This is an outline that is created by you for your own benefit, and it is not usually shared with others unless you are seeking feedback on your work in progress.

A working outline is a rough draft of the main ideas and subpoints of your speech. This working outline will go through many drafts and changes before your ideas are finalized.

As you develop your main points and subpoints, you will want to be mindful of the time limit for the overall presentation. Since most speeches you give in class will be less than ten minutes, too many subpoints or sub-subpoints will likely lead you to exceed your time limit. Also, work to balance the amount of information contained within each main point so it is roughly equal. An outline that has six subpoints for Main Point #1, but only two for Main Point #2 is weighted too heavily towards one.

For some speeches, especially impromptu speeches with very little preparation time, a working outline may be all you need to create before your presentation. However, some situations will require you to formalize your outline so it is presentable to others.

The Formal Outline

A **formal outline** is an outline that contains all the ideas you will cover in your speech, including research you will cite and all the support you plan to use. It is always typed and should be formatted so it has a professional, consistent appearance and is easy to follow. Usually it requires that all content be expressed in complete sentences, not just fragments. The reason for all of this is that this document is created to be shown to others. Often professors, colleagues at work, or others may wish to see the content of a presentation, either for review and evaluation, or because they missed the speech and need to know the content. A formal outline is the written document to accompany a prepared speech.

Because of this, it should also contain a bibliography or **works cited page**, especially for all college-level academic work. It is essential to give proper credit to your sources. A formalized bibliography provides a context for the sources you will cite in your speech and makes it easy for someone who wants to learn more about your topic to find some excellent resources. Your professor may require you to use the guidelines of the Modern Language Association (MLA), American Psychological Association (APA), or another format. Ask your professor for assistance if you do not know how to construct a formal bibliography. A brief guide to MLA citation can be found in Chapter 7.

While they are often prepared for others, formal outlines can benefit the speaker, too. It is a great way to look at your speech as a whole and to make sure the ideas flow logically. The process of creating it will also solidify the information in your mind and allow you to think though each idea as a complete thought, which will help your phrasing of the ideas later on when you speak.

The Speaking Outline

The third type of outline is for your use while preparing and, possibly, delivering your speeches: your **speaking outline**. These are extremely limited notes that are often written on small index cards to help make them less apparent during the presentation, though any type of note will always be visible to the audience.

When preparing your speaking outline, here are some useful tips:

1. *Try orienting note cards vertically rather than horizontally.* This makes them less visually obvious and to replicate the shape of the paper on which you probably wrote your other outlines.

2. *Avoid using more than two note cards.* This helps avoid getting them out of order and making it easy to find the information you are looking for.

3. *Express ideas in key words and short phrases.* This helps avoid the impulse to "read" from the cards.

4. *Write or type clearly and legibly and large enough to read.* Please don't decide to shrink your formal outline down to a tiny font and paste it onto your note cards. This will likely produce disastrous results.

5. *Limit the information on the cards to the bare minimum that you require.* Typically students have trouble remembering numbers, unfamiliar names, and the publication and date of source citations.

6. *Only write notes on one side of the cards.* The audience should not be able to read ahead while you are still delivering your first main point.

It is also essential to keep in mind a few tips about delivering your speech with note cards:

1. *Practice with the note cards you plan to use.* Don't just scratch out what you *think* you will need just moments before your speech.

2. *Do not read extensively from your notes.* Notes can easily become an excuse for looking away from the audience. Don't let them be a substitution for practicing a speech – they are there as a backup for a prepared speaker.

3. *Use them intentionally when needed.* Don't try to hide notes from the audience or peek at the cards. Audiences appreciate a speaker who wants to check her facts or make sure she is quoting someone accurately. Keep the card at your side, and then when you need it, lift it up, look at it, and put it back to your side when you are finished.

4. *Only hold the card with one hand.* Face it, note cards just aren't that heavy. Still, many speakers show their lack of confidence by clutching the cards with both hands or playing with them. Only hold notes in one hand and use your other hand to gesture, when needed.

5. *Use your notes to remind yourself about good delivery.* In addition to the content of your speech, you may wish to write reminders to yourself to smile or make eye contact. You can also indicate places to pause or directions on how to use your voice in a certain area.

6. *Watch out for non-words.* Often when speakers look down at note cards they will also utter a non-word, such as "um" while they look information on their note cards. In Chapter 13 you will learn more about non-words and how to control them. But be aware that non-words have the potential to creep in when you use notes for speaking.

7. *If you have difficulty holding note cards or seeing the cards*, you can always ask your professor for ideas to make an effective choice that accommodates your needs.

Finally, while notes may be allowed for a speech, keep in mind that you may be able to deliver your speech without any notes at all. Many speakers find that, with just a little more practice, they are able to recall what would normally be contained on just two index cards. Speaking without notes is extremely impressive and also improves eye contact and your connection with the audience.

CONCLUSION

In this chapter we have explained the importance of outlining as well as how to structure your speech. This included the functions of an outline, the principles of outlining, and the various types of outlines. As you work on your outline, keep in mind your professor will have different expectations about outlining for specific assignments than may be presented here. Listen carefully for the instructions for each of your assignments. But one thing that both professors and audiences will appreciate is when you keep your presentation well organized.

Speaker's Secret

When typing your formal outlines in Microsoft Word, it can be very helpful to turn off the auto-format function. The program tries to help you make numbered or bulleted lists, but they may not be the ones you need.

FROM FRIGHT TO MIGHT MOMENT

Nervous speakers must be careful not to become too dependent on notes during speeches. It may be a good idea, in fact, to try to deliver your speech without note cards but keep a set of notes in a pocket just in case you need them during the speech. If that time comes, take the notes out with confidence and hold them for the rest of the speech.

SAMPLE MEMORABLE EXPERIENCE SPEECH OUTLINE

INTRODUCTION

I. **Attention Device:** How many of you would place yourselves in a body of water several feet deep, with a dozen animals ranging from 5-7 feet long, weighing up to 400 pounds, who can swim up to 60 mph, and who have been known to kill sharks on their own?

II. **Topic Revelation Statement:** Today, I'll share with you the story of my dolphin swim nine months ago at the Dolphin Research Center in the Florida Keys.

BODY

I. The experience was powerful.

    A. The dolphin swim lasted about 30 minutes, but we were at the facility three hours.

    B. We sat in a classroom and received an informative talk about the facility and lessons on how to communicate with the dolphins.

    C. We were led down to the docks and were introduced to the dolphins.

    D. First we did something called "imitates."

    E. The best part of all was the actual dolphin-swim.

II. There were lessons to be learned.

    A. We can live in harmony with these beautiful, intelligent creatures.

    B. It is crucial to their existence that we all do something to help protect them.

    C. Purchase dolphin-safe tuna.

    D. Cut up plastic rings that come on 6-packs of soda.

CONCLUSION

I. **Review Statement:** Now you know a bit about my amazing dolphin swim.

II. **Lasting Thought:** I strongly recommend this for anyone who is able. I even brought some information with me tonight so that you may plan your own underwater adventure.

Sample Demonstration Speech Outline

Specific Purpose: To inform my audience about how to make throw pillows.

Topic Revelation Statement: Today I will show you how to make your own easy and attractive throw pillows.

INTRODUCTION

I. **Attention Device:** Last week I was in Pottery Barn and they had some gorgeous throw pillows made of velvet. I was going to get them until I saw the price — $60 each. I couldn't afford it, so I did the next best thing — and now I'll show you how to do that, too.

II. **Topic Revelation Statement:** Today I will show you how to make your own easy and attractive throw pillows.

III. **Significance Statement:** Even if you are on a budget, you can still have a home that reflects your taste and style. Your home says a lot about who you are.

IV. **Preview of Main Points:** First we'll go over the items you'll need, then we'll make the pillow case, and then we'll finish the pillow.

BODY

I. First, you should assemble the items you will need.

    A. You'll need to go to a fabric or craft store for most of the items.

        1. I recommend an upholstery store for better fabrics.

        2. Purchase 3/4 yards of fabric for each pillow you want.

        3. Purchase a pillow insert, approximately 14 inches square.

            a. If you have an old pillow you can use its stuffing.

            b. I always use new inserts because I have allergies.

    B. You'll also need thread and a needle or a sewing machine.

II. Now that you have your supplies, we can make the case.

    A. Fold your fabric in half and iron it.

    B. Measure a square 3 inches taller and wider than your pillow insert. Pin the fabric together and trim.<Show pinning and cutting.>

C. Turn the fabric inside out.

D. Sew along the edges about 1/2 inch from the edge. Leave a small opening on one side in the center. <Show sample with hole.>

E. Stick your fingers in the opening and turn it inside out. The good side of the fabric should be showing now.

III. Now that you have a case, you can finish the pillow.

A. Stuff the insert or the stuffing into the opening. <Do this.>

B. Stitch the opening closed with a matching thread.

C. Shape the pillow <Show how to do this.>

CONCLUSION

I. **Review Topic and Main Points:** Now you know how to make a throw pillow. You learned about the items you need, how to make a case, and how to finish it.

II. **Lasting Thought**: So don't just look at designer home fashions and dream. Spend a few minutes and make your own fabulous accessories!

CHAPTER ELEVEN

LANGUAGE

Words are, of course, the most powerful drug used by mankind.
— Rudyard Kipling

On the popular television show So You Think You Can Dance, choreographer Lil'C often stumps viewers with his vocabulary choices. In a June, 2011 episode he remarked to a pair of dancers, "You remind me of how mellifluous the piano is." The confused audience turned to Twitter for a translation using the hashtags #whatthebuck and #Lil'CSAT.

Some speakers use language that is above the heads of the audience (or their own), while others may use language that is inaccurate, vague, or inappropriate. In all of these cases, the words can get in the way of the message they are trying to send. In some cases, the ineffective use of language can also lead an audience to conclude that a speaker is unintelligent, unprofessional, untrustworthy, or uninformed about their topic area. For these reasons, it is vital that you address the issue of language in your speech preparation.

When delivering manuscript and memorized speeches you will have the opportunity to sculpt every word for the best effect. Language matters in extemporaneous and impromptu speeches, too! Because of this, truly great speakers work to improve their use of language all the time so that they can be just as effective with language when unprepared speaking situations arise.

IMPROVING YOUR LANGUAGE CHOICES

None of us are born speaking a language. All language is learned. Improving our vocabulary is a life-long process, since new words enter the lexicon each year. While increasing the quantity of words in our vocabulary is important, improving the quality is just as vital. There are two ways to do this. First, make sure your language is clear, so the listeners understand the message. Second, make sure the language is vivid, so it impacts the audience emotionally.

Language Clarity

Above all, we must be understood immediately when we speak. **Clarity** refers to the accuracy with which an audience understands a speaker's intended meaning. Consider these guidelines for improving language clarity.

Choose familiar words. Familiar words are words well known to the audience. Consider such things as background, interests, and educational level. You may have words in your vocabulary that are not in other people's vocabularies — words that come from your job, hobbies, or sports you play. Such professional terminology is called **jargon**. Similarly, words used in casual conversation with meanings specific to a limited group of people are called **slang**.

The multiple meanings of words cause problems for the public speaker. Many words have a number of meanings. The speaker chooses the words assuming the audience will understand. However, some audience members may think of one of the other meanings of the word and thus be confused. For example, the word "fly" has different meanings to a pilot, a baseball player, a rap musician, and a tailor. If you use a word such as "fly" in a speech, you may have to define it.

Be accurate. Accurate language refers to the correct meaning and usage of a word. If you are unsure of the correct meaning and usage of a word, look it up. Nothing is more embarrassing or more likely to undermine your credibility than misusing a word or making up a word that doesn't exist.

For example, what's wrong with the following sentences?

> Irregardless of the situation, these two nations will never
> be friendly. Their amity goes back centuries.

If you can't find two clear accuracy errors, you'd better identify the words you don't know and look them up!

Be specific. There are words that are vague (or **ambiguous**) and words that are specific (or **concrete**). Vague words describe many possible things, while specific words only refer to one or a few things. Commonly used vague words and phrases include: stuff, a bunch, things, sort of, and fine (as in "I feel fine."). Recently the phrase "back in the day" has emerged as a lazy shortcut to providing a specific time frame for past events.

190

For example, the sentence, "A great many people left the community in 2005," is not as compelling as, "Sixty-five percent of residents left the community in 2005."

Being specific is particularly important in persuasive speeches where you are trying to influence attitudes and behavior. Which of the following sales pitches would you be more likely to act upon?

> **Vague:** Come on down here soon and get some stuff and we'll give you a deal.

> **Specific:** Come to any Circuit Castle before midnight tonight, and we'll give you 20% off the current sale price on all televisions.

Specific, concrete words narrow the number of possible meanings of a word so ambiguity is reduced. For instance, the word "chair" is vague and abstract, but "rocker," "recliner," "chaise" and "stool" are more specific concrete.

Be concise. Concise language refers to using a limited number of words that are not repeated and trimming the fat from the speech. If you choose words that are familiar, concrete, and specific you won't need a lot of them. More words do not mean something is better. In fact, the box on the left reveals that some of the most important documents or speeches in history are very concise.

Vividness in Language

Being understood is great, but you want your message to be remembered. You also want to inspire your audience's imaginations and senses so what you say will stick. Vivid language refers to lively language that makes an impact on the audience emotionally because of interest, energy, and images. It gets the audience involved. Some guidelines include:

Word Counts:

Pythagorean Theorem: 24 words

The Lord's Prayer: 66 words

Archimedes' Principle: 67 words

The Ten Commandments: 179 words

The Gettysburg Address: 286 words

The Declaration of Independence: 1,300 words

US Tax Code for cabbage: 3.8 million words

Avoid Clichés. A cliché is a worn out expression or a stale, trite remark. The first person that said, "It's raining cats and dogs" came up with a clever turn of phrase. Today, however, the phrase is tired. Other examples include, "at the end of the day" and "thinking outside the box."

Use descriptive imagery. There are two types of imagery you can use: literal and figurative:

- **Literal imagery** is the use of words or phrases that trigger images in your listener's mind via direct description. For example, the sentence, "I ate a steak for dinner" is clear. The sentence, "I ate a thick, sizzling, smothered-in-mushrooms, melt-in-your-mouth steak" is memorable.

- **Figurative imagery** involves the use of similes and metaphors. You may recall from an English class that a **simile** is an explicit comparison of two unlike things, using the phrase "like" or "as." The simile occurs frequently in rap music, like Andre 3000's lyric, "shake it like a Polaroid picture." A **metaphor** is an implied comparison of two things that seem dissimilar, usually to relate an abstract concept to something more concrete ("The heart is a lonely hunter.").

Use rhythm. Just like a great song, a great sentence has an effective rhythm. Rhythm refers to the arrangement of words to create certain effects. There are several ways to create rhythm using language.

- **Repetition:** Repeat a phrase to reinforce a point. Representative Richard Gephardt used this technique during the Clinton impeachment hearings in the U.S. House of Representatives when he said, "Let all of us here today say 'no' to resignation, 'no' to impeachment, 'no' to hatred, 'no' to intolerance of each other, and 'no' to vicious self-righteousness."

- **Parallelism:** Arrange a series of words or phrases into a similar pattern. "I came, I saw, I conquered."

- **Alliteration:** Repeat the same first consonant sound in a series of words. "Today's lesson will stress confidence, competence, and compassion."

- **Antithesis:** Contrast two ideas in a parallel structure and suggest there is a choice to be made. In his 1961 inaugural address, John F. Kennedy used this device when he said, "Ask not what your country can do for you; ask what you can do for your country."

Personalize. Get your listeners involved by using words and phrases that hit home, such as the personal pronouns *you*, *yours*, and *ours*. When possible, replace the words people (us), the United States (our country), and college students (students like us). For example, "Thirty-three percent of Californians will be affected by cancer" is not as personal as, "One out of every three people we know will be affected by cancer."

Appropriate Language

The animated television show *South Park* generated national controversy about the use of inappropriate language by children. The children depicted on the show have an understanding about what they find appropriate, and their parents have a very different opinion. Similarly, audiences respond differently to the language in the show. Some find the swearing, sexual references, and shocking terminology to be hilarious; others change the channel.

Appropriate language varies from audience to audience because it refers to language that is right, suitable, and proper for the *occasion*, audience, and speaker. When speaking to an audience, it is very important to be aware that certain words can offend some people, even if they don't bother you. In fact, they may be words you are so used to hearing and saying that you don't even think about them as being potentially offensive.

A good rule of thumb is to avoid any word that could possibly offend someone in the audience. Unless you know the word is okay with every person in your audience, do not use it.

Popular television shows like *True Blood* are known for using especially raw language in order to make the shows authentic. However, in most situations you will encounter, the opposite is true. Discussing sexuality and bodily functions in a non-medical context or using profanity will only make your audience feel uncomfortable. It will prove you are unable to conduct yourself appropriately in professional situations.

Follow a few simple tips for selecting appropriate language:

Avoid using profanity. A very interesting web site hosted by the Cuss Control Academy of Northbrook, IL, at cusscontrol.com, explains what is wrong with profanity in professional situations. They argue, "Profanity imposes a personal penalty. It gives a bad impression, reduces respect people have for you, shows you don't have control, and is considered by many to be immature."

Avoid sexist language. When you make generalizations about women or men, you risk insulting your audience. While some sexist remarks are overt, like saying, "Women can't be presidents of companies," others are more subtle. For instance, always using "he" as a default pronoun, or assuming a nurse in a hypothetical example is a "she" may call attention away from your point and make the audience question your sensitivity to gender issues.

Avoid cultural insensitivity. Even indirect racism can destroy your personal credibility. An example of subtle racism occurred in a speech last semester when a student said that in "his neighborhood" they believe in family values. There was a subtle assumption that other neighborhoods did not have these values. Another student referred to a group as "culturally deprived." All groups have culture. The culture of another group may not be the same as yours, but it is culture nevertheless. It will be impossible for you to have excellent rapport with your audience if you use language that is culturally insensitive.

CONCLUSION

In this chapter we have discussed the importance of language in public speaking. Improving your language choices starts with improving your vocabulary. Second, you need to have clarity and vividness in your language, so the audience enjoys your speech. Finally, appropriateness is essential and includes avoiding profanity, sexist remarks, and cultural insensitivity. Remember words are just as important to a public speaker as numbers are to an accountant.

Speaker's Secret

Oral language is different than written language:
- Oral language is less formal.
- Oral language uses shorter, simpler sentences.
- Oral language allows repetition.
- Oral language emphasizes the sounds of words.

FROM FRIGHT TO MIGHT MOMENT

Vivid language will get your audience caught up in your speech. They will be so interested in your descriptions and word choices that judging you will be far from their minds.

CHAPTER TWELVE

AUDIO AND VISUAL SUPPORT

Now what we got here is a little game of show and tell. You don't wanna show me nothing but you're telling me everything.

— *True Romance*

Sometimes there are things that a speaker alone cannot express with just words, inflection and facial expressions. It can be hard to convey the pain of a hungry child, a sharply fast rate of growth in a company, the complexity in a cell's structure, or the power of a wonderful selection of music. What would you do if you were given the assignment to prepare and deliver a descriptive informative speech about your favorite painting? If your audience has never seen the painting, would you be able to communicate to them the image, color, light, contrast, texture, and emotion? You might, and you should try, but you could also use a little help.

In the following chapter, we will explore learn about the types of audio and visual support and then address why, when, and how you might use these to enhance your speeches.

TYPES OF AUDIO AND VISUAL SUPPORT

Many things fall under the broad category of audio and visual support. Technically it is possible to even have olfactory (smell) or tactile (touch) support, though they are more rare. In general, we will use this term to refer to any support a speaker uses that is not verbal (words spoken by the speaker) or nonverbal (meanings conveyed by the body of the speaker, including facial expressions, tone of voice, gestures, movements, etc).

Listed below are some of the most common types of audio and visual support used by speakers:

Visual Representations

Types of Visual Aids

Visual
Representations

Objects

Media

The type of visual aid you are most familiar with is probably the visual representation. When you give a speech, you often cannot bring in the actual item you are discussing because of size, value, scarcity, or impossibility. For instance, if you wanted to let us know that two million Americans attend rodeo events, while only one million attend professional football games, you can't really bring in three million people to show that comparison to your classmates. Instead, you might create a two dimensional visual representation and share the electronic image via a projector. It may also acceptable to use a traditional poster-style visual in some situations.

Images used in visual representations might include photographs, artwork, or drawings. Data can also be represented visually with a **graph** or **chart**.

A **line graph** consists of lines that are charted on a grid. A line graph is good for revealing trends by showing how information changes over time.

A **bar graph** contrasts two or more sets of data by means of rectangles of varying length. It is good for comparing quantities or magnitudes.

A **pie graph** shows a given whole that is divided into component wedges. A pie graph is excellent for showing proportions. The pie represents 100% and each slice of the pie is a percentage of the whole.

A **pictorial graph** shows comparisons in picture form.

A **flowchart** is a diagram that shows a step-by-step progression through a procedure or system. An **information chart** is material arranged as a series of key points. An **organizational chart** is a diagram that arranges relationships in a hierarchy. A **table** arranges numbers or words systematically in rows and columns.

Objects

Another type of audio or visual support you might use is to show the audience an actual **object**, sometimes called a **prop**. If they are available to you, objects can make excellent visual aids. Showing the actual object leaves nothing for the audience to misinterpret. Of course, it is vital that the object be of an appropriate size to manage (not too big) and visible to everyone in the audience (not too small). Examples of this type of support previously used in speeches by Mt. SAC students include a stuffed vampire bat, a meteorite, and an Australian musical instrument known as a *Didgeridoo* (which she played). Keep in mind there is no need to show people familiar objects they can easily imagine in their mind.

Audio Support

Audio support includes all kinds of presentational aids your audience can hear. A recent student in a public speaking class wrote an informative speech on the history of the jazz scene in Los Angeles in the early 20th century. As part of her presentation, she played short clips of music representing the work of three major artists during her speech. It is vital to check the amplification of any audio aids you use during a presentation before it begins. Many students have tried to play audio clips during their speeches, only to find that the sound from their audio device could not be heard by all members of the audience (or that their battery wasn't completely charged).

Video and Animation

While students who completed their public speaking course in 1975 were largely unable to use moving images in their presentations, it is now possible to easily incorporate a stunning array of interesting video and/or animation into speeches. Speeches can be enhanced by showing powerful video of real-life disasters, informative depictions of complex medical procedures, or entertaining scenes of pets behaving strangely. It is also possible to create custom video and animation to enhance a presentation. Speakers should be aware that these type of resources should be used sparingly. When shown video, audiences can quickly be transformed from engaged listeners to passive viewers. Even the best speakers can have trouble competing for attention with fast-moving visual imagery and driving soundtracks. Remember that public speaking is about making a face-to-face connection with the people in your audience. It can be enhanced by the use of video; video should not replace you as a speaker.

Slideshows

Slideshow programs, such as PowerPoint, have become very popular presentation aids in both education and the business world. Slideshows are able to embed visual images, audio clips, and video clips – though the most common use of slides is to convey text to an audience.

It is tricky to use text as a form of visual support for a speech, because audience members who are asked to read may lose track of ideas that are being spoken at the same time. People also read at very different rates. Of course, reading text also requires that people break eye contact with a speaker for long periods of time

Text is best utilized as a visual when unfamiliar words are being used, such as showing the audience a word in a different language. Occasionally images require short labels. Most often, though, the audience and speaker will be best served when a speaker verbalizes words. An exception to this might be a teaching situation in which a large amount of information must be conveyed in a short period of time. However, it is rarely advisable to use bits of text more than a few words in length. Many speakers who opt to use slides make the error of overwhelming their audiences with text.

Some speakers use slides as a way to hide during presentations, darting off to the side of the room and dimming the lights. A recent lecture at Mt. SAC began with a slide showing a smiling cartoon sun and the words "Good Morning." It is far better to be greeted by a human being than an electronic device. Make sure that you are the source of information, not a series of words and clip art on a dozen screens.

Tip

Limit yourself to 1 slide per 3 minutes of speaking, and do not use slides unless the images can be seen without dimming the light on you.

Handouts

Occasionally it may be appropriate for you to create (or acquire) a handout for each member of your audience that supports your speech in a meaningful way. This could be a simple piece of paper with additional information, or might include a small sample of food, a bookmark, a lucky coin, or even a sample of sunscreen. It can be very distracting to distribute handouts during a presentation, and audience members may be tempted to engage with the handout instead of you, so it is recommended to distribute handouts at the conclusion of a presentation.

ADVANTAGES AND DISADVANTAGES OF AUDIO AND VISUAL SUPPORT

Visual and auditory support can greatly enhance your presentation in a number of ways. Consider the following are **advantages** of using visual or auditory support:

They clarify complex concepts. Many ideas can be made somewhat clearer by the use of visual or auditory support. It may even be necessary for your audience to see an image to achieve clarity. For instance, explaining how a bill becomes a law in the state of California requires a minimum of 5 major steps. A chart or slide listing each step (with an arrow in between each) might help your audience better understand the complicated process.

They can convey powerful emotions. Visuals, in particular, can quickly evoke an emotional response from your audience. Think, for example, of the Save the Children Foundation's advertisements that show images of hungry children. It is one thing for an audience to hear that children are starving, but seeing a specific child and her facial expression often yields a more potent reaction.

They show comparisons. A student recently showed a map of elephant populations across Africa from ten years ago and a second map of elephant populations today. The photographs showed a dramatic difference, and the audience immediately understood the magnitude of the issue.

They help improve recall. Audience members simply remember things better when they have not only heard them but also have seen them. Visual learners are especially helped by visual reinforcements.

They add interest. It is sometimes hard to stay interested in words alone. The mind wanders. Adding audio and visual support can bring new energy, especially to dry topics.

They promote conciseness. Long, drawn out verbal explanations can sometimes be replaced by one well-chosen visual image. A few years ago a Mt. SAC student showed an enlarged picture of a photograph she took after a hurricane in Kauai. The damage was immediately obvious.

They may improve credibility. Well prepared and managed audio and visual support will make you appear both prepared and professional. The opposite is also true. Credibility is immediately lost when you show poorly prepared presentation aids with sloppy work, misspelled words, or grammar errors.

They serve as evidence. An audio or visual aid can function as a form of support for arguments in your speech. Consider how evidence, including crime scene photography and surveillance videos, is often used in courtrooms to prove a person's guilt or innocence. You can strengthen your claims with well-chosen audio or visual evidence.

They assist communication with new speakers of English. Limited English speaking audiences often appreciate visuals, in particular, as it may help them better understand what you are discussing.

Preparing Your Audio and Visual Support

Audio and visual support should be prepared with the same care and professionalism as the content of your speech. With this in mind, review these general guidelines:

Choose audio and visual support that enhances your speech. Any added audio or visual support should serve a specific and identifiable purpose. A picture or graph just for the sake of having one does not enhance the speech.

Use them sparingly. A mistake beginners and some professionals sometimes make is to have far too many types of audio and visual support. It is not necessary to show a poster of an object, hold up the object, show a video of the object, and give everyone in the audience a sample of the object to take home. We recommend between one and three images, sounds, or slides for your classroom speeches and no more than one video clip per presentation.

Each visual image should only contain one major idea. Concentrate on presenting one key point per slide or poster. Limit the number of words to the absolute minimum necessary. If your audience is reading, they aren't listening to you. You can always add information verbally as you display the visual.

Keep the content of visuals consistent and professional. Have a design plan for all posters or slides. Use the same colors, fonts, upper and lower case letters, and styling throughout. Maintain professionalism by choosing a mature color palate (avoid "rainbow" colors), simple fonts, and simple transitions. Avoid meaningless clip art and distracting animations that do not enhance the meaning of the content you are presenting. Unless you are an artist, avoid hand drawing and handwriting on your visual aids. Double check your visual aids for accuracy. Nothing is more devastating to a speaker's credibility than the moment he or she reveals a visual that is scrawled in poor handwriting, filled with grammatical or spelling errors, or colored in with crayon. The quality of your visual aids is a direct reflection of how much you care about your speech and your audience.

Make sure visuals are large. Every audience member should be able to see every piece of information you present. Use bold, easy-to-read lettering, and take out all irrelevant information. Use bold letters and make them larger than you think you need. Test all visuals by standing far away to see how it will be seen by your most distant audience member. Can you see it easily? If not, redo it.

Make sure any poster-style visual aids are sturdy. Never use plain paper. It is too thin and flimsy. The strongest boards – matte board and foam core – are available at any art supply store. These boards will be easier to manage and are less likely to fall off an easel.

Keep in mind the potential needs of all audience members. Some audience members may be unable to hear audio or see images or text, so prepare in advance to provide interpreting, closed-captioning, or other resources so everyone can benefit from your audio and video support.

Many people use PowerPoint (presentation slideshows) ineffectively. Gary Chapman of the LBJ School of Public Affairs at the University of Texas has summarized what he calls a list of "The Ten Sins of Powerpoint." They include overloading slides with too much text, revealing the speaker's poor sense of design, using slides throughout the speech, and serving as a "crutch" for speakers to avoid engaging with the audience. You can review Chapman's whole list of "sins" at http://www.utexas.edu/lbj/21cp/syllabus/powerpoint_tips.htm

No matter what type of support you choose to use, you must prepare and use it correctly.

USING VISUAL AND AUDIO SUPPORT DURING YOUR SPEECH

Using this type of supporting material can be frustrating if you aren't comfortable with technology. They also pose some risks to presenters. Computers, projectors, tablets, audio players, Internet connections – they are all susceptible to complications and, at times, failure. Every precaution should be made to insure that your presentation won't be diminished by your use of audio or video.

Planning a few things in advance can help tremendously. If you are using something electronic, you will need power. Check in advance to see if you will have available power and carry an extension cord for remote presentations just in case. Also keep extra batteries and projector bulbs handy. Many a great PowerPoint has fallen prey to a "clicker" with a dead battery. Also – practice the technique with the actual equipment you will use during the speech and then pre to pre-test any and all mechanical systems before you speak.

During your speech, make sure that you follow the basic steps for using your visual and audio support effectively. Your professor will likely demonstrate some of these techniques in class, but here are a few good tips to get you started:

Make sure every person can see or hear them. Don't block visuals with your body while you are displaying them. Test audio levels, keeping in mind that acoustics in a room full of people may be different than in an empty room.

Control the moment when the audience sees a specific visual image. Nothing zaps the power of a carefully constructed moment in a speech when the visual support shows up too early or too late. Conceal any visual items (props, electronic images, videos, etc) until the exact moment the audience should be aware of them – and then conceal them again when you move on to a new subject.

Talk to your audience, not your visuals. Maintain eye contact with the audience and avoid the urge to turn and look at your visual like a spectator. It is helpful to see how the audience reacts to your visual support (such as a video clip) so you know if they understand the meaning and purpose.

Do not dim the lights for extensive periods during your speech. Your audience will be more easily distracted and likely to sleep. Make sure you are always well-lit for your speech, even if it means that you must stand a bit further from your screen.

Do not use the blackboard/dry erase board. Unless there is specific rhetorical reason for doing so, creating visuals during a speech makes the speaker appear unprepared and unprofessional.

Explain the purpose and source of all audio and visual support to the audience. Also add any essential details that are not clear.

Avoid passing an item around while you are speaking. Speakers sometimes choose to show the audience an object too small to pass the back row test, then try to solve this problem by circulating the item. This can be disastrous as it pulls attention from you to the item and invites the audience to talk to one another during your presentation.

CONCLUSION

Visual and audio support are excellent ways to impress and educate your audience. We have covered the advantages of using this type of support as well as some basic types of presentational enhancement. Most importantly, you now have important tips at your disposal for creating visual and audio support and managing it during your presentation. If you follow this advice, your speech will be not only a treat for the ears, but also a feast for the eyes.

Speaker's Secret

Creating audio and visual support for your speech can be quite time consuming. Don't let that take away from time you should be spending on your speech and speech delivery! If you spend all your time editing a video for your speech, your speech itself may suffer. Audio and visual support is exactly what the name implies: support for the main source of meaning in your speech: you!

FROM FRIGHT TO MIGHT MOMENT

Professional looking visual aids show the audience you are concerned about them and will help them form a positive impression of you. In addition, visual aids give you a breather, because people are focusing their attention on something other than you.

CHAPTER THIRTEEN

DELIVERY

People have to talk about something just to keep their voice boxes in working order so they'll have good voice boxes in case there's ever anything really meaningful to say.

— *Kurt Vonnegut, Jr.*

While the topic and content of a speech are certainly important, the manner in which you deliver your speech can drastically alter your audience impact. Remember from Chapter 1 that **interference** is an element in the communication process. A speaker with excellent delivery skills can minimize distracting verbal and non-verbal behaviors that might interfere with an audience's grasp of a message. Additionally, advanced delivery skills can help a speaker to be more entertaining and emotional. A skilled speaker can also emphasize key concepts and ideas. This will further improve the overall experience for the audience.

HOW TO CHOOSE A DELIVERY STYLE

The first delivery issue you should consider when preparing your speech is the style. There are **four delivery styles of speeches**: manuscript, memorized, impromptu, and extemporaneous. While speeches may involve a combination of these, the best choice is to have a clear style of delivery selected for each speech.

Manuscript Delivery

The first method involves speaking from a **manuscript.** When delivering a speech from a manuscript, the speaker writes out every word of the speech in advance and then reads from the script during the performance. The expectation is very high that the content will be strong since the speaker has had a chance to sculpt every single word.

When delivering a speech with a manuscript, it is essential that you still perform the speech, not just read it out loud. The tone of your voice must be conversational and energetic, and you must make eye contact with the audience. As we will discuss later in this chapter, eye contact does not mean flashing your eyes in the direction of the audience a few times each minute. Manuscript speeches should be rehearsed many times so you are very familiar with the speech and have even memorized some important sections, like the beginning and the end.

Most speakers never get to use the fancy, transparent teleprompters that politicians and celebrities use. You will likely be holding your speaking notes in your hands, which can limit your ability to gesture. Because of this, make sure that your manuscript itself is easy-to-use and professional looking. A final challenge is that you may be standing behind a lectern, which conceals part of your body and creates a nonverbal barrier between you and your audience.

Manuscript speeches are good to use in situations where every word counts, when what you're saying is complicated, or in situations when your emotions could get the best of you. When delivering a eulogy, for instance, you might need a script to keep you focused.

Memorized Delivery

The second style of speech delivery is memorized. When you perform a memorized speech, you write it out word-for-word and deliver it with no notes.

It is very time consuming to memorize a speech, and even a well-memorized speech can be hard to recall when you are under the stress of performing. Sometimes speakers who memorize their content deliver it in a very flat tone with a blank expression. These speakers may find that because they are concentrating on what word to say next, they lose their connection with the audience.

Memorized speeches can be very effective when speakers know their material well enough to deliver it convincingly and connect with the audience. It can be very exhilarating when you speak with the confidence of knowing what you will say next and the freedom of delivering the speech without notes. You can focus on your listeners, see their facial expressions, and respond to their reactions.

For most situations in your life, you probably won't have the time to memorize an entire speech. However, if you plan to deliver a speech multiple times it may be worthwhile to memorize it so you can refine your delivery.

If you plan to use the memorized style, develop a strategy for memorization. Every person has his or her own techniques, but a few strategies have worked for students in the past. Some have chosen to memorize one sentence of the speech at a time, repeating all of the other memorized sentences as they learn each new one. Other students have chosen to record their speeches to tape or iPod and listen to them repeatedly until they know the lines. The most advisable option is to start by speaking extemporaneously (see below) with no notes and record yourself giving the speech. Listen back as you review your manuscript to see which ideas you missed. Your first performance will probably be short and include very few ideas from the speech, but keep repeating this exercise again and again. You will begin to recall more and more ideas, then supporting ideas, then specific phrasing. The advantage of this method is that it helps your mind learn the ideas in the speech, not just the words of the speech, so your eventual delivery should sound more natural.

Impromptu Delivery

The third way to deliver a speech is **impromptu**. Impromptu speaking occurs when the speaker has limited preparation time. The speaker prepares an outline of the speech during the brief preparation time, if any is given at all. Then, he or she develops the subpoints and creates the wording while speaking.

Impromptu speaking is the most frequently used speaking style in our everyday lives. You will use these skills to answer tough questions asked by job interviewers or clients. You will also use the impromptu style when making unexpected presentations during professional or community meetings.

Impromptu speaking, when done well, can be very impressive. As you know from experience, when a person is able to come up with something good in an impromptu situation, it is very impressive to others. This may be the reason improvisational comedy is so popular. Remember, though, that you shouldn't intentionally choose the impromptu style if you are given time to prepare. That choice is likely to hurt your credibility as you will look less prepared than you should be. This style should be saved for only those situations where you must prepare your presentation in little to no time.

Competition speech, known as **forensics**, allows students to compete in an event called Impromptu Speaking. Students are typically given a quotation and are asked to speak for approximately five minutes after just two minutes of preparation. While it is challenging at first, speakers who practice improve quickly. Most competitors deliver thoughtful, interesting, and organized speeches. Participating in forensics can be a great way to hone your impromptu skills through more practice.

Even though impromptu speaking is spontaneous, it is possible to prepare. Techniques are further addressed in Chapter 17.

Extemporaneous Delivery

The last method of speech delivery is **extemporaneous**. In this type of delivery, you prepare the complete content of your speech, including a very thorough outline, but do not write the speech out word-for-word. You will rehearse the speech several times and become extremely familiar with the material, then deliver the speech for an audience with the use of notes.

This style of delivery has many advantages. For one, you tend to sound very natural and conversational because you are developing words and phrases naturally. The content can be altered based on audience analysis during the speech. If the audience seems bored with one section, you can proceed to your next main point. If they seem interested in a particular area, you can elaborate.

After you become skilled at researching and organizing your speeches, you will find preparing an outstanding speech using the extemporaneous delivery method can be done quickly and professionally. Though there are many different strategies for preparing an extemporaneous speech, two things you should always remember are to know your subject thoroughly and practice your speech. With these two tools, it will be much easier to take the general ideas from your notes and speak "off the cuff."

If you are interested in becoming a teacher, you will probably become very familiar with this delivery style. If you think a six to eight minute informative speech is difficult to perform with just a few notes, notice that your professors can lecture for an entire class period with just a page or two of notes!

For this course, your professor will likely assign a delivery style for each speech assignment. After you leave class, you will have to make that decision on your own. Be sure to weigh the advantages and disadvantages of each delivery style.

DELIVERY TECHNIQUES

In Chapter 3 you were introduced to a few basic delivery techniques for speaking. Now we will address some more advanced techniques that involve your voice and body.

Using Your Voice

If your speech could be compared to a symphony, then your voice would be the instrument which plays the written notes. It is a highly flexible instrument and is capable of a wide range of vocal variety. It is also a delicate instrument, requiring careful use.

Projection

For beginning speakers, the most essential vocal technique is **projection**. For communication to occur it is essential that every audience member be able to hear every single word of your speech. This is achieved with **vocal projection**, sending your voice to different areas of the room. With a microphone and amplifier, projection is easily achieved. In many speaking situations, however, you won't have any support for your voice other than your own lungs and vocal cords. Projecting your voice requires good control of your breath and the use of your diaphragm muscle. According to communication consultants Cyndi Maxey and Jill Bremer's 2004 book *It's Your Move*, breathing from the diaphragm allows your lungs to expand more, giving you greater oxygen to put power behind your words. To see if you are speaking with your diaphragm, place your hand near the top of your stomach. Breathe out sharply and say "ho ho ho." If you feel a muscle tensing, you are correctly using your diaphragm.

Volume Variety

Another vocal characteristic related to projection is **volume variety**. Variety in volume assists the audience in maintaining interest and involvement in what is being said, and helps to emphasize key concepts. In his famous speech, "I Have a Dream," Dr. Martin Luther King, Jr. used volume to accent and compliment his message. Lowering his voice to almost a whisper or raising it to a high crescendo has kept audiences past and present mesmerized by the delivery of his message. When students watch this speech, they sometimes will physically move their bodies closer to the television screen when he speaks softly, demonstrating how involved they are with him as a speaker. At the moments when he is loud and demonstrative, audience members can be seen sitting at attention ready to respond to his message. Though many speakers increase their volume for emphasis, few take advantage of the power of quiet moments. If you attempt this technique, remember you still need to project your voice out to everyone in the audience, even if your overall tone is quiet or hushed.

Pitch

Pitch is the placement of your voice on a musical scale, and **pitch variety** refers to a speaker's use of a range of high and low notes while speaking. In the same way we tend to like melodies in music that move up and down the musical scale, we also prefer speakers whose voices employ pitch variety.

Using a somewhat lower pitch than your typical speaking voice can help to emphasize a serious point, demonstrate anger, or add richness to descriptive language. It also adds **closure** to a sentence or an idea. If you have a chance to review recordings of your speeches, listen to hear how frequently you let your voice drop in pitch. You may notice your voice dropping at the end of every sentence, or even in the middle of sentences. This can make your speech hard to listen to, because ideas are not linked - they are constantly being "closed." Of course, one of the most obvious places to use a drop in pitch to create closure is the last phrase of your speech.

Using higher notes during your speech can demonstrate excitement, positive emotional feelings, and add a sense of energy to your speech. Be careful, though, speaking at too high of a pitch or sustaining a high pitch for too long can be an irritation to your audience.

The opposite of a voice with pitch variety is a **monotone** voice. A monotone speaker uses very little pitch variety. This type of speaking is usually very low energy, doesn't emphasize the most important ideas in the speech, and doesn't hold the audience's attention very well. A famous example of a monotone speaker is Ben Stein, who you might recognize from commercials or as the economics teacher in the classic film *Ferris Bueller's Day Off.* He asks questions to the class and then tries to elicit a response by droning, "Anyone? Anyone?" No one responds.

Rate

Rate is the cadence or speed of word delivery in your speech. At a minimum, it is essential that you speak at a reasonable rate for audience comprehension.

There are some unfortunate stereotypes connected with the rate at which people speak. A slow talking person who hesitates a lot is sometimes perceived as less intelligent. At the same time, speaking slowly can be very effective when delivering emotional messages or explaining difficult or technical concepts. It can even make you seem more confident. Speaking at a fast pace can be effective when you are trying to motivate an audience, because the energy can be exciting. However, speakers who constantly speak at a fast rate can seem nervous or even untrustworthy.

In general, the best speakers will have **rate variety** within each presentation. Changing your rate helps hold the interest of the audience, while giving them time to catch up and reflect upon your most important ideas.

Pausing

Pausing is the use of silence in your speech. It can be uncomfortable to be silent while standing in front of an audience, so pausing may be the single most underused vocal technique. Not only does pausing allow the audience to catch up and react to what has been said, it also creates interest and allows for powerful nonverbal messages to be shared more clearly. Do not be afraid of silence. In our fast paced modern society, people expect there to be noise all the time. The uniqueness of silence allows you the power to bring their attention back to you and your message.

Additionally, a split-second pause before a word emphasizes it as important by creating a slight break in your speaking rhythm. You can use this technique in combination with volume and pitch to bring great variety to your delivery. Try reading the following sentence out loud and hesitate slightly before you say the word "essential." Notice how it highlights the word.

> It is essential that every college student take a public speaking course.

The opposite of a silent pause is the vocalized pause, in which we use non-words to avoid silence. **Non-words** are sounds like "um" and "uh" that find their way into our vocabulary during a speech. These filler sounds crop up because we are afraid of using silence in our delivery, so we make pointless sounds to keep the audience listening. The irony is that these sounds actually distract an audience from listening.

Non-words can also be words that we think are real words, but they are used during a speech like a filler word. Common examples of these are:

Like	**And**
So	**Stuff**
Well	**Basically**
Y'know	**Really**
Okay	

These words weaken our content because they are meaningless when used as fillers or in excess. You may not be aware that you are using non-words in your performances. Ask a classmate or review your speech on video to check. If you use a lot of them, deciding to make an effort to avoid these words is the first step to eliminating them from your speeches. Also be careful when you look at your note cards. This is a very common time when speakers will say, "Ummmmmm." When you feel the urge to use a non-word during a speech, just pause. Chances are it's a natural, necessary break in the idea you are discussing. Your delivery will go from cluttered to compelling!

Pronunciation

Pronunciation is the culturally agreed upon sounding of words. There is an expectation that people will pronounce words correctly, and the more education one has the greater this expectancy. For example, when interviewing for scholarships or jobs, one mispronounced word can be the difference between being declared the recipient or losing out. This applies equally to public speaking. When the audience realizes you have mispronounced a word, including a person's name, they may lose respect for you and begin to doubt the accuracy of other things you are saying. It is your responsibility as a speaker to know how to pronounce all the words and names in your speech confidently and without hesitation.

Articulation

Articulation is the clarity with which word sounds are uttered. The opposite of articulation includes slurring or mumbling words. Articulation allows you to be clear and understood so there is no miscommunication. Clarity connotes strength. Slurred speech connotes weakness or disinterest.

Many speakers do not realize they are articulating poorly, because everyday speech allows for a lot of latitude in articulation. We hear a friend ask us "Wajawaneet?" and we know that they mean, "What do you want to eat?" When we speak in front of an audience, they are probably not as familiar with our voice and speaking style, and would not understand that same phrase.

Being articulate may require you to overemphasize the movement of your mouth, lips, or tongue. You should also pay attention to how clearly you separate each word while you speak and avoid letting words run into one another. Articulation is also a great way to slow your rate of speech. Speakers who speak too quickly often slur their words, so careful attention to articulation is the first step to achieving a more conversational rate. To practice articulation, try giving parts of your speech with a pen or pencil held horizontally with your teeth. You will have to speak very clearly to overcome the obstacle of the pen.

Vocal Health

One of the worst things that can happen to a speaker is losing his or her voice. Illness is obviously a potential cause of a scratchy or lost voice, but other factors can also damage your voice — sometimes permanently. **Smoking** is a very common reason for vocal problems, particularly because of the importance of strong, deep breaths to project your voice. Over time, smokers' voices often become scratchy and coarse. Also, **overuse** of your voice can lead to a damaged voice. Shouting or talking for an extended period of time can cause hoarseness because of the wear and tear on your vocal cords. The effect of this damage is increased for speakers who do not support their voices by properly using their diaphragm muscle and instead try to create volume by tightening their vocal cords. Dr. Michelle Yagoda, a leading ear, nose, and throat physician, writes in her 2005 pamphlet *The Professional Voice: Steps Toward Optimal Vocal Health*, that the use of blood-thinning agents, like **aspirin**, as well as **alcohol** and **exposure to cold temperatures** can compound strain on vocal cords.

Over time, a lack of attention to your vocal health can lead to permanent vocal damage, including the development of small nodes on the vocal cords that may be irreversible. In 2011, musician Adele strained her voice so badly she was forced to reschedule several months' worth of concert dates. People with vocal damage are sometimes forced to write on a note pad rather than speak to avoid irreversible damage.

If you have a sore or scratchy throat, try to keep it warm and drink warm liquids to soothe it, such as tea with lemon. If your throat itches, instead of coughing, try to swallow. Avoid using products that numb the soreness in your throat. If you can't feel the pain and start talking, you might further damage your throat and pay for it later. In general, make sure you drink plenty of liquids to keep your throat and mouth from drying out, and get plenty of rest before giving a speech.

If you are really serious about improving the overall health and strength of your voice, consider taking an introductory voice and diction or vocal music class. These courses typically teach proper breathing techniques and will present exercises to help develop the quality and range of your voice.

Using Your Body

When you are in front of an audience, your body position, movement, and expression are an integral part of your performance. For some speakers, effective body movement during a speech is a tremendous challenge. Often, speech anxiety manifests itself in the form of shaking hands, wiggly toes, funny facial expressions, and averted eyes. With some practice, however, it can be relatively easy to improve this aspect of performance. As you work on the techniques described below, be sure to use a partner, friendly audience member, or a video of yourself so you can have accurate feedback about your progress.

Posture

Posture is the physical placement of the body in the speaking situation. It is important because it conveys a sense of strength or weakness. Before you even utter words, the audience observes your body language. The physical manner in which you carry yourself reveals your perception of yourself. **Good posture** involves a straight back, shoulders rolled backwards, head held up straight, and weight balanced evenly on top of a centered torso. This type of stance sends a message to the audience that you are confident, poised, and prepared. Bad posture in which the speaker is slouched or leaning sends a number of negative nonverbal messages, including a lack of confidence, a lack of poise, and a lack of credibility.

Controlled Movement

There are two types of body movement during a speech: unintentional and controlled. **Unintentional movement** includes fidgeting, clasping or wringing of hands, swaying, and pacing. These movements are somewhat acceptable in everyday conversation, but are magnified when you stand in front of an audience, creating a distraction from your message. They also make you appear nervous, weak, or unprofessional. Instead, speakers should work toward **controlled movement**. Controlled movements can include transitional walking and gestures.

Transitional walking occurs when a speaker takes steps to nonverbally signal a change in the tone or topic of the speech, such as the transitions between main points. Always walk in the same way you would naturally take steps, but keep in mind these tips:

1. *Walk parallel to the audience.* Avoid backing away from them or walking toward them, unless it is for strong dramatic effect.

2. *Always talk and walk at the same time.*

3. *Look at someone in the direction you are walking.*

4. *Start with the leg that is in the direction you are headed.*

5. *Never speak to just a portion of your audience.* When you reach your new destination, reorient your whole body so you are still facing the entire audience.

6. *When you are done walking, stop.* Don't wander.

7. *Never move while you are making a key point.* Your nonverbal message ("transition to new idea") will contradict your verbal message.

If you are disabled or injured and are unable to walk transitionally, consider making comparable transitional body movements, if possible. This should be done if your speech is longer than just a few minutes. In general, though, the movement should not become a major distraction to the content of

214

your speech. If mobility is challenging for you, stay in one place for your performance and focus on your vocal delivery and facial expressiveness to add interest and create a sense of transition.

Gestures

Gestures are controlled hand movements. They are important because they add expression, emphasis, and clarity. Natural gestures are fluid and have a definite beginning and ending. They should be firm, confident and used to emphasize a specific word or concept. Placement of gestures is important. Gestures are usually delivered above the waist. Gesturing too low can be distracting and calls attention away from your face and voice. Avoid too much repetition of the same gesture because it makes your speech seem over-rehearsed and unnatural. Avoid touching your hands together, playing with your note card, or holding a pen.

If you are not comfortable making gestures yet, just relax your arms at your sides while you speak. This may seem awkward, but it looks very natural to the audience and helps them focus attention on your face and eyes. Avoid holding an arm bent at your waist, putting your hands in your pockets, hiding your hands behind your back, crossing your arms, or grabbing your arm with your hand.

Facial Expressions

Facial expressions are the movements of various parts of the speaker's face. Be aware that your face reveals many inner thoughts and feelings. Therefore, try to feel confident and your face will show it. Match your expressions to the tone of the speech. Eyebrows, lips, eyes, and even your nose can all add interesting accents to your words as you speak. At a minimum, your face should reflect your interest in your topic. It's surprising how many speakers appear to be bored by their own speeches!

Remember from Chapter 3 the importance of a speaker's **smile**. A smile radiates warmth and is calming to the audience. They are better able to establish a connection with you as a speaker because you appear friendly. Even if you are speaking about a very serious or controversial subject, you can begin your presentation with a smile. Making friends with the audience is even more crucial in these instances.

It has been said that the eyes are the windows to the soul. The expression **eye contact** indicates that the primary way you make a contact with the audience is by looking at them and having them look back at you. An over-reliance on notes prevents this relationship. Hair falling in your face, wearing sunglasses, or wearing a hat or cap prevents this relationship.

Though it is not always the case in other cultures, in the United States the overwhelming expectation is that speakers will make **sustained eye contact** with their audiences. Speakers who avoid eye contact may be considered more nervous and less credible than other speakers. In general, work to sustain eye contact with each member of your audience *for a complete thought or idea*. Once the thought is completed, find the next person and begin the next idea. It is very challenging to deliver an entire speech using sustained eye contact. However, sustained eye contact will be extremely effective for you if you are willing to spend time mastering this technique.

CONCLUSION

In this chapter, you have learned the importance of using your voice and your body to enhance your speech. These skills are more advanced than the ones you were introduced to in Chapter 3, but you probably have more experience as a speaker now and are ready to expand your skills. Many of the techniques take time to perfect, so try to incorporate them into your presentations little by little and keep working hard at developing outstanding delivery!

Speaker's Secret

Most speakers think that they are ready to speak when they have mastered the content of their speech, but in reality the audience will only listen to the content of most speeches if the delivery is not distracting. Don't forget to give yourself ample time to rehearse your delivery for best effect.

FROM FRIGHT TO MIGHT MOMENT

The secret to outstanding delivery is to talk *with*, and not *to* your audience. If you think of the audience as your friends, there will be less to worry about!

CHAPTER FOURTEEN

INFORMATIVE SPEAKING

The beginning of knowledge is the discovery of something we do not understand.

— *Frank Herbert*

In our world of smart phones, wireless Internet, and 24-hour news networks, a steady stream of facts and data is literally at our fingertips. We live in the age of information — an age in which technology increasingly helps us exchange messages in new and creative ways — but technology can only do so much. Often, we are responsible for crafting our own informative messages. Sometimes, we must deliver them live and in person.

If you have ever given someone directions, told someone how to make a particular food dish, presented a report, or taught any type of lesson, then you have been an informative speaker. You no doubt realized the difficulty of being clear and understandable when delivering complicated messages to a general audience. You may have also realized that some messages often go beyond merely informing and actually try to influence audiences. So, what precisely is informative speaking?

THE GOAL OF INFORMATIVE SPEAKING

As its name suggests, the goal of informative speaking is to inform, enlighten, teach, or educate the audience. We often evaluate informative speeches by asking ourselves a simple question: Did I learn something from this presentation?

Consider how the goal of informing differs from the goal of persuading an audience. Persuasive speakers aim to change or influence an audience. They may wish to challenge what a person thinks or alter the way in which he or she behaves. Informative speakers, on the other hand, are interested in *passing along factual information*. To clarify this concept, consider the topic area of air pollution. A persuasive speech on this topic might address the harmful effects of air pollution and then urge audiences to buy electric cars or carpool. Conversely, an informative speech might report on the amount of pollution in our air or how electric cars operate. Notice the goal in the second set of examples is not to change or influence what the audience feels or the way they behave. Rather, the primary goal is to educate listeners.

While both informative and persuasive speeches impart knowledge, the primary difference between the two is the speaker's *motive* for sharing the knowledge. As you move through the stages of speech construction, ask yourself, "Why do I want to give this audience this information?" Sometimes without realizing it, we construct persuasive arguments in supposedly informative messages. If, for example, you were discussing a controversial issue such as cloning and you informed the audience of all of the potential dangers of the practice, your speech would become an argument against cloning. Only if you also present the possible benefits of the research would you have a balanced informative speech.

Are you wondering why it matters if there is overlap between informative and persuasive information? Is it just a picky public speaking class rule? Consider this real life scenario:

You go to a college-sponsored counseling seminar to learn about which courses to take to complete your Associate's Degree. You expect to hear about all options available to you from a non-biased source. However, the person hosting the seminar only talks about why you should take extra psychology classes to prepare you for a degree in psychology. Obviously this isn't the session you signed up for.

A familiar example of a persuasive message hidden in an informative framework is the so-called "infomercial," commonly seen on late-night television. These 30 or 60-minute programs supposedly inform us about all the features of a great new product, but they do not really give us all the information, do they? Will they share the fact that their product is made of low-grade plastic? That it does not include a vital component (sold separately)? Or that it only works in certain climates? Be a little skeptical when listening to informative presentations. And remember, your audience may also be listening skeptically when you speak. Don't let that last statement alarm you; although they may be listening cautiously, there are strategies you can use that will make your audience want to hear your message.

THE THREE GOLDEN RULES OF INFORMATIVE SPEAKING

RULE # 1: BE THOROUGH

When your primary goal is to educate, a careful and comprehensive discussion of your topic is vital. An informative speaker who leaves the audience with unanswered questions or unclear explanations has not been effective.

A common reason why informative speakers fail to be thorough is that they try to teach too much, and the result is usually a "half-baked" speech. They fill their time with a seemingly endless stream of words, and they either never actually make a point, or they make so many that the audience is left confused. In such a situation, the annoyed audience reacts to the speaker much like a judge responds to long winded attorney, asking, "Just where are you going with this?" You are better off thoroughly teaching a few things well, than superficially covering a wide range of topics. Make sure that you appropriately narrow your topic and sufficiently focus your main points so that you can cover the subject completely in your allotted time frame. If you can articulate the purpose of your informative speech clearly in a single sentence, you are probably on the right track. If you cannot reduce your speech to a sentence, you probably have a speech that will "spray" a lot of information, much of which will miss the target.

RULE #2: DON'T BE BORING

It's sad to say, but sometimes people are boring when presenting educational messages. Not everyone is mindful of the state of mind of an audience while delivering a speech. To avoid a disengaged audience, be sure to choose the right topic for your speech. Always be more concerned about what your audience already knows than what you already know. You cannot be informative if an audience already knows the information you are presenting. If the audience does have some general knowledge of your topic, you will need to provide something surprising or more in-depth. Once you have selected the right informative topic, consider the following two concepts that can help you avoid boring public speaking:

Need to Know

Do your audience members **need to know** the information you will be presenting? In other words, is it significant? Great speakers present information in a way that makes knowledge attractive. One way to do that is by including information that has a significant financial, medical, cultural, educational, or other important impact on the lives of their immediate audience.

Neat to Know

Besides being significant, information should also be interesting or **neat to know.** In other words, the facts of your subject should immediately spark curiosity when you mention them. For example, a student recently delivered an informative speech on the "Invisibility Cloak" — a military invention which reflects light rendering airplanes completely invisible. With its military benefits, the invisibility cloak is something we clearly "need to know" about. The added attraction of invisibility makes the topic even more exciting and "neat to know."

Great informative topics, which fulfill both the need and neat to know, are sometimes hard to find. You will need to do a lot of thinking, talking with people, reading, and listening to find a true gem that is both important and fascinating. For a further challenge, try to find a topic that excites your public speaking professor! After seeing hundreds of informative speeches a year, it will be difficult to find a topic that he or she has not yet heard, but it could happen.

Once you have sparked our curiosity through your dynamite topic, hold onto it by choosing vivid examples, telling exciting stories, and speaking with animated vocal delivery and facial expression. Show the audience just how exciting and interesting your information is by the level of interest you show towards your topic and by the enthusiasm you demonstrate in your own delivery style. Show that you have thought of their needs by the information you share and the organizational method you use.

RULE #3: GET ORGANIZED

Former President Woodrow Wilson was once quoted as saying that it took him two weeks to prepare a ten-minute speech, one week to prepare a one-hour speech, and that he could be ready on the spot for a two-hour speech. At first it seems odd that the shortest speech takes the most time to prepare and the longest speech takes the least amount of time. Think about it, though. Most of us can talk off the top of our heads with little preparation for a long time. If we are given a definite amount of time to make our point, though, we really have to focus our thoughts and synthesize our ideas. As Wilson explained, when you have time constraints, "Every word must be brilliant. Every line must be a winner. Only thoughts that will register the greatest impact are acceptable." Don't let the length of your informative speech or your familiarity with the topic trick you into thinking that organization is not important.

One of the first things beginning professors learn is that effective instruction cannot happen without proper organization. Students grasp information better when it is presented in a structured format. Here are some common organizational frameworks for each type of informative speech. (Many of these structures are described in greater detail in Chapter 8.)

A speech of description, especially when it concerns a place such as a city or a country, is often organized using a **spatial structure**. For example, in a speech vividly describing "The Splendor of Maui" you could use a map and divide the area up into two to four geographic regions. Each region could function as a main point in your presentation.

A speech of demonstration is also called a "How-To" speech and often makes use of a **chronological**, step-by-step organizational pattern. Each step becomes a main point of the speech. If there are too many steps to make each one a main point, consider how you might group steps into phases. For example, if you were demonstrating how to make a type of food dish, you might first discuss the preparation phase, then the actual cooking phase, and finally, the serving phase. Speeches about events in history or biographical speeches about a specific person often use the chronological structure, as well.

A speech of explanation, which helps the audience to understand how something works mechanically or systemically, often uses the **structure-function sequence**. This is an organizational pattern in which your first main point describes the different components of your topic. The second and, if needed, third point explains the applications (or uses) of the subject. For example, in your first main point you describe the features of a digital camera; in your second main point you explain how it creates digital pictures, and in main point three, how the photos can be shared online.

A speech of revelation uncovers new information about concepts or objects like discoveries, theories, and inventions, and is often organized using a **topical pattern**. In the topical pattern, the speaker chooses the most important topics to cover regarding a subject. Follow the steps from Chapter 8 to help you create main points for this type of speech structure.

These categories are not completely distinct from one another. Your speech may belong to just one or maybe all of these categories. Regardless of the type of speech you present, make sure to keep in mind the three golden rules of informative speaking so that your speech will be as engaging as it is educational.

CONCLUSION

In this chapter we have explained the function of informative speaking and we offered a few guidelines for doing it well. Informative speaking does not have to be boring. Remember that each of us has the capacity to become a professor simply by preparing and enthusiastically delivering a thorough, organized speech packed with relevant and novel information.

Speaker's Secret

Visual aids can be very effective when it comes to informing people. Many people learn new information better if they can see it as well as hear it. For even greater effect, get your audience involved. Retention of material is almost twice as high if people do something as well as see or hear it.

FROM FRIGHT TO MIGHT MOMENT

The fear of being boring is a concern for many speakers, but if your informative speech contains lots of personality, stories, and humor, you can be confident your audience will respond positively to your performance.

SAMPLE EXPLANATION INFORMATIVE OUTLINE

Specific Purpose: To inform my audience about the delicious legacy of In-N-Out Burger

INTRODUCTION

Attention Device: May 10, 2011 was a special day for Danielle DeInnocentes. The Texas resident was so overcome with emotion that she burst into tears, stating, "I've waited eight years for this." Danielle wasn't crying over her wedding day or the birth of her first child. Instead, The Dallas Observer of May 11, 2011 noted that what got Danielle so worked up was getting her first In-N-Out burger at the grand opening of the Frisco, Texas location. If you're like me, you probably don't cry every time you eat In-N-Out. Most of us in Southern California probably take for granted these restaurants that are all around us. But it's still my favorite fast food.

Topic Revelation Statement: Today, I would like to inform you about a cornerstone of Southern California's culture, In-N-Out Burger.

Significance Statement: The 2009 book In-N-Out Burger describes the restaurant as a "cultural institution," and it might be one of your favorite places to eat. But if that's not enough, Consumer Reports of June 30, 2011, named In-N-Out Burger both the best fast food burger and the best fast food restaurant out of 53 that were tested.

Preview of Main Points: So let me tempt your appetite by first, outlining the history of In-N-Out. Then, I will explore some of the unique cultural elements of the restaurant and its following. Finally, I will cover the secret (or not-so-secret) menu.

BODY

I.   In-N-Out has a rich history rooted in Southern California.

   A.   The restaurant started out as a small, local burger chain.

      1.   Husband and wife team Harry and Esther Snyder opened the first In-N-Out in 1948 in Baldwin Park, California.

      2.   According to the In-N-Out company website, accessed on January 10, 2012, the Snyders' motto on founding the restaurant was, "Give customers the freshest, highest quality foods you can buy and provide them with friendly service in a sparkling clean environment."

      3.   Up until his death in 1976, Harry Snyder managed the company and its 18 locations, all in Southern California.

   B.   Harry's son Rich took over in 1976 and began expanding the restaurant to over 90 locations by the early 1990s.

C. The company expanded geographically from the 1990s to the present.

    1. The previously cited book In-N-Out Burger reveals that the restaurant spread to Las Vegas and Northern California starting in 1992.

    2. In the 2000s, In-N-Outs opened in Arizona and Utah.

    3. In-N-Out's most recent expansion is to Texas. The Dallas Morning News of October 7, 2010 notes that the chain will build eight new restaurants in the Dallas area.

TRANSITION: Now that I have given you a brief overview of In-N-Out's history, let's examine the cultural elements that make In-N-Out so unique.

II. In-N-Out has several elements that set it apart from other fast food chains.

A. The restaurant's exclusivity has brought it loyal fans.

    1. The Los Angeles Times of May 7, 2009 describes In-N-Out's fans as a "cult" because of their devotion to the chain.

    2. With only 258 restaurants in the nation and a menu that never changes, people from outside of California are eager to get a taste of In-N-Out.

    3. According to the Los Angeles Times August 14, 2002, when the first In-N-Out opened in Scottsdale, Arizona, there was a four hour wait to order food, and news helicopters covered the event.

B. The restaurant has drawn attention for its religious elements.

    1. The most well known religious aspect are the Bible verses printed on the packaging for food and drinks at In-N-Out.

        a. The Deseret News of December 26, 2009 observes that the chapter and verse, but not the actual words, are printed on the edges of cups, burger wrappers, and tray covers.

        b. This practice was started in the 1980s and continues today.

    2. According to the previously cited Los Angeles Times, the Bible verses are were begun by former CEO Rich Snyder, a devout Christian, and are still printed in his memory.

C. In-N-Out attracts a large celebrity following.

    1. D Magazine March 2011 reports that chef Julia Child once had In-N-Out brought to her room when she was sick in the hospital.

2. The Sunday Mail, April 20, 2008, reports that celebrity chef Gordon Ramsay liked In-N-Out so much when he tried it the first time, that he got in his car after finishing his burger and went through the drive-thru so he could order the same meal to go.

3. Basketball player Ron Artest told The Orange County Register of January 24, 2011 that the only reason he chose the Lakers over other teams was so he could eat In-N-Out.

TRANSITION: Now that I've told you how In-N-Out has such a unique culture surrounding it, let me finally tell you about what might be the most interesting part of the restaurant…its secret menu.

III. In-N-Out has a special menu that only insiders know about.

    A. The "secret menu" is a variation on the traditional In-N-Out food.

        1. According to the A Hamburger Today blog, March 3, 2011, the official In-N-Out menu only has single and double hamburgers and cheeseburgers, fries, sodas, and shakes.

        2. However, loyal customers know that the restaurant will modify the menu items or make special items upon request.

            a. According to the In-N-Out website's "Not-so-secret menu" page, customers can order a grilled cheese.

            b. You can also order items like a Neapolitan shake or a Wish burger, which is a vegetarian option.

    B. The most famous secret menu item is "animal style."

        1. The previously cited Serious Eats states that an animal style burger includes Thousand Island spread, mustard grilled patties, and extra grilled onions.

        2. Animal style fries include spread, cheese, and grilled onions.

        3. The previously cited D Magazine states rumor has it that "animal style" was named by the cooks at one In-N-Out after a group of unruly customers would come in and regularly place the special order.

    C. There are some large burgers that can be ordered on the secret menu.

        1. The official secret menu allows ordering a 3x3 or 4x4. This is three or four patties and slices of cheese.

        2. Whatupwilly's blog of January 23, 2006 chronicles the largest In-N-Out burger ever made, a 100x100 constructed at the Las Vegas In-N-Out in 2004.

        3. After this incident, the chain restricted the largest size of a burger to 4x4.

CONCLUSION

Review of Topic/Main Points: Today, I have tempted your tummies by informing you about one of my favorite restaurants, In-N-Out. First, I outlined the history of the company, then I explained some of its interesting cultural elements. Finally, I let you all in on the secret In-N-Out menu.

Lasting Thought: The next time you eat In-N-Out, you probably won't burst into tears like Danielle DeInnocentes. But before you bite into that juicy double-double, think about what a unique part of California culture we have in this fast food chain.

WORKS CITED

Arave, Lynn. "In-N-Out Serves Burgers with a Side of Scripture." *Deseret News*. Deseret Media Companies, 26 Dec 2009. Web. 16 Jan 2012.

Arellano, Gustavo. "Ron Artest: Only Reason He Plays for the Lakers is In-N-Out." *OC Weekly*. OC Weekly, Ltd., 24 Jan 2011. Web. 16 Jan 2012.

Hiltzik, Michael. "In-N-Out: Can Perfection Survive?" *Los Angeles Times*. Los Angeles Times, 07 May 2009. Web. 16 Jan 2012.

"History." *In-N-Out.com*. In-N-Out Burger, n.d. Web. 16 Jan 2012.

"In-N-Out Burger Beats McDonald's in Consumer Reports Fast Food Ratings." *Consumer Reports*. Consumers Union of U.S., Inc., 30 Jun 2011. Web. 16 Jan 2012.

Lopez-Alt, J. Kenji. "The Ultimate In-N-Out Secret Menu (and Super Secret Menu!) Survival Guide." A Hamburger Today. *Serious Eats*, 2 Mar 2011. Web. 16 Jan 2012.

Luna, Nancy. "Attack of the Double-Double." *D Magazine*. D Magazine, Inc., March 2011. Web. 16 Jan 2012.

McNichol, Tom. "The Secret Behind a Burger Cult." *The New York Times*. The New York Times Company, 14 August 2002. Web. 16 Jan 2012.

Perman, Stacy. *In-N-Out Burger: A Behind-the-Counter Look at the Fast-Food Chain that Breaks All the Rules*. New York: Harper Business, 2009. Print.

Rallo, Nick. "Woman Cries Over In-N-Out Burger. This is Getting Weird." *Dallas Observer*. Dallas Observer, LLC, 11 May 2011. Web. 16 Jan 2012.

Robinson-Jacobs, Karen. "In-N-Out Burger Plans up to 8 Restaurants for D-FW, Major Distribution Center for Texas Hub." *Dallas Morning News*. Dallas Morning News, 07 Oct 2010. Web. 16 Jan 2012.

Scott, Jill. "Gordon Ramsay Admits Secret Passion for Fast Food Burgers." *Sunday Mail*. Scottish Daily Record and Sunday Mail, Ltd., 20 April 2008. Web. 16 Jan 2012.

"Secret Menu." *In-N-Out.com*. In-N-Out Burger, n.d. Web. 16 Jan 2012.

Whatupwilly. "In-N-Out 100x100." *Whatupwilly.com*, 23 Jan 2006. Web. 16 Jan 2012.

Sample Revelation Informative Outline

Specific Purpose: To inform my classmates about how scientists are using the properties of the naked mole rat to improve humans' life and health.

INTRODUCTION

Attention Device: The popular Disney kids show Kim Possible introduced the world to a tiny little guy named Rufus the Naked Mole Rat who loved to tag along on Kim's adventures and seemed impossible to kill. He even got his own song with the lyrics, "What is that? That freaky thing! It's a Naked Mole Rat." What is that freaky thing is a pretty legitimate question when you first look at a naked mole rat. They are pretty wrinkly, and you might think they're ugly, but these cute little critters are getting quite a bit of attention from scientists.

Topic Revelation Statement: In the next few minutes, I will inform you about the amazing scientific discoveries of an animal almost no one knows, the naked mole rat.

Significance Statement: Some informative topics might cure cancer, others reverse aging, and still others save victims of heart attacks and strokes. My topic does all three…and more. And he's cute. The medical mysteries of the mole rats led Bioscience Technology Online, December 15, 2009 to proclaim them "the new lab rat of choice," as researchers rush to unlock the amazing biological properties of what some consider one of the ugliest animals.

Preview of Main Points: Well I'll defend the naked mole rat's honor by first introducing you to this curious creature. Then, I'll explain how they can make your life better. And finally, I'll reveal how it might make your life longer.

BODY

I.   So let's meet the naked mole rat.

    A.   The naked mole rat has some very unique characteristics.

        1.   McClatchy-Tribune News Service, December 27, 2009 says the hairless animals resemble tiny, shriveled sausages.

        2.   Add in the fact that they're nearly blind, have buckteeth, and don't grow more than three inches long, and you've got a recipe for one scary animal.

        3.   These critters are indigenous to the Horn of Africa – specifically Sudan, Kenya, and Ethiopia.

        4.   They are the only cold blooded mammal known to humans.

    B.   The Chicago Tribune, December 20, 2009 tells us that the mole rats live in tight-knit colonies of up to 300 members, deep underground.

1. They are the only mammals known to live with a social structure similar to insects.

2. They are led by a queen, who is the only female in the tribe unlucky enough to reproduce, and she does so with one to three suitors of her choosing.

3. BBC Two's program "Friends and Rivals" of March 2011, reports that in these colonies, each rat has a specialized task: Guard, or worker.

    a. Guards are basically looking out for the Mole Rat's number one predator: snakes.

    b. Workers spend all their time tunneling underground in search of food.

        i. The Zoological Society of San Diego Website, updated daily, reports that some mole rats' tunnels can become as long as three football fields.

        ii. In proportion to their size, that's like someone of average height tunneling 48 miles!

C. The tunnels where the mole rats live are a key part of their intrigue.

1. These tunnels have temperatures reaching up to 90 degrees and a toxic mix of sulfurous air.

2. The air contains less than five percent oxygen and would kill almost any other animal.

3. But the mole rats thrive in this toxic environment. According to Asian News International, February 24, 2009, they live to be around 30 years old, far more than the typical 3 years for their rodent counterparts.

TRANSITION: Now that I've explained how the mole rat is one curious and ugly creature, let's explore how scientists are hoping to exploit some of its traits to make our lives better, namely that mole rats don't feel pain or age.

II. The mole rat has two unique properties that could benefit humans.

A. Mole rats don't feel pain.

1. The mole rats' living conditions gave researchers the first clue that they don't feel pain. The previously cited Chicago Tribune notes that the air in the rat's burrows is highly acidic, but the rats show no reaction.

2. National Geographic February 1, 2008 reports that subsequent studies confirmed this by injecting the mole rats with acid and chili pepper powder. But instead of burning the rats, there was no response.

3. The Chicago Daily Herald, November 29, 2009 notes that Dr. Thomas Park of the University of Illinois Chicago has discovered that the Naked Mole rat doesn't have a neurotransmitter known as Substance P.

  a. Substance P is found in all other mammals.

  b. This neurotransmitter is responsible for creating burning pain sensations.

 4. The previously cited Daily Herald claims that researchers across the country are now closely studying substance P in humans in hopes of using it to fight chronic pain syndrome.

B. Mole rats also age very slowly.

 1. At the age of 30, they live about 10 times longer than their rodent counterparts.

  a. The previously cited Chicago Daily Herald mentions that they frequently show no signs of aging until 25.

  b. The mole rats also do not suffer from age related conditions such as osteoporosis, menopause, or mental failure.

 2. The San Antonio Express-News of February 19, 2009, observes that mole rats' proteasomes are extremely efficient.

  a. Proteasomes are the part of the cell that eliminates waste and damaged proteins, keeping the cell healthy.

  b. In fact, the previously cited Asian News International claims that even a Mole Rat has twice as many healthy proteins as a normal rat.

 3. Scientists hope to exploit the mole rat's protein structure.

  a. The hope is that researchers can use the mole rat's protein efficiency to create better anti-aging treatments for humans.

  b. According to Science Daily, March 5, 2009, they also hope to reproduce the mole rat's protein disposal to treat neurodegenerative diseases such as Parkinson's, Alzheimer's, Huntington's, and Lou Gehrig's disease.

TRANSITION: Now that we've examined how the mole rats might improve our lives with their pain free and anti-aging properties, let's move on to my final point where I'll tell you how the mole rats might make our lives longer.

III. The mole rat has two additional properties that can help humans live longer.

A. Mole rats are impervious to cancer.

 1. Mice have a very high cancer rate.

  a. In fact, The New York Times, October 27, 2009 notes that in some strains, 90% of them die from tumors.

        b.   But there have been no documented cases of cancer in naked mole rats.

    2.   The previously cited Daily Herald reports that researchers at the University of Rochester have isolated a gene present only in mole rats called P16.

        a.   This gene prevents cells from reproducing when they cluster together.

        b.   Because cancer usually results from uncontrollable cell growth, duplicating the mole rat's genetic defenses may be the key to developing new cancer treatments for humans.

B.   Mole rats can survive without oxygen.

    1.   While living in their underground tunnels, mole rats experience extreme hypoxia, or oxygen deprivation.

        a.   Heart Disease Weekly of December 20, 2009, reports that Naked Mole Rats' brains can last in this oxygen starved environment for half an hour.

        b.   In fact, the mole rats' brains function six times longer than mice with low oxygen.

    2.   The Hindustan Times, December 1, 2009, explains that this may be because the mole rats' neurons retain a fetus' ability to survive in the womb without oxygen for their entire adult lives.

    3.   Scientists hope to duplicate this survival ability to use in humans who experience hypoxia when suffering a stroke or heart attack.

CONCLUSION

Review of Topic/Main Points: This concludes your tour of the underground world of the naked mole rat. First, we met the little critters and discovered some of their habits. Then we explored how they could make our lives better by reducing pain and aging, before finally understanding how they can help us live longer by fighting cancer and surviving without oxygen.

Lasting Thought: You might not love the naked mole rats like I do, but you have to admit, they're kinda cute. And more importantly, this resilient rodent shows it's full of endless…possibilities.

WORKS CITED

"Friends and Rivals." Trials of Life. *BBC Two*. BBC, 23 Mar 2011. Web. 27 Dec. 2011.

Hock, Lindsay. "Introducing the New Lab Rat of Choice." *Bioscience Technology Online*. Advantage Business Media, 15 Dec 2009. Web. 10 Jan 2010.

"Mammals: Naked Mole Rat." *San Diego Zoo's Animal Bytes*. Zoological Society of San Diego, n.d. Web. 10 Jan 2010.

"Mole Rats May Unravel the Secret to Long Life." *Asian News International*. Al Bawaba (Middle East) Ltd., 24 Feb 2009. Web. 10 Jan 2010.

Mullen, William. "For Scientist, Answer to Chronic Pain Therapy Lies in a Dark, Stinky Tunnel." *McClatchy-Tribune News Service*. McClatchy Tribune Information Services, 27 Dec 2009. Web. 10 Jan 2010.

Mullen, William. "They Got a Face Only a Scientist Could Love: Researcher Studies Naked Mole Rats." *Chicago Tribune*. Tribune Publishing Company, 20 Dec 2009. Web. 10 Jan 2010.

"Naked Mole Rats May Offer Tips for Surviving Stroke." *Hindustan Times*. HT Media Ltd., 1 Dec 2009. Web. 10 Jan 2010.

Roach, John. "Naked Mole Rats Unable to Feel Burning Pain." *National Geographic News*. National Geographic Society, 1 Feb 2008. Web. 10 Jan 2010.

Tumiel, Cindy. "Scientists Spill Secrets of Mole Rat's Longevity." *San Antonio Express-News*. Hearst Communications Inc., 19 Feb 2009. Web. 10 Jan 2010.

"University of Chicago; Naked Mole Rats May Hold Clues to Surviving Stroke." *Heart Disease Weekly*. NewsRx, 20 Dec 2009. Web. 10 Jan 2010.

University of Texas Health Science Center at San Antonio. "Naked Mole Rats May Hold Clues to Successful Aging." *Science Daily*. Science Daily LLC, 5 Mar 2009. Web. 10 Jan 2010.

Wade, Nicholas. "The Lifespan of a Rodent May Aid Human Health." *New York Times*. New York Times Company, 27 Oct 2009. Web. 10 Jan 2010.

Weber, Paul J. "Scientists Gaining Insight From Strange Little Rats." *Daily Herald*. Daily Herald, 29 Nov 2009. Web. 10 Jan 2010.

232

SAMPLE INFORMATIVE REVELATION SPEECH OUTLINE

Specific Purpose: to educate my classmates about new research on saliva

INTRODUCTION

I. **Attention Getter:** In 1903, Dr. Ivan Pavlov published his groundbreaking research in which he conditioned dogs to salivate on cue by ringing a bell. As far as most of you are concerned, this is probably the most interesting research ever conducted involving saliva. Dr. Irwin Mandel said it best when he stated, "Saliva doesn't have the drama of blood, the integrity of sweat or the emotional appeal of tears." But it's time for people to start paying attention to the forgotten bodily fluid — saliva.

II. **Topic Revelation Statement:** Today, I will inform you about new research being conducted on saliva, with potentially life-saving results.

III. **Significance Statement:** The *Los Angeles Times* of January 21, 2002 reports that over 25 million Americans suffer from saliva deficiency, with potentially disastrous consequences for your mouth, teeth, and breath. What scientists are discovering about saliva could have widespread benefits in everything from fixing bad breath to preventing AIDS.

IV. **Preview of Main Points:** First, we'll uncover some of the basic facts about saliva. Then, we'll investigate some saliva related problems. Finally, we'll turn our attention to some promising saliva research that'll have you drooling.

BODY

I. There are many interesting facts about saliva.
    A. Let's begin by defining saliva.
        1. Saliva is a complex secretion formed mainly from the salivary glands.
            a. According to a brochure published by the *American Academy of Otolaryngology*, titled *Salivary Glands: What's Normal, What's Abnormal*, we have hundreds of salivary glands in our throats and mouths.
            b. The major glands are located near the upper teeth, in front of the tongue, and on the floor of the mouth.
            c. The *Augusta Chronicle* of September 11, 2001 reports that these glands can produce up to 3 pints of saliva per day.
        2. Saliva is mostly water, but *Hormonal Update* in a story posted on October 19, 2001, notes that saliva also contains hundreds of enzymes, proteins, minerals, blood cells, and bacteria.
    B. Saliva is one of the body's most important fluids.
        1. *Chemist and Druggist* of March 31, 2001 explains that saliva is like your body's natural mouthwash.
            a. It protects your mouth by neutralizing acidic foods.

       b.   It sweeps away bacteria that cause cavities and tooth decay.

    2.   The previously cited *Los Angeles Times* reports that saliva also eases digestion, prevents bad breath, and makes speaking easier.

  C.   Saliva was once viewed negatively.

    1.   Centuries ago, doctors believed that saliva contained evil spirits released by the brain.

    2.   They would also poison patients with mercury to cause saliva to pour out of patients' mouths.

II.   There are a several common problems associated with saliva.

  A.   It is possible to have too much saliva.

    1.   The *Practitioner* of October 12, 2001 points out that there are a small number of people who suffer from sialorrhoea, or "excessive saliva production."

    2.   Sialorrhoea is caused by menstruation, early pregnancy, weakening of mouth muscles from Parkinson's Disease, epilepsy, and other disorders.

  B.   A total lack of saliva is also possible.

    1.   The August 13, 2001 *Chattanooga Times* explains that Sjogren's syndrome is an illness in which the body's immune system attacks and destroys the salivary glands.

    2.   The cause of Sjogren's syndrome is still not known, but is currently being researched.

    3.   Sufferers of Sjogren's syndrome often use artificial saliva.

       a.   The previously cited *Chemist and Druggist* claims that it mimics the feel of saliva.

       b.   However, it is missing the proteins and enzymes that real saliva provides.

  C.   Xerostomia, or dry mouth, is the most common saliva disorder.

    1.   According to the *Pittsburgh Post Gazette* of March 21, 2000 xerostomia is a side effect of more than 500 prescription drugs including anti-depressants, anti-histamines and acne medications.

    2.   Dr. Athena Pappa, Professor at Tufts University School of Dental Medicine notes that people with dry mouth have ten times the normal amount of bacteria in their mouths.

    3.   The *Ayr Advocate* of August 9, 2000 says that dry mouth sufferers are turning to water, candies, and sugarless gums to return their saliva production to normal.

III. There is a great deal of new research about saliva.

  A.   Saliva is being used in law enforcement.

    1.   The British government, according to the February 19, 2001 *Press Association*, says that saliva is more reliable and convenient than blood for testing.

    2.   A pamphlet on saliva by *National Institute of Dental and Craniofacial Research* points out that saliva contains pieces of your DNA.

       a.   A few drops can reveal whether you've had too much to drink or have been using illegal drugs.

       b.   Dried saliva on a postage stamp or envelope can even be used to identify who sent a letter.

B.   Saliva's proteins are being isolated and used to create new drugs.

   1.   Scientists were inspired by animals licking their wounds.

      a.   *Beyond 2000* of March 14, 2001 says that researchers have discovered a new protein in saliva called secretory leukocyte protease inhibitor, or SLPI.

      b.   SLPI can accelerate the healing of wounds.

      c.   This research is being used to develop treatments for patients with non-healing wounds and for day-to-day cuts and scrapes.

   2.   Scientists have also discovered the protein histatin.

      a.   The May 1, 2001 *Drug Discovery and Technology News* says that histatin is being used against oral lesions associated with HIV.

      b.   *PR Newswire* of January 8, 2002 also reports that histatin is being tested against viral infections associated with cystic fibrosis.

   3.   Finally, a January 7, 1998 press release from the Cornell University Medical College reports that they are focusing on a component of saliva that blocks HIV growth and are working on a drug that prevents HIV transmission.

CONCLUSION

I.   **Review of Topic and Main Points:** Now you know some of the basic facts about saliva, some saliva related problems, and the latest research on the matter.

II.   **Lasting Thought:** Ivan Pavlov did produce one of the most famous psychological discoveries of all time, but that was not what he set out to do. Pavlov was a biologist, and his famous experiment began as an attempt to understand how saliva helped dogs digest food. One hundred years later, scientists are still learning more about the fascinating properties of saliva. Sure it sounds gross, but try getting through a speech without it.

WORKS CITED

Barrett, David. "Police to Pilot Saliva Drug Test." *Press Association*. n.p., 19 Feb. 2001. Web. 20 Mar 2002.

Casano, Peter. "Salivary Glands: What's Normal, What's Abnormal." *American Academy of Otolaryngology*. 2002. Web 20 Mar 2002.

"Demgen Scientists Publish Antibacterial Activity of P1 13D Against Cystic Fibrosis Infections." *PR Newswire*. n.p., 8 Jan. 2002. Web 21 Mar 2002.

Donohue, Paul. "A Life Without Saliva and Tears is Miserable." *Chattanooga Times* 13 Aug. 2001: D4. Print.

"Dry Mouth Can Lead to Tooth Decay." *Ayr Advocate* 9 Aug. 2000: 14. Print.

"Histatin Tested Against Candidiasis." *Drug Discovery Technology News* 4.5 (2001). Web. 20 Mar 2002.

McIntosh, Shirley. "Physical, Mental Conditions Can Aggravate Dry Mouth." *Augusta Chronicle* 11 Sep 2001: A15. Print.

Mestel, Rosie. "The Gland Tour: How Saliva is Made." *Los Angeles Times* 21 Jan 2002: S6. Print.

Mestel Rosie. "The Wonders of Saliva." *Los Angeles Times* 21 Jan 2002: S1+. Print.

"Salivary Diagnostics." *National Institute for Dental and Craniofacial Research.* National Institute of Health, 2000. Web. 20 Mar 2002.

Parker-Pope, Tara. "Is Your Mouth as Dry as a Desert?" *Pittsburgh Post-Gazette* 21 Mar 2000: C4+. Print.

"Salivary Hormone Monitoring." *Hormonal Update* 2.1 (2001). Web. 21 Mar 2002.

Sung, Peggy. "Study Shows Component of Saliva is Very Effective in Blocking AIDS Virus." *Weill Medical College of Cornell University*. Cornell University, 7 Jan 1998. Web. 20 Mar 2002.

"The Gob-I Desert." *Chemist and Druggist* 31 March 2001: 25+. Print.

"The Role of Saliva in Oral Health Problems." *The Practitioner* 12 Oct. 2001: 841+. Print.

"Tongue Bath." *Beyond 2000.* n.p., 14 Mar 2001. Web. 20 Mar 2002.

SAMPLE INFORMATIVE REVELATION SPEECH MANUSCRIPT WORLD'S FAIRS TYLER ADAMS, 2000

INTRODUCTION

This year, the world focused its attention on one city for a global event that brought together 156 of earth's nations. This multi-billion dollar undertaking was attended by millions of people from all corners of the globe. You probably read about it in newspapers and magazines, and saw it on TV — unless you live in the U.S. No, I'm not giving a speech about the Olympics — heaven knows we've had our fill of Bob Costas. The event I'm talking about is Expo 2000 — the most recent World's Fair held this June through October in Hannover, Germany.

For 150 years World's Fairs have showcased the most amazing and far-reaching cultural and technological advances - just like an informative round ...but on a slightly grander scale. According to the *Bangkok Post* of August 13, 2000 attending the World's Fair is like traveling ahead in time. Since 1851, nearly a billion people have seen the future at a world exposition. Yet we may not realize the staggering impact they have had and are still having. That's where I come in.

Today I'll first take you back in time and examine the history of International Expositions. Next measure the impacts past World's Fairs have had on our present. Finally I'll take you on a brief tour of the future, as was unfolded at Expo 2000 and consider the U.S. government's shocking decision not to participate.

BODY

Some say that the World's Fairs were in a way the first real Internet. Not in the computer sense — but in the way they drew millions to a common space occupied by people from around the world sharing the most advanced technologies, ideas and culture - with global impacts. The first World's Fair, held in London in 1851, focused on one main exhibition hall, the still standing Crystal Palace. Over 17 thousand exhibitors demonstrated their world wide wares.

The Fair was conceived by English nobleman Sir Henry Cole, ostensibly to promote harmony among all the peoples of the world. But Erik Mattie notes in his 1998 sociological overview, *World's Fairs*, that the market exposure the fair provided for British products was also a strong motivating factor. Over the nest few fairs, though, public attendance grew and the focus shifted. New products were still featured but it was now their entertainment value that was paramount. This increased importance of entertainment was evident in the 1893 Chicago World's Fair which saw the advent of a separate amusement area featuring the world's first ever Ferris Wheel. And as the turn of the century... turned, and official body was organized to govern universal expositions. Since 1931, the Bureau International des Expositions, BIE for short, has established the dates and locations of World's Fairs. There is no set time interval between fairs. Sometimes years go by without a fair, and sometimes multiple fairs are held in the same year. This was the case in 1939, when the seminal New York World's Fair was held at the same time as an International Exposition hosted by San Francisco to celebrate the completion of the Golden Gate Bridge.

There is no questioning the popularity of World's Fairs — even the first one in 1851 drew an attendance of over 6 million people and was participated in by 28 countries. While attendance to fairs has varied over the decades according to locations and the political and economic environment at the time, recent expositions have garnered as many as 64 million visitors and involved as many as 156 nations. World's Fairs provide unique opportunities to the hosting location, such as increased tourism and outlandish, but inescapable, hotel rates. The host can also benefit culturally. The Architectural Record of this July notes that Expo 2000 was also intended to encourage Germans to be more tolerant of foreigners. A noble goal ...if only Germany had pursued it back in the `30s.

World's Fairs do not only affect their hosts. Let's move on and see how they impact the whole world.

<Show visual #1> These distinctive structures may look familiar to you, but do you know where they are? Ok, it's a trick question. The Trylon and Perisphere, theme buildings of the 1939 World's Fair were demolished soon after the fairs closing. This is the case with most World's Fair structures - they are meant to last only a short while. World's Fairs, like time, are fleeting - if you don't see them during their run, you never will. But there are occasional survivors.

<Visual #2> The Unisphere, built for the 1964 expo, now stands on the exact same ground once occupied by the Trylon and Perisphere. Another surviving, and frankly butt-ugly, structure is the nearby watchtowers <Visual #3>, which you may have seen almost crush Will Smith in the movie "Men in Black." So close, but yet, so far. Across the country is Seattle's most distinctive landmark. The Space Needle <Visual #4> did not, contrary to popular belief, fall from space. It was constructed from the ground up for the 1964 World's Fair. The U.S. pavilion at Expo '67 took the form of a giant geodesic dome <Visual #5>. While most Americans have never seen this Montreal landmark, you might be familiar with its evil clone at Disney's Epcot Center, itself an evil clone of the 1939 New York World's Fair.

Paris, France. City of Lights ... City of Love. It's most famous landmark: <Visual #6> La Tour Eiffel - built not out of love but for, say it with me, the World's Fair, this one in 1889. Arguably the world's most recognizable edifice, the Tower was also intended as a temporary structure. Strange as it may seem this landmark was originally thought to be unsightly and even monstrous by artists, architects, and those picky Parisians. The fact that the tower is now looked on as a symbol of French national pride is evidence of Gustave Eiffel's triumph of innovative design, and also bears testament to the ability of World's Fairs to reshape our perception of the world.

Culture and art have also been influenced by World's Fairs. Since Amsterdam in 1883, the fairs have featured exhibits of both contemporary and historical societies from around the world. For those of us who are more likely to participate in less intellectual - and more tasty - aspects of culture, it is interesting to note that Belgian waffles, iced tea (the beverage, not the rapper), and the ice cream cone all made their debut at World's Fairs. While the world waits for contact from space aliens, the first contact the common man made with extraterrestrial matter was at...the World's Fair. In Osaka in 1970 the public was able to experience a new aspect of culture by visiting a moon rock exhibit.

By far, the most influential aspect of World's Fairs has been in the area of technology. In the days before the Discovery Channel, World's Fairs provided a way for people to experience future innovations that were not yet attainable to the average person. The elevator, the escalator, the sewing machine, and even the Ford Mustang all premiered at World's Fairs, as did false teeth and artificial limbs. However, the types of inventions that have been the most notable are those dealing with communications - now that seems relevant. Ever since the telegraph was demonstrated at the inaugural fair in London, World's Fairs have showcased the next step in electronic communication. That's right, television, which has had at least a slight global impact, made its public debut at the 1939 New York World's Fair, and I think you'll agree with me that the world has never been the same.

OK class, let's review. World's Fairs are huge, popular, and important. So why after 150 years of participation was the U.S. a no-show in Hannover? Before we answer that question, let's look at what Expo 2000 was all about. The Malaysia Business Times, August 74, 2000 says that the expo aimed to "open people's minds to issues, ideas, visions, and concepts which can help mankind respond to the challenges of the new millennium."

According to the June 9, 2000 *Irish Times*, the fair grounds were rather large — about the same size as Monaco — that's a lot of space. The most popular sites at Expo 2000 included the Japanese pavilion which was made out of recyclable paper, and the Dutch pavilion which looked like some kind of huge club sandwich with a live forest in the middle. Entertainers at the fair included Carlos Santana and Britney Spears.

Expo 2000 came under criticism from the international press because it failed to reach, or even come close to, its projected attendance of 40 million. However, the *Jakarta Post* of September 7, 2000 points out that the problem was with the unrealistic projection, not with attendance. Expo 2000 was also criticized on October 8, 2000 by the New Zealand paper *The Dominion* for losing money, and *The Scotsman* of this September 6th claimed that it was such a bomb that the 2,000 prostitutes who came to town for the event gave up and went home.

It's important to note though, that World's Fairs have historically lost money. World's Fairs aren't organized to make a profit, they are put on to promote cooperation, harmony, and the future. Sadly — for the US — it came down to money. *U.S. News and World Report* of June 5, 2000 explains that after expensive Expos in '92 and '98, Congress passed a law disallowing the use of tax dollars for World's Fairs. They expected corporate sponsors to front the money, but the Fortune 500 didn't bite. Consequently, impoverished Ethiopia had a presence at the Expo but, according to the *San Diego Union-Tribune* July, 30 2000 with just weeks before opening and a huge Pavilion space reserved in the center of the Fair — we bailed out. The only presence the wealthiest nation on earth had was through commercial ventures like IBM, McDonald's, and Microsoft.

According to the *Baltimore Sun* of July 12, 2000 US non-participation conveyed all kinds of messages to the world — none of them positive. It may even partially explain our negative trade balance. At a minimum, it says that we *aren't* the world.

Also as a result of our non-participation, very few Americans attended and there was almost no media coverage of this enormous global event in US media. So did we miss anything?

> The first live interaction between humans and a colony of Artificial Intelligence machines.

The first public German apology for the holocaust and a memorial to its victims

A scientifically-based projection of all major technological breakthroughs expected in the next 100 years and theories about their cultural and environmental impacts.

So in answer to my earlier question, YES, you missed A LOT. And that's just a sampling. There's no way I could tell you about everything at the expo in 10 minutes. Remember, it's the SIZE of MONACO. If you would like more information on Expo 2000, surf on over to www.expo2000.de where you can take an interactive tour of the Fair that was.

CONCLUSION

Today we have looked back at the history of World's Fairs, examined the effects they have had on our present, and taken a glimpse of the future represented by Expo 2000.

The most sought after collectible from the 1939 World's Fair is a lapel pin that proclaimed: "I have seen the future." The next World's Fair is slated for 2005 in Seto, Japan. Whether or not the US chooses to participate, I have no doubts that people who attend will once again see the future.

<Editor's Note: This is a speech that was written in manuscript form and memorized for use in intercollegiate forensics (speech) competitions. Tyler performed this speech in Prague, Czech Republic and won the International Championship for Informative Speaking in March 2001. >

FIFTEEN

PERSUASIVE SPEAKING

Speech is power; speech is to persuade, to convert,
to compel.

— *Ralph Waldo Emerson*

Every day we are bombarded with messages that try to influence the way we think and behave. Apple commercials try to sell us the latest i-device. Public service announcements urge us to stay away from drugs. Politicians campaign to win our votes. Each of these scenarios is an example of a persuasive appeal. Soon, you will have to construct your own persuasive speech with its own specific appeal.

Although persuasion comes in many different forms, at the heart of each message is the desire to influence an audience. **Influence** is a broad term that can mean a dramatic change on the part of listeners or simply a subtle reinforcement of the way they already think or act.

PERSUASIVE GOALS

Persuasive speeches inherently seek to influence audiences in one or more ways.

Belief-based speeches ask audiences to consider their fundamental beliefs about whether something is true or untrue ("Second hand smoke causes cancer.").

Attitude-based speeches ask audiences to consider whether something is right or wrong ("Human cloning is immoral.").

Behavior-based speeches ask audiences to consider their personal actions and whether a specific behavior should be stopped, adopted, or changed

("Do not adopt a pet until you are financially able to care for it.").

Policy-based speeches ask audiences to consider altering an existing policy (such as a rule or law) or to help create a new policy ("The California three-strikes law should be repealed.").

CHOOSING A PERSUASIVE TOPIC

As you choose a persuasive topic, there are a few important guidelines to keep in mind.

First, consider **the persuasive goal of your speech**. You should ask yourself, "what does my audience think/feel/do now," as well as, "what do I want them to think/feel/do after my speech?" This is important because one topic could have several persuasive angles. For example, a speech on the topic of medical marijuana may seek to change listeners' beliefs ("There is no medical evidence to support marijuana's medicinal benefits") as well as behaviors and policies ("Vote for the total legalization of medical marijuana"). A clear statement will help focus your arguments and will effectively narrow down a topic that could be too broad.

Second, make sure your persuasive goal is **feasible** for the audience. Part of audience analysis in persuasion is asking yourself if your audience can actually make the change you are requesting. For example, knowing that many college students are struggling financially, persuading them to take an expensive vacation is probably unwise. Similarly, consider a fairly common topic: "donate blood." If anyone in your audience has had a recent tattoo or piercing, doesn't meet the weight requirements, or is homosexual, they are automatically excluded by the Red Cross. You might convince them that donating blood is a great idea, but you are likely to leave them frustrated that they cannot follow your advice.

Finally, many students are tempted to take on large, controversial issues such as abortion or assisted suicide. But realistically, highly controversial topics are difficult when your goal is to influence audience members. They require an audience member to completely re-evaluate his or her belief system. The beliefs people have about religion and politics are often so strongly held that they are unlikely to be altered significantly after a speech of just a few minutes. If you want to change your audience's mind on a controversial subject, look for a small shift that would be easier for them to make. For example, instead of persuading them to support a total ban on the death penalty, consider instead arguing that all death row inmates be allowed a full review of their cases with DNA evidence and reputable legal representation.

When discussing controversial topics, influencing an audience can be extremely difficult. This is especially true if audience members are firmly opposed to your position. Persuasion is easier said than done. But it's not impossible. In fact, several centuries ago, one of the most famous thinkers in Western philosophy had quite a bit to say about it.

ARISTOTLE AND PERSUASION

One of the first people to discuss the idea of persuasion formally was the ancient Greek philosopher Aristotle. Aristotle was a student of Plato and tutor to Alexander the Great. Aristotle's many books include *Poetics*, *Metaphysics*, *Politics*, and *Rhetoric* — in which he delineates the three major aspects of persuasion: pathos, logos, and ethos.

Pathos

In Aristotelian theory, **pathos** refers to the emotional appeal inherent in much of persuasion. When we become emotionally involved in a speaker's message, we are more likely to be influenced.

Think for a moment about the recent "Truth" public service announcements dealing with cigarette smoking. Many use fear or disgust to get the message across such as those that display a pile of body bags or that list the actual ingredients in cigarettes. Sympathy is also a common appeal. When ads focus on the innocent victims of second-hand smoke, sadness is evoked to create influence.

The idea is quite simple. Emotion creates engagement in an audience. As speakers, we can generate and employ many different types of emotional appeals including, but not limited to:

Fear	**Humor**
Anger	**Patriotism**
Sympathy	**Excitement**

Pathos works because these emotions spur us to action. How many times have you taken an action because you were angry, or done something because a friend or family member made you feel guilty? Negative emotions like sadness or fear make audiences uncomfortable, and they can be encouraged to take action to get rid of those emotions. Similarly, positive emotions like love or acceptance make audiences feel good, and they can be persuaded to take action to perpetuate or recapture those feelings.

So, how does a speaker generate these emotions in audience members? One method is to use supporting materials that have an emotional punch. Real-life stories about people experiencing hardship and/or joy may reach the hearts of listeners. Also, using specific words that have an emotional quality can generate pathos. Instead of saying, "Today my topic is dog bites," search for more emotional language like, "Today we'll uncover a menace threatening our playgrounds and neighborhoods: vicious, unleashed dogs." Finally, your delivery can create pathos. Emotion is contagious. In your speaking style you should demonstrate the emotion you want audience members to feel. If audience members see the speaker becoming angry, sad, fearful, or excited, chances are good that they will start to feel the same emotions.

Logos

Emotion alone is not enough to ethically persuade an audience. Speakers must also use **logos**, or what we refer to today as **logical appeal.**

A logical speech is one that appeals to our sense of reason by using well-substantiated arguments. In simple terms, an **argument** is any claim that is supported by evidence. For example, in a student speech on auto mechanic fraud, the speaker made a claim in her introduction that this was a significant problem, worthy of her audience's attention. She supported this claim by providing not only emotional examples about real people who were victimized but also statistics from reliable sources about the number of people affected each year. Using numerical evidence as well as stories, she supported her claim and proved it was a significant topic.

The Three Tools of Persuasion According to Aristotle's Rhetoric:

Pathos: Emotional proof in which you use meaningful delivery and real-life examples to reach our hearts.

Logos: Logical proof in which you research and clear arguments to appeal to our sense of reason.

Ethos: Personal proofing which you use your own character and competence to create an aura of credibility

When we take a position and back it up with evidence on the basis of facts, observations, and other supporting evidence we use the reasoning process. In essence, reasoning is just drawing a conclusion based on the evidence. As an audience member, if you feel the evidence backs up the claim, you are more likely to be persuaded. If a speaker said the reason we have a gang problem in Los Angeles is because not enough gang members get up in the morning and have a bowl of Cheerios, and you decided that evidence was ridiculous, you would not be persuaded. But on the other hand, if a speaker said the reasons were because of a lack of parental supervision, high dropout rate in high school, a lack of after-school activities, peer pressure, drugs, poverty, and racial tension, you would probably agree with that and would be persuaded.

As you can see from the preceding examples, for an argument to make sense, it must not only use research and evidence, but also be constructed logically. Some forms of **logical argument construction** include:

Cause and effect: For example, "Since 90% of smokers experience some kind of health problem, we can logically assume that cigarettes cause serious health risks."

Inductive reasoning: These arguments begin with specific instances and move to a general claim. "Students, workers, and parents all report they experience unexpected drowsiness which harms their ability to perform simple tasks throughout the day. Obviously, sleep deprivation is a problem that affects many different types of people."

Deductive reasoning: These arguments start with a general claim and move to a specific conclusion. "Ours is a society based on the idea of individual freedom and non-discrimination. Thus, traffic officers who commit racial profiling by pulling over African Americans without cause are violating some of the foundations of American society."

These are just a few ways to construct arguments in your speech. There are many more. Your instructor may talk about others during class.

As a final note about logos, be sure to steer clear of any **logical fallacies** as you put together your arguments. Some logical fallacies include:

Bandwagon: "Everybody's buying real estate; so should you!"

Tradition: "We've never given pluses and minuses with letter grades at our college; we shouldn't start doing it now."

Hasty generalization: "Three students at our college experienced car robberies last semester. Campus crime is a huge problem here."

False dichotomy (offering only two choices when there are other options): "Either you support the right for all women to terminate their pregnancy or you are totally opposed to abortion in all instances."

Ethos

Ethos is the final aspect of persuasion discussed by Aristotle. Ethos refers to the credibility of the speaker. Research indicates the more credible a person is perceived to be by an audience, the more persuasive power he or she will wield.

Advertisers use ethos all the time to sell products. Take, for example, Olympic figure skating medalist Michelle Kwan and her involvement with Disneyland, Kraft Foods, Visa, and other products. Michelle's professional credentials combined with her likeable personality make her an extremely effective spokesperson. Unfortunately, most of us do not have the immediately recognizable ethos of Michelle Kwan. We must work harder to establish credibility during our speeches.

The first step is discovering the two general questions audience members ask themselves when determining a speaker's credibility:

1. Is the speaker an expert, or at least competent to speak on a subject?

2. Does the speaker possess an honest and likeable character?

The fact that Michelle is a great skater is not the only reason why she is such a credible spokesperson. There are lots of great athletes. Michelle has also supported charitable organizations, earned her doctorate, and served as a special U.S. Ambassador. For many people, she is perceived to be likeable, sincere, and trustworthy.

Once you realize that credibility is made up of a speaker's **perceived expertise and character**, you can begin to analyze how certain aspects of speech making affect our individual credibility.

You can establish your expertise on a topic in a variety of ways. The most obvious is relating any relevant personal experience. If you have familiarity with your topic or a personal story to share, that instantly tells an audience that you are someone they can trust. If, however, you don't have a strong personal connection to your topic, the next best way to establish your expertise is to be well informed. Your use of quality research and supporting materials on a topic lets an audience know that you have learned all that you can about your subject. Finally, your speaking ability conveys your expertise to the audience. If you are well organized and speak with confidence, your audience is more likely to assume that you are trustworthy.

Your can also influence how the audience perceives your character in several ways. The most obvious should be a strong adherence to the ethics of speech making including avoiding plagiarizing words or ideas. You can also accomplish this by approaching your audience with a friendly, sincere attitude. Remember in Chapter 3 the ways to show an audience that you care. That simple act of caring about your speech and your audience can help them see you as a likeable speaker. Finally, you can also make language choices that connect you to your audience. Use **inclusive language** such as "we" and "our," instead of language that separates you from your audience, such as referring to them as "you."

ORGANIZING PERSUASIVE SPEECHES

Thus far, we have discussed persuasion from a theoretical standpoint. Let's move to some of the specifics of this speech by taking a look at three different ways to structure a persuasive speech.

Method One: Three Reasons

The **three reasons** structure is the most simple of the patterns we will discuss. Just because it is simple, however, does not mean it is ineffective. In this type of speech, the speaker makes a claim and then supports that claim using three separate reasons. Consider the following rough outline:

> **Topic:** Capital Punishment
>
> **Claim:** Capital punishment is an ineffective means of punishing criminals in our society.
>
> **Reason One:** Capital punishment does not deter crime.
>
> **Reason Two:** Capital punishment costs more money than imprisonment.
>
> **Reason Three:** Capital punishment is inherently racist.

Of course, this is a very brief outline. In a formal outline, each of these points would need to be supported with convincing subpoints and appropriate research. However, this example does demonstrate how each reason individually supports the overall claim. Together, these three reasons have the potential to create a convincing argument.

Method Two: Problem/Cause/Solution

The problem/cause/solution speech is an intermediate pattern for persuasive speeches which, like its name suggests, first convinces listeners that there is a problem worthy of their attention, then uncovers the factors that are responsible for the problem, and finally outlines specific steps that will fix the problem. Each step is a main point of your speech, and each is crucial to the overall appeal you are creating. Here's another rough outline to consider:

Topic: Hand washing

Claim: The lack of hand washing is a serious health hazard in the United States.

Main Point One (Problem): Many people do not wash their hands regularly, and this harms our society.

Main Point Two (Causes): People don't take the time to wash their hands because they do not know the potential health hazards.

Main Point Three (Solutions): If businesses, organizations, and individuals followed a few simple hand washing guidelines, we could stop this health hazard.

Again, this is very brief and needs much more development. For a more detailed example of this structure, please refer to the sample speeches at the end of this chapter.

You may think the Problem/Cause/Solution structure requires a lot of informational steps before getting to the persuasive part (solutions). However, sometimes persuasion involves giving a lot of information and allowing audience members to draw some of their own conclusions. The persuasion is subtle, not aggressive. You need to take time to develop the problem and its causes for the audience instead of just jumping up and telling them what they should do and believe.

Method Three: Monroe's Motivated Sequence

Let's now consider an advanced persuasive structure that builds upon many of the concepts introduced in the Problem/Cause/Solution format. Allan Monroe was a speech professor in the 1930's whose five step psychological approach to persuasion has certainly stood the test of time.

His approach is so influential, in fact, that it even bears his name: **Monroe's Motivated Sequence.** This approach was detailed in the 1969 version of his book *Principles of Speech Communication.*

Step One: Capture the Attention of the Audience

This should be painfully obvious by now. If listeners are not paying attention to a speaker, there is no way that speaker can create influence. Your introduction must make audiences want to listen to you.

Step Two: Create the Need for Change

Before audience members will change their beliefs, attitudes, or behaviors, a speaker should tell them why change is necessary in the first place. Persuasive speakers often describe the inadequacy of the present situation to accomplish this step. For example, if you were trying to persuade listeners to drink more water, you must first demonstrate that most people do not drink enough water, and that this lack of water in our diet creates a number of health hazards. In a Problem/Cause/Solution speech, the need step corresponds to both the problem and cause areas.

Step Three: Satisfy the Need

Now that the audience has been primed to see that change is necessary, they are ready for a specific plan that will fulfill these needs. The satisfaction step does just that. Often, the satisfaction step details several proposals that communities, institutions, and people can adopt that will satisfy the need and thus fix the problem. To continue with our example about drinking water, you might detail the ways in which schools, businesses, and peers could adopt specific policies that would encourage citizens to drink eight glasses of water every day. In a Problem/Cause/Solution speech, the satisfaction step is similar to the solution area.

Step Four: Visualize the Results

Audience members like to know that if they do what the speaker recommends, positive outcomes will ensue. In the visualization step, the speaker explains the benefits a listener will experience if they implement the plan outlined in the satisfaction step. In our speech about water consumption, you might describe how drinking eight glasses of water every day decreases our chance for cancer and heart disease, aids our bodies in digestion, and improves the overall quality of our skin.

Step Five: Call to Action

Finally, the audience is ready for your specific persuasive plea. The call to action should be personal and easily accomplished by everyone in your audience. The call to action in our water speech is clear: drink eight glasses of water every day, and encourage your friends and family members to do the same! In a speech that follows Monroe's structure, the call to action will probably occur somewhere in your conclusion. Often, speakers use the call to action as the last line of their speech.

Monroe's Motivated Sequence is a more complex organizational structure than either the Three Reasons or Problem/Cause/Solution approach. As you decide the most appropriate structure for your speech, consider your topic as well as your persuasive goal. Topics that seek to influence beliefs or attitudes are often best suited to the first approach. If you want to directly influence listener actions and behaviors, you may want to use the Problem/Cause/Solution structure, or, if you're feeling brave, you may want to give the five steps of Monroe's Motivated Sequence a try.

CONCLUSION

In this chapter, we have taken a look at the theoretical foundations of persuasion as well as practical applications of this theory. Be responsible as you use persuasion in your life. Ideally, your persuasion will help others make good choices that improve their lives, or the lives of others. If you are asking others to think, feel, or act differently only to serve your personal wishes – you may need to reconsider your message.

Speaker's Secret

Sometimes persuasive speakers go overboard and start yelling at their audience. While it's good to care about your topic, most people don't respond to scolding. You can be influential while still being our friend. No matter how serious the subject matter, a smile and pleasant demeanor will make audiences more prone to accept your message.

FROM FRIGHT TO MIGHT MOMENT

Persuasive speaking is all about influencing the audience. Instead of worrying about your own fear, focus on the various ways in which you might impact your audience. Speakers in the past who argued for civil liberties or against social injustice changed millions of lives. Aren't we glad they fought through their fear

SAMPLE PROBLEM-CAUSE-SOLUTION PERSUASIVE SPEECH OUTLINE

Specific Purpose: To persuade my audience to take action against individuals who commit financial aid fraud known as Pell Runners

INTRODUCTION

Attention Device: Laurie Wolf, executive dean of student services at Des Moines Area Community College received a strange call from a student asking when his financial check would be disbursed, but it didn't stop there. The same student called her office 15 times in one day demanding his Pell Grant check. Curious, Wolf pulled his student-aid record to discover that he had been given aid from seven other colleges. When she requested transcripts, he vanished! Wolf told the Chronicle of Higher Education, August 28, 2011 that this student was probably a "Pell Runner," a scam artist who bounces from college to college, staying just long enough to receive a Pell Grant refund before disappearing.

Topic Revelation Statement: Today, I hope to persuade you that it's time to tackle the problem of Pell Runners, or students who defraud the Pell Grant system.

Significance Statement: Kevin Lineberry, assistant director of student financial services at Forsyth Technical Community College, told The Daily Tar Heel on Sept. 8, 2011, "This is a long-term pervasive problem in the financial-aid system, particularly at community colleges." And CTI Careersearch on Sept. 7, 2011 states, "nearly $700,000 in Pell Grant money was received by students who never completed coursework."

Preview of Main Points: First, we will discover the problem of Pell Runners, then we will outline its causes, before finally exploring some solutions to protect the financial aid system on which so many of us rely.

BODY

I.   Pell runners might sound like a science fiction film, but the problem faced by colleges is very real.

    A.   The problem is simple to define.

        1.   According to the Department of Education website last updated on August 8, 2011, "A Federal Pell Grant, unlike a loan, does not have to be repaid, with the maximum Pell Grant for the 2011-12 award year being $5,500."

            a.   Students apply for and receive a Pell Grant just like most financial aid.

            b.   But once the college receives the Pell Grant, and subtracts the cost of tuition and fees, a student receives the remainder as a refund, which is supposed to pay for educational expenses.

c. Nothing in the grant requires the students to actually complete their coursework.

2. So Pell runners enroll in a school with low fees – like a community college – receive a sizable refund check, then drop or fail their classes.

   a. The next semester, or year, these runners move on to another low cost college for free money.

   b. As one college financial aid officer told Marketplace Radio of May 31, 2011, "Teachers on some campuses say they know when the checks come in because it's a lot easier to find a parking space."

B. But the effects extend well beyond the money these fake students receive.

1. Students who actually receive financial aid will receive less.

   a. Education Week of April 11, 2011 reported that in the current political climate, Pell Grants are likely to be targeted by Congress for cuts.

   b. Fraud is one of the justifications used to cut aid.

2. On top of cuts to programs, Pell runners are causing increases in tuition.

   a. The previously cited Chronicle of Higher Education notes that, the Pell Grant fraud rates at some colleges in Louisiana were as high as 12 percent.

   b. So the state Legislature passed a bill that will gradually double tuition at the state's technical colleges.

3. Probably the most devastating impact is on students like you and me, when Pell Grant runners take seats in classes they never intend to complete.

   a. Consider that the Los Angeles Times of March 31, 2011 notes that California's community colleges are slashing 400,000 students and thousands of classes.

   b. If Pell runners are taking up seats in classes that could go to other, more serious students, then they are keeping people like you and me out of classes, and maybe out of college altogether.

TRANSITION: Now that we know how Pell runners are damaging our colleges, let's inspect the roots of this devastating problem.

II. There are two contributing causes to Pell Grant fraud.

A. One of the major reasons why Pell Runners are so successful is because community colleges do not do a good job of keeping or sharing their records.

1. The previously cited CTI Careersearch states, "Part of the overarching problem with stopping Pell runners is that community college systems do not have a way or do not take the time to track previous academic records."

2. Because they don't monitor activity at other colleges, it's easy for students to bounce from school to school without attracting much attention.

   a. Kevin Lineberry told the previously cited Chronicle of Higher Education, "A student who has issues at Forsyth Tech can transfer to another community college and still continue to receive financial aid."

   b. The community college system, especially here in California, makes it harder to keep track of students.

      i. It's very common for a student to take classes at multiple colleges while trying to complete a degree.

      ii. That means it becomes much harder for a college to distinguish between a student who is completing their education and one who's taking advantage of the system.

B. The flexibility and poor accountability of the Pell Grant program is the second reason Pell runners can game the system.

   1. The Pell Grant basically functions as "free money" for students who receive it.

      a. A student can receive Pell Grants for 18 semesters.

      b. That means that a Pell Runner receiving the full award could fraudulently receive nearly $50,000 over the course of nine years.

   2. According to the previously cited Education Week, "the number of Pell Grant awards increased from about 690,000 students to 1.1 million." The explosion of numbers has made them harder to track.

   3. But as Community College Spotlight, June 2, 2011, states, students are supposed to spend the money on books or living expenses.

      a. But students don't have to account for how they spend the money. So it gets used for cars, clothing, and Christmas gifts.

      b. The lack of accountability makes it absolutely easy to 'abuse' the grant, as well as making it difficult to decipher how much grant money is lost to fraud.

TRANSITION: But now that we've grasped the causes, it's time to do something about this fraud that is so damaging to students and our colleges. So let's explore some possible remedies for this issue.

III. There are several ways to solve the problem of Pell runners.

   A. First, colleges need to begin linking students' grades and attendance to the receipt of financial aid.

      1. The previously cited Chronicle of Higher Education cites the example of Northern Virginia Community College.

         a. NVCC places students with poor academic histories on academic warning status.

         b. If they don't make academic progress, they can be placed on suspension and denied the remainder of their Pell Grants.

      2. Community colleges can also distribute the grants in increments instead of one large check.

         a. The Chronicle of Higher Education notes that some community colleges in California split financial aid checks into two disbursements.

         b. The second check comes after the "census date," when faculty have to verify a student is attending their class.

   B. Second, we can reform the Pell Grant Program itself.

      1. The previously cited Education Week suggests raising the eligibility requirement for Pell Grants from 12 units to 15.

      2. Others have suggested limiting years of eligibility from nine years to six years of undergraduate study.

      3. Another reform suggestion would limit the availability of Pell Grants for certain schools.

         a. Students enrolled in schools with weak records of student success would either be ineligible for grants or receive lower amounts.

         b. The idea behind implementing higher standards is to allow the Pell Grant Program to continue to assist honest and goal oriented students while putting an end to the abuse of this grant.

   C. We, as students, have a responsibility to do something to save this the program.

      1. First, we can raise awareness on campus by informing fellow students and faculty to be on the lookout for abuse.

      2. Second, contact your Financial Aid Office to ask about their policies on the Pell Grant and encourage them to either adopt multiple disbursements or carefully check students' prior records.

3. Finally, you can take a more active role by lobbying and/or joining your school's Associated Students and proposing legislation that would add multiple disbursements to financial aid checks.

CONCLUSION

Review of Topic/Main Points: Today we discovered the problem of Pell Runners. First, we filled out our FAFSA and discovered the problem. Then we waited in line for hours while examining some causes, and finally we got our award check and celebrated with some solutions to this fraud.

Lasting Thought: Financial aid helps so many students achieve their dream of a college education, and it is deplorable that some shady students jeopardize aid for us all. Mom always said, "there's no such thing as a free lunch," and it's time we prove she's right. It took Laurie Wolf 15 phone calls from a Pell runner to figure out there was a problem. Let's hope this knowledge allows us to answer the call and make a change.

WORKS CITED

Adams, Caralee. "Enrollment Jumps Linked to Growth of Pell Grants." *Education Week*. Editorial Projects in Education, 11 April 2011. Web. 20 Sep 2011.

"Federal Pell Grant Program." *U.S. Department of Education*. U.S. Department of Education, 2 Aug 2011. Web. 20 Sep 2011.

Field, Kelly. "Education Department Chases 'Pell Runners' Who Threaten Aid Program." *Chronicle of Higher Education*. The Chronicle of Higher Education, 28 Aug 2011. Web. 20 Sep 2011.

Jacobs, Joanne. "'Pell Runners' Abuse Grants." *Community College Spotlight*. Teachers College of Columbia University, 2 Jun 2011. Web. 20 Sep 2011.

Marshall-Genzer, Nancy. "Some Lawmakers Target Pell Grants for Cuts." *Marketplace*. American Public Media, 31 May 2011. Web. 20 Sep 2011.

O'Neill, Maggie. "Schools Crack Down on Pell Grant Runners." *CTI CareerSearch*. QuinStreet, Inc., 7 Sep 2011. Web. 20 Sep 2011.

Rivera, Carla. "California Community Colleges to Slash Enrollment, Classes." *Los Angeles Times*. The Los Angeles Times, 31 March 2011. Web. 20 Sep 2011.

Will, Madeline. "Government and Colleges Crack Down on Pell Grant Fraud." *The Daily Tar Heel*. DTH Publishing Corporation, 8 Sep 2011. Web. 20 Sep 2011.

SAMPLE PERSUASIVE SPEECH OUTLINE: MONROE'S MOTIVATED SEQUENCE

Specific Purpose: to persuade my classmates to support efforts to get students involved as election poll workers.

INTRODUCTION

I. **Attention Device:** Hanging chads. Butterfly ballots. Recounts. These are words most Americans didn't know prior to the 2000 presidential election, but are very aware of now. As the Florida recount dragged on for nearly a month, Americans also learned a great deal about the flaws in our voting process. Counting errors, confusing ballots, and polling places that opened late and closed early were just a few of the issues that prompted calls for voting reforms. An issue that has remained for Florida and the rest of the states, though, is the difficulty of getting qualified people to work elections to cut down on errors.

II. **Topic Revelation Statement:** In fact, with a national shortage of qualified poll workers and the growing presence of technology in elections, college and high school students are an untapped resource of election workers. Today, I hope to persuade you to become part of the solution.

III. **Significance Statement:** Beverly Moore, director of the Warren County Board of Elections, told *The Cincinnati Enquirer of September 29, 2002,* "It seems like there should be a better way. The bottom line is poll workers are the backbones of elections."

IV. **Preview of Main Points:** To see how we all can strengthen this backbone, let's first examine the need for more qualified poll workers. Second, we'll examine the plan to have more students working elections. Finally, I'll help you visualize the benefits of increased student participation in elections.

BODY

I. The current system for recruiting poll workers is failing. (NEED)
    A. There is a severe poll worker shortage.
        1. According to *The Sarasota Herald-Tribune* of November 1, 2002, there is difficulty finding poll workers because they have to work 14 hour days and are paid very little.
        2. The results, according to the previously cited *Cincinnati Enquirer,* are that "mixed in with dedicated people ...you get a lot of warm bodies that have no business being there."
        3. Poll workers also often quit if they are confused or if trouble arises.
    B. The shortage of qualified poll workers creates several problems.
        1. According to *The Washington Post,* September 14, 2002, polling places open late if workers don't show up and have to close early if people quit.
        2. Additionally, lack of familiarity with computerized voting systems affects voters.

      a.   The *Chronicle of Higher Education* on December 13, 2002, notes that the typical poll worker is about 70, and intimidated by computers. They may leave if they get frustrated.

      b.   This can lead to delays and errors in both voting and counting votes.

II.   There is a large untapped source of poll workers available. (SATISFACTION)

   A.   Local governments should allow and encourage high school and college students to work polls.

      1.   *The Washington Post* of August 29, 2002 notes that most students will work for the $6 per hour a poll worker is paid, and don't mind putting in a 14 hour day.

      2.   Students may also volunteer to receive community service credit at their high schools or colleges.

      3.   Most students have basic computer skills and familiarity with technology.

   B.   States will need to amend their laws to permit younger workers.

      1.   The previously cited *Washington Post* reports that most states require poll workers to be over 18 and registered voters.

      2.   18 states, however, have lowered their requirements to allow 16 and 17-year old students to work polls in some capacity.

      3.   The previously cited *Cincinnati Enquirer* also claims that some states have instituted minimum GPA requirements to make sure they are getting the best students for their workers.

III.   Student poll workers are an easily workable solution. (VISUALIZATION)

   A.   Several states and communities have already successfully implemented this policy.

      1.   Don Samuels, member of a voting task force, estimated in the *Sun-Sentinel* of September 21, 2002, that thousands of high school seniors would be helping out during the 2002 Florida elections.

      2.   Long Beach, California has allowed 16 and 17-year old students to serve as poll workers since 1997 with great success.

   B.   Bringing students into politics can help reduce student apathy.

      1.   Students are unlikely to participate in politics.

         a.   According to *The Saint Louis Post-Dispatch* on January 10, 2002 the percentage of 18-year olds voting reached its lowest level ever in the 2000 election.

         b.   *The Daily Princetonian* on December 9, 2002, claims that a recent survey indicates students would rather do community service than get involved in politics.

      2.   Jane Elmes-Crahall, a professor of communications at Wilkes University, told the *San Bernardino Sun* of November 7, 2002, that students care very passionately about issues, but are disconnected from the political process.

      3.   Working at polls helps reconnect students with politics.

         a.   Students can witness our democratic process in action.

         b.   They can also read about relevant issues for the election in which they work.

    c.   R. Michael Alvarez, professor of political science at Caltech, told the previously cited *Chronicle of Higher Education* that bringing students to the polls will have a long-term impact on their involvement in the political process.

CONCLUSION

I.   **Review of Topic and Main Points:** We have seen the dramatic need for new poll workers by first understanding the shortage of qualified workers. Then, we noted that students represent an untapped source of election officials. Finally, we discovered that this process has the potential to revitalize youth participation in politics and has already experienced some success.

II.   **Call to Action:** That's where we come in. As college students, we have the unique opportunity to inform ourselves about the political process and serve our communities. So consider the following actions. Volunteer in your precinct for the next election. Recruit friends, family, and fraternity, sorority, and club members to help, also. If younger students are not allowed to work polls where you live, lobby to have those laws changed.

III.   **Lasting Thought:** The right to vote for 18-year olds was a hard fought battle. It's time we proved that we can make a valuable contribution to the political process.

WORKS CITED

Binette, Chad. "Florida's Poll Workers' Jobs Getting Tougher." *Sarasota Herald Tribune* 1 Nov 2002: BS1+. Print.

Blunt, Matt and Gerald Tirozzi. "Young Workers Could Solve Poll Problems." *St. Louis Post-Dispatch* 10 Jan 2002: B7. Print.

Huriash, Lisa. "Voting Task Force Enlists Students, City Workers." *Sun-Sentinel* (Ft. Lauderdale, FL) 21 Sep 2002: 6A. Print.

Jenkins, Colleen. "Too Young to Vote but Old Enough to Run an Election." *The Washington Post* 29 Aug 2002: A20. Print.

Keating, Dan. "Fla. Vote Uncovers a Problem: Overwhelmed Poll Workers." *The Washington Post* 14 Sep 2002: A06. Print.

Lipsky-Karasz, Daniel. "Harvard Study: Students Choose Community Service Over Politics." *Daily Princetonian* 9 Dec 2002. Web. 4 Feb 2003.

Olsen, Florence. "Researches from Caltech and MIT Track Improvements to Voting Process." *Chronicle of Higher Education* 13 Dec 2002: 38+. Print.

Schroeder, Cindy. "Need Ongoing for Election Workers." *The Cincinnati Enquirer* 29 Sep 2002: 1B+. Print.

Silva, Andrew. "Young Voters Care About Issues, But Turned Off By Partisanship." *San Bernardino Sun* 7 Nov 2002. Web. 4 Feb 2003.

CHAPTER SIXTEEN

SPEAKING OUTSIDE THE CLASSROOM

Oh my God, you guys, I seriously do not have a speech prepared whatsoever. I'm shaking right now.
— *Christina Aguilera, at the Grammy Awards*

When many people think of public speaking, they imagine a famous politician or business executive standing at a lectern in front of a huge audience or TV cameras recording the event as the speaker delivers a formal speech from a manuscript or a teleprompter. Situations such as these are certainly public speaking events, but they are just a few examples in a long list of the occasions for which people speak to audience. Each day, ordinary people deliver important speeches in commonplace situations for a variety of reasons.

Many students feel that they will never need to give a formal speech. After all, not everyone will become a politician, corporate giant, celebrity, or religious figure. The tools you have learned to deliver effective informative and persuasive speeches, however, are essential building blocks to any form of public speaking. Even if you never deliver the State of the Union Address, you will likely need to perform a presentation for your job, give a toast at a best friend's wedding, deliver a eulogy at a funeral, or simply tell a story to a group of people at a party. Interestingly, these short speeches can be the most difficult to master and deliver effectively. This chapter will focus on the types of speeches you will most likely give throughout your lifetime and provide step by step instructions to writing these speeches.

SPECIAL OCCASION SPEECHES

Most important events have a speaker. Graduations, weddings, and funerals are just a few examples. Because each special occasion is unique, the specific requirements and expectations for each speech will vary from situation to situation. However, special occasion speeches still have one of the three major goals of public speaking: to inform, to persuade, or to entertain.

Special Occasion Speeches to Inform

Speech of Introduction

Most featured speakers are introduced to the audience before they speak. If you find yourself giving a **speech of introduction**, it is up to you to set the stage for a successful performance. The primary goal of this speech is to inform the audience about the speaker. Here are a few tips for a successful introductory speech:

Research the speaker. Consult his or her resume or arrange a short interview to ensure you have the most accurate and updated information available. Focus on the speaker's achievements in your speech to build up his or her ethos. You may also want to find out something about the speech topic. Be sure to give the audience any information they need to fully understand the speaker's presentation.

Don't steal the spotlight. Remember, audiences are not there to see you. Your speech should be short and focused exclusively on the speaker.

Don't mix up information. It's easy to mix up dates, years, or names of awards when preparing a speech of introduction. To avoid this, simply review your speech with the person you are introducing for accuracy.

Speak extemporaneously. If you need a set of brief notes, use them. But keep your delivery natural and conversational. Do not read from a manuscript.

Step by Step – Speech of Introduction

1. Quickly establish the nature of the occasion.
2. State three or four critical pieces of information regarding the speaker.
3. Announce the topic of the speaker's speech.
4. Welcome the speaker.

Sample Speech of Introduction:

"As our student government continues to grow, so do our opportunities. Many of you have expressed interest in the exploring these opportunities. You are all here today as student leaders ready to learn about new avenues in which you can represent our student body. Today, I am pleased to welcome Dr. Cynthia Ramirez, Vice President of Academic Affairs. Dr. Ramirez has worked with community colleges for over 28 years and here at our college for over 10 years. Dr. Ramirez has been actively involved in helping student groups organize their efforts and realize their potential. Recently, Alpha Gamma Sigma raised over $10,000 following Dr. Ramirez's guidance. Knowing that we are looking for ways to expand our representation, she has volunteered to talk with us about becoming involved in a variety of school wide committees. Let's give a warm welcome to Dr. Cynthia Ramirez."

Award Presentation Speech

When an organization or institution honors someone with an award or gift, someone has to present the award. The **award presentation speech**, like the introductory speech, is designed to primarily inform. Here are a few tips for a successful speech:

Keep the winner a surprise. Talk about the award first and get the audience curious. Build this suspense by discussing the award and reasons why this person won before you announce the winner's name.

Clarify the nature of the award. What does it honor? Why is it given? Are there any past recipients you might mention?

Explain the recipient's qualifications and traits. Be sure to praise the winner so that the audience understands why this person is so deserving of the award.

Make sure your speech is short and to the point. Remember to stay focused on the recipient and the reason for the award presentation.

Step by Step — Award Presentation

1. Discuss the award and its history.
2. Discuss the donor or source of the award.
3. Explain briefly how the award came to be.
4. Talk about the criteria for winning the award.
5. List the ways the recipient met this criteria.
6. Mention the rigor of the selection process, if applicable.
7. Finally, announce the name of the recipient.

Sample Award Presentation Speech:

"The Tan Award was first given in 1999. Mrs. Tan was a Professor of Communication for 30 years. When Mrs. Tan decided to retire, she also decided to continue to touch students' lives. The avenue for this became a scholarship award that recognizes exceptional communication students. The criteria for this award are not easily met. However, one applicant met and exceeded the criteria this year. This student has a 4.0 grade point average, is actively involved in student government, and a member of the Forensics team. The award winner this year won several medals at various speech tournaments, including the gold medal for informative speaking at the national championship tournament. While Mrs. Tan is now living in the beautiful state of Hawaii, she personally reviewed each applicant's qualifications and sent the following statement about this applicant: 'There is one student who clearly exemplifies this award. He uses his speaking skills in every aspect of life, and has excelled in more areas than many of us hope to. Congratulations to Damon J. Hill — this year's winner of the Tan Award.'"

Acceptance Speech

If you ever win the Nobel Prize, or are simply honored as employee as the month, you may be expected to give an **acceptance speech.** Here are a few tips for a memorable speech:

Be gracious. Thank the presenter, acknowledge the organization that sponsors the award, and, if you feel it's appropriate, thank the people in your personal life that helped you reach the achievement. If other people were nominated, you may want to mention them, as well.

Choose the right delivery style. If you have been nominated or know beforehand you will win, you may want to prepare an extemporaneous speech. You do not want to appear too assured, however. Award winners who sound overly prepared can seem arrogant or self-obsessed. Audiences like speeches that are genuine and heartfelt.

Keep it short. If you've ever watched an awards show on television, you know that long acceptance speeches can be boring. You may not have an orchestra that will cut you off if you speak too long, but you will see some glazed eyes if you are long-winded.

Step by Step - Acceptance Speech

1. Briefly thank the person or group giving the award.

2. Share your feelings about the award.

3. Acknowledge those that helped you receive the award.

4. Finish with a positive statement.

Sample Acceptance Speech:

"Thank you Mrs. Schroeder for this award. I am so honored that you are proud of my performance at the Community College Association. I have to thank Samantha for teaching me everything there is to know about the Accounting Department. She taught me how to take my book knowledge of accounting and apply it specifically to the interests of the Community College Association. I hope that one day I can mentor a new employee the way she mentored me. Thank you all for making my time here a joy instead of a job."

Special Occasion Speeches to Persuade

Persuade may seem like too strong a word to accurately describe the next two speeches. However, both are designed to influence, inspire, and move an audience. In that sense, they are persuasive in nature.

Eulogy

The **eulogy** is a speech is delivered at a funeral to memorialize a person who has died and help audience members reconcile their emotions. Here are a few tips for a tasteful speech:

Write the speech on behalf of the whole audience, not just yourself. Remember you are just one person who knew the deceased. Try to account for, or at least acknowledge, each of the different roles and relationships in this person's life. One way to begin to accomplish this is to interview other people so you share memories from a variety of perspectives. As you think about the structure of a eulogy, consider using a chronological pattern to help you account for the entirety of the deceased's life. Finally, if other people are speaking, you may want to coordinate your speeches so they don't overlap in content.

Use a manuscript. Remember, when emotion might get the better of you, a manuscript will help you maintain control and composure. If you are delivering a eulogy, no one will think less of you for using a script. Even with a word-for-word script in hand, you may experience a swell of emotion that could make speaking difficult. Crying or taking a moment to compose oneself during a eulogy is not a sign of weakness, nor is it considered dropping the ball. It is just a natural response to a difficult, emotional situation.

Be sure the eulogy is appropriate. Appropriateness is crucial in emotional contexts like a funeral. Use of humor may be fine in one eulogy, and not another. Also, a funeral is not the right time to divulge secrets or awkward moments from a person's life. Being sensitive and appropriate means taking into account the circumstances of the person's death and the religious or spiritual dimensions of the funeral, and then using your common sense about the type of eulogy you will deliver.

Step by Step – Eulogy

1. Introduce the deceased through the story of his/her parents. When they met, married, and gave birth to the deceased.

2. Include the births of the deceased's sisters and brothers, if any. You can also include any stories that you've collected from siblings about their childhood.

3. As you recount the years of the deceased, incorporate his/her accomplishments, interests, activities, or life changes that occurred during that time frame. This should include their schooling, career, relocations, marriage(s), births of children and grandchildren, etc.

4. Again, you can incorporate positive, appropriate stories from close colleagues, friends, and family members in the appropriate years.

5. You don't have to talk about a person's death or the reason they died in the conclusion. Instead, you can conclude with a positive note or summation of the person they were.

Sample Eulogy:

"Stephen Mindle was born to Michelle and Ted Mindle two years after they married. Ted was a professional football player, and Michelle was a television sports announcer. They met while she was covering a Super Bowl game that Ted's team actually lost that year. However, together they won with the birth of Stephen, who would bring many winning occasions to them. Stephen was an only child, yet he had many "aunts and uncles," as he called them, who thought of him as their child. By the age of 5, Stephen was able to hear a person speak, and imitate their voice almost perfectly. He was the youngest winner of Dramatic Interpretation at the National Forensic League speech competition for high school students. After high school, he went directly into professional voice-over work and created the voices for many of Disney's beloved characters.

"He received 6 Oscars for his talented animation work. Everyone loved him for his ability to make people smile and realize the day was brighter because he had entered their life on that given day. Dr. Ron Adenza, the principal where Stephen attended high school, told me that Stephen would often help the booster club by calling parents asking for donations imitating the voice of many Hollywood stars. The parents were always amazed at the connection of celebrated stars that were spokespersons for the school. Those assembled here today are better people because of our lives crossed paths with Stephen Mindle. He will be remembered because of his kindness, love, friendship, but most of all, we will remember those voices that will continue as long as there is a movie or cartoon that his voice was a character. Stephen you are a bright shinning star to us and we will miss you."

Epideictic Speech

This is a speech delivered to praise or condemn someone or something. Epideictic speeches are delivered in situations such as a retirement dinner in which you might, for example, praise a longtime co-worker or at a political rally in which you might speak for or against a candidate for office. Here are a few tips for a successful speech:

Remember Aristotle. Epideictic speeches are essentially persuasive speeches. As such, they must be grounded in ethos, pathos, and logos. Instead of simply expressing your opinions, take time to carefully research and structure your speech, and then deliver it using the tools discussed in this class. And don't forget the power of pathos; consider emotional appeals, including humor.

Craft your language carefully. The best epideictic speeches make strong use of vivid, clear, and appropriate language. You may also want to consult quotation books to find particularly inspirational words from other people.

Since epideictic speeches vary broadly, there is no easy step by step formula. Remember to meet the appropriate time limit of the speech, clarify whether you are praising or condemning the person or event, organize your speech, use emotional examples, and give facts as well as opinions.

Special Occasion Speeches to Entertain

Toast

A **toast** is a speech of thanks or well wishing given with drink in hand, often before dinner celebrations like weddings and anniversaries. If you are a social person or attend business dinners, you may find yourself giving a toast at a moment's notice. Toasts can be given simply to recognize and thank the host for the evening. Fortunately, toasts can be very easy to write as long as you make them simple and positive in tone. There are several ways to organize a toast. For example, a storybook style description of a couple's romance may work well for some weddings, while a very formal and traditional approach will work well at others. Here are some general guidelines for toasts:

Stand. Make sure to give your toast with your glass in hand.

Place the glass appropriately. Keep the glass at waist level until you raise it at the very end of your toast.

Talk equally about all people who are receiving the toast. No matter what the occasion, or who is in the audience, always remember to talk equally about everyone you are toasting.

Be positive. Only share positive statements, characteristics, or stories.

Make it personal or emotional. When delivering a toast, focus on ways to use humor, excitement, or personal opinions to make the speech meaningful.

Involve your audience. Always refer to the people sitting at the table in your toast so everyone feels involved in the moment.

Keep it short. People are hungry, after all.

Bad **Sample Toast:**

"I've never done this before. I'm so nervous. Here it goes. I can't imagine a better couple. I don't think that Matt or Kristin would have found a better match if they looked forever. I've heard that there is a 50% chance a couple will get divorced. Well, I don't think that Matt and Kristin need to worry about that. I took Kristin and Matt camping with my family one weekend and she had to dig a hole to go to the bathroom. I'll never forget when she fell into the hole – what a mess! Matt had to help her out of the hole. May you both help each other out of holes of crap throughout your life!"

That toast was clearly an example of a bad toast! The speaker started by dropping the ball. The toast is filled with negative language and negative examples. Further, the speaker told a humiliating story. Who wants to hear potty humor right before eating? Sadly, that was a real toast given at a real wedding. Let's make some simple changes following the steps listed below:

Step by Step – Toast:

1. Explain your relationship to the honoree.

2. Thank the parents/organizers of the event (if needed).

3. Pick one or two values or characteristics this person exemplifies (one is best).

4. Tell a humorous, positive, and specific story showing how they embody this characteristic.

5. Note how this value makes them a wonderful business partner, couple, colleague, etc.

6. End with a congratulatory line and lift your glass as you say it.

Good **Sample Toast:**

"I am honored to be Kristin's Matron of Honor. I have known Kristin since high school and we have been best friends since the day we met. Through our friendship, I've had the chance to meet Matt and witness their relationship grow into what it has become today — a marriage. I would like to thank Kristin's parents, Mr. and Mrs. Smith and Matt's parents, Mr. and Mrs. Jones, for their support throughout their relationship and the effort, thought, and love they have given to this wedding. Matt and Kristin are perfect for each other. Matt's spontaneity keeps Kristin's life exciting, and Kristin's practical thinking keeps Matt grounded. I saw how much they complemented each other one weekend on a camping trip. Having never been camping, Kristin was out of her element. Matt realized she would enjoy it and encouraged her to try it. All weekend he taught her the art of camping, fishing, and having fun without electricity. When Matt realized he didn't pack matches to start a fire, Kristin quickly provided matches from her well-stocked backpack. I remember watching them work and play together and seeing how they made an amazing team. Matt, may you keep Kristin's life full of adventure. Kristin, may you always be practical so that your adventures go smoothly. You really know how to light a fire – so keep it burning! Here's to Matt and Kristin — an amazing team!"

After Dinner Speech

An **after dinner speech** is a funny, entertaining speech on a light topic often delivered after a luncheon or dinner. Here are some suggestions:

Make sure your speech has a point. Unless you are Kevin Hart, a consistently funny speech is hard to craft. Be yourself, give a speech that has a message, and throw in humor when it seems appropriate.

Pick the right topic for the occasion. This is true for any speech, but after dinner speeches have some special requirements. Since this is an environment in which people are expecting to be entertained, make sure your topic is light and not offensive. Try to find a topic area that is new and creative, has some significance to your audience, and one that will not be unappetizing while people are seated around a table with food.

Most after dinner speeches are formal speeches that will inform or persuade the audience. The occasion will dictate the length, and the audience will evaluate how effectively the speaker chose the content, delivery, and impact.

Keynote Speech

You may be asked to give a **keynote** speech at some point in your lifetime. This speech is usually used at the beginning or end of a conference or convention. The word "keynote" really describes the goal of this speech: to present a significant idea intended to set the *tone* for the rest of the meeting or event, to inspire the participants, to summarize the message given during the conference, or to inspire the participants to apply this message. Although there are no set guidelines for a keynote speech, the goal is to inspire or to generate enthusiasm among participants. Here are some suggestions:

Decide what message you want to send. When asked to be a keynote speaker you can ask for suggestions on the message. The event organizer may have a theme for the event or outcome goal in mind.

Be structured. Structure your speech using the speech organization model (i.e., introduction, body, and conclusion). The following are examples of structures that have been used in keynote speeches:

Themes:	Discipline, Persistence, Teamwork
Principles:	Risk, Virtuosity, Originality
Lessons Learned:	How to Compete, How to Commit, How to Collaborate
Journey:	From one place to another

Practice, Practice, Practice. Being a keynote speaker is both an honor and a lot of responsibility. You will be setting the mood for the event. You should approach this speech the way this book has taught you to approach your classroom speeches.

EVERYDAY SPEAKING OCCASIONS

There will be other speaking situations in your everyday life that may not be as momentous as the situations described on the last few pages, yet they are still important. Each of the following speeches will present different challenges, but skills you learn in this class can prepare you to handle each one of the following confidently and effectively:

At school:	teach, deliver a lecture, tell a story, lead a ceremonial event
At place of worship:	preach, deliver a sermon, teach
At court:	argue your case, listen to the opponent, testify
At your business:	deliver sales presentations, run a meeting, interview, be interviewed
At the legislature:	debate, testify, hold a press conference
At the theater:	be a responsive audience member, act, direct

CONCLUSION

This chapter is intended to remind us that public speaking does not occur only in a speech class. In the years to come, you will likely find yourself preparing a toast or speech for a special occasion. Having this book on your shelf should prove to be helpful and will allow you to refer to these guidelines. On special (as well as not so special) occasions, we deliver real-world presentations to many types of audiences. Consider this class as a laboratory in which you experiment with different skills and concepts to prepare you for all the speeches you will encounter outside the classroom.

Speaker's Secret

The speeches you prepare during this course won't necessarily resemble speeches you will be asked to give outside of the classroom. However, the skills and experience you gain from these classroom speeches can easily be applied to nearly every speaking situation you will encounter throughout your life.

FROM FRIGHT TO MIGHT MOMENT

We fear the unknown. Public speaking is an unknown experience for most people. You can lessen this fear by speaking as often as possible, not just in this class, but in real-world situations you encounter.

SAMPLE HERO SPEECH MANUSCRIPT

INTRODUCTION

If you asked him, he'd tell you that he never really liked teaching, or teenagers, or anything, really. Most of the other kids in my class called him words like grouch, or grinch, or a lot worse. Even I didn't like him for a long time — especially how he always smelled like Swisher Sweets cheap cigars. But, by the end of 11th grade, Mr. Largent turned out to be the most important and influential teacher I ever had. I'd like to tell you why I consider him to be a hero in my life.

BODY

Classic Literature is pretty far from the mind of your average teenager, and that's who I was at the start of 11th grade. I didn't have a care in the world, except for what kind of car I would buy as soon as I could save the money. Third period was English Lit with Mr. Largent, and while he would mumble aloud from Homer, we'd all pass notes and watch the clock. Sometimes he'd try to get us involved or excited about the book we were reading, which for most of the term was The Odyssey, but the tide was definitely against him in that classroom. Sometimes I felt sorry for him and pretended to listen, but I never thought to let him actually enter my mind and make any additions or improvements. And then one day he just snuck right in.

At the end of The Odyssey, the main character Odysseus comes home to his wife after being gone for years. While he was gone he wasn't exactly faithful, either. For our final assignment of the class, Mr. Largent asked us to write something different than we'd done before. He wanted us to think about our own lives and write about someone who may have left us for a period during our lives - even for a short time - and how we felt about them coming back. I thought about writing about my dog, Bo, who left when I was in sixth grade, but I couldn't. My hand just started writing about my dad.

He left me and my mom when I was a freshman and never came back. He had only called twice since, and other than that we just heard about him from people we knew, kind of like Odysseus. What was supposed to be a three page paper was becoming a twelve page paper as I wrote and wrote. I argued first that the wife should not take him back for any reason, and then that he should never have come home at all. But by the end, through tears, I decided that she'd take him, of course, just like we'd take my Dad if he ever showed up again. As embarrassing or humiliating as it might be, you want the person more than your pride. And after I wrote my paper, I wrote my Dad a letter telling him that I always hoped he'd be a part of my life, and that he could always come back to me, and that I hope he does.

CONCLUSION

I haven't heard from my Dad yet, but I got a really wonderful note on my paper from Mr. Largent. He said that my essay was one of the best he's ever had, and that he was glad that an ancient story could still mean something to a teenage girl today. I know it doesn't seem like a lot, but Mr. Largent made me realize that everyone has something to teach us, and that we should always learn things that are presented to us in school - because you never know when it will suddenly jump out of the past and hit home.

CHAPTER SEVENTEEN

IMPROMPTU SPEAKING

It takes me more than three weeks to put together a good impromptu speech.

— *Mark Twain*

You don't always have three weeks to prepare a speech. More often than you might believe, you will be called upon to give a speech on the spur of the moment. You might be at a meeting and the person who is supposed to introduce the guest speaker is caught in traffic. Suddenly, you are giving an impromptu speech of introduction. You are at work, and the business changes to a topic about which you are very passionate. Suddenly, you want to speak, be understood, and move people to your side of the issue. One of the most common types of impromptu speaking is the job interview. In these situations, and many more, you will be thankful that you have training in impromptu speaking.

These impromptu situations will require you to call upon much of what you have learned so far in this public speaking class, and they will require you to add a few new techniques, as well.

Impromptu speeches occur when a speaker has little or no preparation time. The speaker must prepare a quick mental outline and choose his or her exact wording for the speech as the speech is in progress. For many, this can be a very intimidating type of speaking, even though we do it every day.

Regardless of what the impromptu situation is, there are two important things your speech should have: organization and supporting materials. This chapter will discuss both of those elements, as well as give you some strategies on how to deliver and prepare for an impromptu speech.

Organizing Your Impromptu Speech

Impromptu is no different than any prepared speech you might give in that your message will be easier for your audience to understand if it is well organized. Because you have very little time to prepare your organization, it will probably not be as detailed as it has been in speeches where you have prepared outlines with subpoints and extensive supporting details. A common mistake impromptu speakers make is speaking without structure and rambling on too long. A solution to this problem is using a solid structure for each impromptu speech you deliver.

As with all speeches, make sure your speech has an introduction, body (with main points), and conclusion. A very simple outline will work well for impromptu speaking. While developing an organizational pattern might seem like it would complicate your speech, it will actually provide clarity for your audience. The following very basic speech structure is a good guideline to keep in mind:

Introduction:

I.   Attention Getter

II. Topic Revelation Statement

III. Preview of Main Points

Body:

I.   First Main Point

II. Second Main Point

III. Third Main Point

Conclusion:

I.   Review of topic and Main Points

II. Lasting Thought

To assist you in selecting your main points, many of the organizational structures of speeches we discussed in Chapter 8 can be quickly applied to an impromptu speech. Additionally, some simple impromptu main point structures you may wish to try include:

Past, Present, Future	**Costs, Benefits**
Biography, Accomplishments	**Pros, Cons,**
Greatest Accomplishment	**International, National, Local**

SUPPORTING YOUR IMPROMPTU SPEECH

When doing a persuasive or informative speech, much of your support comes from outside sources. You may rely somewhat on personal experience, but, as we discussed in Chapter 15, a primary way to build ethos comes from the use of experts and research. In an impromptu situation, however, you don't have the luxury of time to do research and find great supporting materials like statistics, comparisons, and testimony.

You do, however, have the great resource of your mind at your disposal. Everything you know is part of the arsenal of ideas available to you for an impromptu speech. Sources include books you have read, theories you have learned in class and elsewhere, movies you have seen, biographies, novels, stories, and articles you have read, and much, much more. Your personal experiences and stories also provide a great source of supporting materials. Consider a job interview where the employer asks you to discuss your greatest strengths. A personal story that illustrates whatever skill you choose is the best way to support your idea. Whatever support you choose, your mind is your greatest asset when tackling an impromptu situation.

Preparation: Your Mind is a Great Storehouse of Knowledge

Contrary to popular belief, you can prepare for impromptu speaking. In a sense, all of your life is preparation for it.

In order to prepare in advance of a speaking day for this unique type of speaking, it is helpful to do an **inventory of your knowledge**. You will probably be surprised at the vast storehouse of information in your mental archive when you take the time to reflect. Unfortunately, unless we keep this information well organized, we won't have quick access to it in impromptu situations.

There are many ways to organize your knowledge. Whichever method you choose, the key is to figure out how to use the knowledge you have. For example, you might think of a list of movies you have seen as possible examples. It's one thing to have seen a movie, and another to use it in a speech. So think of speech themes or topics for which you might use it as an example. Let's say you've seen the movie *The Lion King*. If you're going to include it in your list of usable examples, you'd want to figure out what sorts of speech topics/themes the movie links to (betrayal, revenge, love, friendship, tolerance, destiny, etc.). This helps you find ways to connect concepts in your mind and discover new ways to apply common knowledge that you have. Check out the activity at the end of this chapter to get you started.

You can also prepare for impromptu speeches by **anticipating possible topics** you might be asked to discuss. For instance, you might invest just a little time thinking in advance about the questions a job interviewer will ask you or imagining possible clients you could encounter while at a conference. This little time you spend anticipating and preparing could have a big payoff when you have just the right answer or product pitch on the tip of your tongue.

DELIVERING IMPROMPTU SPEECHES

By their very nature, impromptu speaking situations are unpredictable, and therefore, can create stress and anxiety in a speaker. Somehow, though, many people are able to deliver impromptu speeches calmly and confidently without ever breaking a sweat. How do they do it? Well, many professionals will tell you they simply choose to **seem confident**, even if they don't feel confident. You can seem confident by maintaining eye contact, speaking slowly, controlling your body movement, and smiling.

Also, if you want to improve as an impromptu speaker, you need to work on your **fluency**, or the smoothness with which the right word comes out of your mouth at the right time. Because you are "making it up as you go along," you might also be more prone to "umm," "uhhh," and other non-words in impromptu speeches. It is especially important in these situations to think about your non-words and use pauses if you need to collect your thoughts or develop an idea. If you're in a job interview or other setting where you are not given separate time to prepare your speech, resist the urge to start talking immediately. Instead, collect your thoughts for 10-15 seconds, and then begin speaking. By doing this, you are less likely to start with "ummmm" or trip over your words as you introduce your main ideas. Practicing impromptu speeches is actually a great way to improve your overall fluency as a speaker, since it forces your mind to work more efficiently to select appropriate language. With more practice, your skill at talking about a topic spontaneously will improve.

Finally, it is important to be **succinct** when you are giving impromptu speeches. When you are out of ideas, review and conclude your speech. Since you haven't rehearsed your speech, you may not have a good sense of how much time has passed since you began. If you hear yourself repeating an idea you already shared, it's time to wrap it up.

Mental Preparation Before the Speech

Try this thought process:

1. Choose a topic (unless one was given to you) and formulate a position on that topic.

2. Choose your organizational structure.

3. Review your storehouse of knowledge for some concrete examples, facts, and reasoning to support each main point.

4. Develop an attention device so it can be used at the beginning of the speech as well as part of the conclusion.

5. Mentally review parts 1-4, then deliver the speech.

SKILL-BUILDING IMPROMPTU SPEECHES

Different instructors like to use different types of topics for this classroom assignment. Creative options allow this assignment to take on many forms. Some common examples you may encounter include:

Quotations and proverbs. Your instructor might choose a proverb that expresses the values of a particular culture. He or she might also choose a quotation from a famous philosopher or even a funny movie quote or song lyric. You can look at the end of this chapter to find some sample quotations for practice speeches. If you encounter a topic like this, remember that most quotations give some kind of advice or a philosophy on life. Try to develop a thesis or position related to that philosophy and then support that with your examples as main points.

Abstract concepts or single words. A second type of impromptu topic for classroom use is single, abstract concepts or words. They are interesting because they are open to many interpretations. Imagine giving a speech on any of the following: truth, lying, dignity, generosity, greed, faith, hope, charity, patriotism, freedom, power, dictatorship, privacy, good, evil, justice, rich, poor, and beauty. As with a quotation, if you get a broad and simple topic like this, try to develop a thesis statement related to your word that you can defend and support with examples. This will provide your speech with structure that might not be apparent from the very broad topic.

Objects. Sometimes professors opt to give a student an object as a topic. One common way you may encounter this is through a "grab bag," where your professor puts a bunch of items into a box or bag and has you pull one out as your topic. You could get anything ranging from a pencil to a deck of cards to a brick. These types of topics can be challenging, but remember the earlier advice to develop a thesis. If you get a concrete object, ask yourself questions like "Why do people use this object?" or "What importance does this have for me or society?" Those questions might help you develop a focus for your speech and think of supporting examples.

Item to sell. Some public speaking professors ask students to pretend to sell an item as their impromptu assignment. Topics could include: sell an original invention, sell a car, sell a product, sell a private school college education, sell makeup, sell tickets to a concert, sell a computer, and sell clothes. In this case, remember the persuasive techniques from Chapter 15 to help you organize your speech. Monroe's Motivated Sequence is a great way to organize an impromptu sales speech.

CONCLUSION

In this chapter, we have discussed how to handle situations where you are given little or no time to prepare your speech. The most important elements to remember are the organization of your speech, support for your ideas, and fluency of the words used. Impromptu speaking might seem a bit scary at first because it is unpredictable, but if you can develop the skill of impromptu speaking, you will find it helps you in all other aspects of your life, and you will be a master at thinking on your feet.

Speaker's Secret

Practice what you speak! You know more than you think you know. Do a little archaeological exploration of your own brain to dig up facts and stories you learned years ago, then use this information in an impromptu speech.

FROM FRIGHT TO MIGHT MOMENT

Impromptu speaking may seem, at first, to be the most frightening type of speaking. However, you now know that it is the type of speaking you do every day, and that you can prepare and practice even for an impromptu speech.

SAMPLE IMPROMPTU SPEECH OUTLINE

Topic: "Keep true to the dreams of thy youth." (Schiller)

INTRODUCTION

I.   **Attention Device:** What do Bill Clinton, Oksana Baiul, and Tom Hanks have in common?

II. **Topic Revelation Statement:** I was given the quotation, "Keep true to the dreams of thy youth."

III. **Preview of Main Points:** Today we will examine three individuals who made the dreams from their youth come true. First, in politics, we will discuss Bill Clinton. Next, in the arena of sports, we will see how Oksana Baiul made her ice skating dream come true. Finally, we will look to the world of entertainment and discover how Tom Hanks was able to fulfill his dream.

BODY

I.   **Bill Clinton** met President Kennedy when he visited the White House as a young man. On that day, he decided he would be President of the United States.

II. **Oksana Baiul,** as a young child in Russia, wanted to be a figure skater. Even though she had much hardship, including the loss of her parents, she didn't quit. One day, she found herself on the victory stand at the Olympic Games.

III. **Tom Hanks** saw a play when he was young. He was amazed that people earned their living acting and on the spot decided that he would do the same.

CONCLUSION

I.   **Review of Topic and Main Points:** I have discussed the topic, "Keep true to the dreams of thy youth." We saw how Bill Clinton in politics, Oksana Baiul in sports, and Tom Hanks in entertainment didn't lose sight of their childhood dreams.

II. **Lasting Thought:** The next time you are asked what do Bill Clinton, Oksana Baiul, and Tom Hanks have in common, you will know that it is that they persisted and made their dreams come true.

IMPROMPTU QUOTATIONS

"Oh yes, the past can hurt. But you can either run from it, or learn from it."
–Rafiki, The Lion King

· ·

"It takes a great deal of bravery to stand up to your enemies, but a great deal more to stand up to your friends."
–Professor Dumbledore

· ·

"Some people can't believe in themselves until someone else believes in them first."
–Good Will Hunting

· ·

"All you can do in life is try to solve the problem in front of you."
–Mean Girls

· ·

"The brave may not live forever, but the cautious do not live at all."
–The Princess Diaries

· ·

No legacy is so rich as honesty.
–William Shakespeare

· ·

The more you find out about the world, the more opportunities there are to laugh at it.
–Bill Nye

· ·

Truth is beautiful, without doubt; but so are lies.
–Ralph Waldo Emerson

· ·

If you don't know where you are going, any road will take you there.
–Lewis Carroll

· ·

He who strikes the first blow admits he's lost the argument.
–Chinese Proverb

· ·

Silence is one of the hardest arguments to refute.
–Josh Billings

· ·

If you don't love what you do, you won't do it with much conviction or passion.
–Mia Hamm

· ·

The only victory that counts is the one over yourself.
–Jesse Owens

The only disability in life is a bad attitude.
– *Scott Hamilton*

. . . .

All the arguing in the world can't change the decision of the umpire.
–*Lou Gherig*

. . . .

All you ever talk about is becoming a pro hockey player, but there's a problem – you're not any good.
–*Terry, Happy Gilmore*

. . . .

Don't talk about the next step until you've climbed the one in front of you.
–*Norman Dale, Hoosiers*

. . . .

One must not tie a ship to a single anchor, nor life to a single hope.
–*Epictetus*

. . . .

If you have a wounded heart, touch it as little as you would an injured eye.
–*Pythagoras*

. . . .

The beginning is the half of every action.
–*Greek Proverb*

. . . .

You should never wear your best pants when you go to fight for freedom.
–*Chinese proverb*

. . . .

While forbidden fruit is said to taste sweeter, it usually spoils faster.
–*Abigail Van Buren*

. . . .

Nothing that costs only a dollar is worth having.
–*Elizabeth Arden*

. . . .

Opportunity is missed by most people because it is dressed in overalls and looks like work.
–*Thomas Edison*

. . . .

Each success only buys a ticket to a more difficult problem.
–*Henry Kissinger*

. . . .

Experience is the name everyone gives to their mistakes.
–*Oscar Wilde*

APPENDIX A
SPEECH ASSIGNMENTS

ICEBREAKER SPEECH ASSIGNMENTS:

ASSIGNMENT	**Time Warp Speech**
OBJECTIVE	To present a short speech like you might be asked to give 5-10 years from now (or an except from that speech)
TOPIC	Open, but don't give a speech about what you plan to do in 5-10 years, be yourself in 5-10 years delivering a speech somewhere.
SUPPORT	As needed
TIME RANGE	2-3 minutes
DELIVERY STYLE	Appropriate for the imagined situation
NOTES	Note cards permitted, if appropriate for the imagined situation.
VISUAL AIDS	None
ATTIRE	Appropriate for the imagined situation
HINTS	Be creative. Aim high! Sample topics used by previous students include, "My Academy Award Acceptance Speech," "Arguing to the PTA to Get a Stop Sign in Front of My House," and "Talking to a Second Grade Class about My Job."

ADDITIONAL
INFORMATION

MY SPEAKING DATE _____

ASSIGNMENT	**Speech Fear Speech**
OBJECTIVE	To share with the class your experiences with speech anxiety, including possible origins for the anxiety and your plan to overcome it
TOPIC	You are the topic.
SUPPORT	As needed
TIME RANGE	2-3 minutes
DELIVERY STYLE	Extemporaneous
NOTES	One note card permitted
VISUAL AIDS	None
HINTS	Don't be too tough on yourself. As you prepare, keep in mind that speech anxiety impacts a great majority of people.

ADDITIONAL
INFORMATION

MY SPEAKING DATE _____

ICEBREAKER SPEECH ASSIGNMENTS, CONT'D:

ASSIGNMENT	**Introduction Speech**
OBJECTIVE	To interview a classmate for 5-10 minutes, learning information about his or her life experience, then to introduce that person to the class as though he/she was about to be the guest speaker for the class today.
TOPIC	A classmate
SUPPORT	Facts, stories, explanations, and/or testimony from your classmate
TIME RANGE	60-90 seconds
DELIVERY STYLE	Extemporaneous
NOTES	One note card permitted
VISUAL AIDS	None
ATTIRE	Casual
HINTS	Don't be vague. Use interesting details. Make the person you will be introducing sound as interesting as possible.

**ADDITIONAL
INFORMATION**

MY SPEAKING DATE _____

IMPROMPTU SPEECH ASSIGNMENTS:

ASSIGNMENT   **Simple Topic Speech**

OBJECTIVE   To offer the audience insight or simple wisdom about your topic

TOPIC   A word or short phrase to be drawn randomly

SUPPORT   Personal experience and knowledge

TIME RANGE   2-3 minutes

DELIVERY STYLE   Impromptu

NOTES   One note card permitted

VISUAL AIDS   None

ATTIRE   Casual

HINTS   Don't let not knowing the topic overwhelm you. If you don't panic, the ideas will flow easily when you prepare.

ADDITIONAL INFORMATION

MY SPEAKING DATE _____

ASSIGNMENT   **Quotation-based Impromptu Speech**

OBJECTIVE   To offer the audience insight into a particular quotation or saying

TOPIC   A quotation to be drawn randomly in class (may be from a famous person, song, book, movie, etc.)

SUPPORT   Personal experience and knowledge

TIME RANGE   2-3 minutes

DELIVERY STYLE   Impromptu

NOTES   One note card permitted

VISUAL AIDS   None

ATTIRE   Casual

HINTS   Try to break the quotation down to a simple idea or phrase. It will make it easier to think of support.

ADDITIONAL INFORMATION

MY SPEAKING DATE _____

IMPROMPTU SPEECH ASSIGNMENTS, CONT'D:

ASSIGNMENT	**Impromptu Sales Speech**
OBJECTIVE	To persuade the audience to buy a product or service
TOPIC	Provided to you in class
SUPPORT	As needed
TIME RANGE	2-3 minutes
DELIVERY STYLE	Impromptu
NOTES	One note card permitted
VISUAL AIDS	None
ATTIRE	Casual
HINTS	Have fun and be creative!
ADDITIONAL INFORMATION	

MY SPEAKING DATE _____

INFORMATIVE SPEECH ASSIGNMENTS:

ASSIGNMENT   ## Speech Introduction Speech

OBJECTIVE   To perform and refine the introduction to your informative speech

TOPIC   Your informative introduction

SUPPORT   As needed

TIME RANGE   30-90 seconds

DELIVERY STYLE Extemporaneous

NOTES   One note card permitted

VISUAL AIDS   Only permitted if part of the introduction

ATTIRE   Casual

HINTS   Memorize at least the first line of your introduction so you can begin by looking at your audience for a whole thought.

**ADDITIONAL
INFORMATION**

MY SPEAKING DATE _____

ASSIGNMENT   ## Informative Demonstration Speech

OBJECTIVE   To teach your audience how to do something they probably do not already know how to do

TOPIC   Your choice

SUPPORT   As needed

TIME RANGE   4-6 minutes

DELIVERY STYLE Extemporaneous

NOTES   Two note cards permitted. Notes discouraged, as your hands will probably be busy.

VISUAL AIDS   If appropriate for topic

ATTIRE   Casual

HINTS   Food is great, but be sure to practice the whole speech with food preparation before you arrive. Unprepared demonstration speeches tend to go very overtime.

**ADDITIONAL
INFORMATION**

MY SPEAKING DATE _____

INFORMATIVE SPEECH ASSIGNMENTS, CONT'D:

ASSIGNMENT	**Informative Revelation Speech**
OBJECTIVE	To organize, support, and deliver a researched informational speech
TOPIC	Should be something new and unique, but also relevant to your audience. Teach us something we did not know about before listening to your speech. See sample topic lists in Appendix C for ideas.
SUPPORT	Minimum of 6 sources must be cited during the speech. Sources must be current and credible.
TIME RANGE	5-8 minutes
DELIVERY STYLE	Extemporaneous
NOTES	Two note cards permitted with writing on one side only
VISUAL AIDS	Ask instructor
ATTIRE	Professional appearance
HINTS	
ADDITIONAL INFORMATION	

MY SPEAKING DATE _____

ASSIGNMENT	**Cultural Informative Speech**
OBJECTIVE	To educate your audience about an unfamiliar culture, subculture, or an aspect of a culture
TOPIC	Your choice
SUPPORT	Minimum of 5 sources to be cited in the speech, including 1 interview.
TIME RANGE	5-8 minutes for individual speech; 12-15 minutes for group presentation
DELIVERY STYLE	Extemporaneous
NOTES	Two note cards permitted with writing on one side only
VISUAL AIDS	Ask instructor
ATTIRE	Appropriate for topic
HINTS	Dig deep. Avoid making stereotypical assumptions about a culture.
ADDITIONAL INFORMATION	

MY SPEAKING DATE _____

PERSUASIVE SPEECH ASSIGNMENTS:

ASSIGNMENT   **Personal Action-Changing Persuasive Speech**

OBJECTIVE   To persuade your audience members to take a specific action or change a specific behavior

TOPIC   Your choice; avoid topics that are obvious or too difficult for audience members to accept

SUPPORT   Minimum 6 sources to be cited in the speech. Sources must be current and credible.

TIME RANGE   6-8 minutes

DELIVERY STYLE   Extemporaneous

NOTES   Two note cards permitted with writing on one side only

VISUAL AIDS   Optional

ATTIRE   Professional

HINTS   Be sure to include appeals to ethos, pathos, and logos.

ADDITIONAL INFORMATION

MY SPEAKING DATE _____

ASSIGNMENT   **Policy-Changing Persuasive Speech**

OBJECTIVE   To persuade your audience members that a government or organization should take a specific action and/or change an existing law or policy

TOPIC   Your choice; avoid topics that are obvious or too difficult for audience members to accept

SUPPORT   Minimum 8 sources to be cited in the speech. Sources must be current and credible.

TIME RANGE   8-10 minutes

DELIVERY STYLE   Extemporaneous

NOTES   Two note cards permitted with writing on one side only

VISUAL AIDS   Optional

ATTIRE   Professional

HINTS   Be sure to include appeals to ethos, pathos, and logos. Choose a policy that has some impact on your audience.

ADDITIONAL INFORMATION

MY SPEAKING DATE _____

PERSUASIVE SPEECH ASSIGNMENTS, CONT'D:

ASSIGNMENT	**Monroe's Motivated Sequence Persuasive Speech**
OBJECTIVE	To persuade your audience members to take a specific action, change a specific behavior, or support a specific policy
TOPIC	Your choice; avoid topics that are obvious or too difficult for audience members to accept
SUPPORT	Minimum 6 sources to be cited in the speech. Sources must be current and credible.
TIME RANGE	6-8 minutes
DELIVERY STYLE	Extemporaneous
NOTES	Two note cards permitted with writing on one side only
VISUAL AIDS	Optional
ATTIRE	Professional
HINTS	Be sure to use all 5 steps of Monroe's Sequence. See Chapter 15 for details.
ADDITIONAL INFORMATION	

MY SPEAKING DATE _____

ASSIGNMENT	**Group Sales Presentation**
OBJECTIVE	To develop a new product or service and seek financial backing from a corporate venture firm with a persuasive presentation
TOPIC	Your product and why they should give you money
SUPPORT	As needed
TIME RANGE	18-22 minutes
DELIVERY STYLE	Extemporaneous
NOTES	Two note cards permitted per group member with writing on one side only
VISUAL AIDS	Required
ATTIRE	Professional
HINTS	Make your presentation interactive. Don't just have each group member speak for 5 minutes in turn.
ADDITIONAL INFORMATION	

MY SPEAKING DATE _____

SPECIAL OCCASION SPEECH ASSIGNMENTS:

ASSIGNMENT   **Memorable Experience Speech**

OBJECTIVE   To organize and deliver a speech about a past experience

TOPIC   May be serious or humorous, but must be meaningful and vivid

SUPPORT   Your experience and observations

TIME RANGE   2-3 minutes

DELIVERY STYLE   Extemporaneous

NOTES   One note card (optional)

VISUAL AIDS   None

ATTIRE   Casual

HINTS   Consider these topic areas: most embarrassing moment; my longest minute; biggest surprise of my life; narrow escape; strangest coincidence.

ADDITIONAL INFORMATION

MY SPEAKING DATE _____

ASSIGNMENT   **Hero Speech**

OBJECTIVE   To thoughtfully write and revise a short speech commemorating someone who has been a personal hero in your life

TOPIC   A specific person, not yourself

SUPPORT   Your own opinions and experiences

TIME RANGE   2-3 minutes

DELIVERY STYLE   Manuscript

NOTES   Manuscript

VISUAL AIDS   None

ATTIRE   Casual

HINTS   Be detailed and specific. Avoid clichés. Make delivery notes on your manuscript.

ADDITIONAL INFORMATION

MY SPEAKING DATE _____

SPECIAL OCCASION SPEECH ASSIGNMENTS, CONT'D:

ASSIGNMENT	**Pet Peeve Speech**
OBJECTIVE	To prepare and deliver a short speech about something that irritates you, and will also be of interest to your audience
TOPIC	Your choice
SUPPORT	Your opinions and experiences
TIME RANGE	2-3 minutes
DELIVERY STYLE	Manuscript
NOTES	Manuscript
VISUAL AIDS	None
ATTIRE	Casual
HINTS	Humor can be very effective. Make delivery notes on your manuscript.
ADDITIONAL INFORMATION	

MY SPEAKING DATE _____

ASSIGNMENT	**Movie Review**
OBJECTIVE	To present a summary and review of a film
TOPIC	A film (Choose one that is not obvious or cliché.)
SUPPORT	Your opinions and a clip from the film
TIME RANGE	3-4 minutes
DELIVERY STYLE	Extemporaneous
NOTES	One note card per person
VISUAL AIDS	Required (short video clip)
ATTIRE	Casual and/or appropriate
HINTS	Remember why people read movie reviews - to decide if they want to see the film. Pick a film you think people probably haven't seen.
ADDITIONAL INFORMATION	

MY SPEAKING DATE _____

Skill-Building Speech Assignments:

ASSIGNMENT	**Oral Interpretation**
OBJECTIVE	To perform a selection of poetry, fiction, or a scene from a play written by someone else
TOPIC	Literature
SUPPORT	None
TIME RANGE	2-3 minutes
DELIVERY STYLE	Manuscript
NOTES	Manuscript
VISUAL AIDS	None
ATTIRE	Casual, no costumes
HINTS	Choose a selection with lots of energy and interesting characters. Children's literature is very fun for this assignment.
ADDITIONAL INFORMATION	

MY SPEAKING DATE _____

ASSIGNMENT	**Supporting Materials Speech**
OBJECTIVE	To support a single thesis/argument with at least five kinds of supporting materials
TOPIC	Your thesis
SUPPORT	Five different types
TIME RANGE	2-3 minutes
DELIVERY STYLE	Extemporaneous
NOTES	One note card with writing on one side only
VISUAL AIDS	If chosen as a type of support
ATTIRE	Casual
HINTS	
ADDITIONAL INFORMATION	

MY SPEAKING DATE _____

SKILL-BUILDING ASSIGNMENTS, CONT'D.

ASSIGNMENT: **Declamation Speech**

PURPOSE: To analyze a significant historical speech and to perform an excerpt of that speech using advanced delivery skills.

Constructing the Speech:

1. Find a complete transcript of a speech given by an important American leader. To help you locate a speech, you may refer to the "Ripples of Hope: Great American Civil Rights Speeches" collection which can be found in the Credo Reference database on Mt. SAC library website. You will also need additional outside research about the speaker and the speech delivered.

2. After reading the complete transcript and outside research, construct a speech that identifies:
    a. speaker: background, achievements, personal qualities, etc.
    b. message of speech: theme, purpose, argument, etc.
    c. audience for the speech
    d. feedback: immediate response to the speech as well as historical implications

3. Using these four elements, analyze why this speech is considered important to American history.

4. Perform a short section of the speech using advanced delivery skills.

Suggested Outline:

Introduction
I.   Attention Device: perform one line from your chosen speech
II. TRS: Introduce the speaker and the title of the speech
III. Preview of Two Main Points

Body
I.   Analysis
    A.   Speech Model
        1.   Speaker
        2.   Message
        3.   Audience
        4.   Feedback
    B.   Answer question: why is this speech considered an important historical speech?
II. Performance: perform a short segment of the section of the speech using advanced delivery skills.

Conclusion
I.   Summary of main points as well as a recap of the historical importance of speech
II. Lasting Thought

Guidelines

Time: 4-6 minutes total (3-4 minutes for analysis, 1-2 minutes of speech performance)

Research: At least one outside source (verbally cited).

Notes: One notecard permitted for analysis. Speech performance must be memorized.

Delivery: Advanced skills. Professional Attire.

Index